America's Gothic Fiction

America's Gothic Fiction

The Legacy of *Magnalia Christi Americana*

Dorothy Z. Baker

The Ohio State University Press
Columbus

Library of Congress Cataloging-in-Publication Data
Baker, Dorothy Zayatz.
America's gothic fiction : the legacy of Magnalia Christi Americana / Dorothy Z. Baker.
  p. cm.
Includes bibliographical references (p.) and index.
ISBN-13: 978-0-8142-1060-4 (cloth : alk. paper)
ISBN-13: 978-0-8142-9144-3 (cd-rom)
1. American fiction—History and criticism. 2. Religion and literature. 3. Mather, Cotton, 1663–1728. Magnalia Christi Americana. 4. Mather, Cotton, 1663–1728—Influence. 5. Puritan movements in literature. 6. Horror tales, American—History and criticism. 7. Gothic revival (Literature)—United States. 8. Religion and literature—United States—History. 9. National characteristics, American, in literature. I. Title.
PS166.B35 2007
813.0872—dc22
                  2007012212

Cover design by Fulcrum Design Corps, LLC
Text design and typesetting by Juliet Williams
Type set in Minion Pro
Printed by Thomson-Shore

The paper used in this publication meets the minimum requirements of the American National Standard for Information Sciences—Permanence of Paper for Printed Library Materials. ANSI Z39.48–1992.

9 8 7 6 5 4 3 2 1

Contents

ॐ

Acknowledgments

ゆや

My work on the legacy of Cotton Mather owes an immense debt to many scholars whose studies on American historical narrative and American historical fiction provided the foundation for this book. In addition, I could not possibly list the countless colleagues whose ready ears, bibliographic leads, and astute observations sustained and enriched my work. I would especially like to thank Jane Donahue Eberwein, Wyman H. Herendeen, John Lienhard, Steven Mintz, Nancy Lusignan Schultz, Roberta F. Weldon, and Lois Parkinson Zamora for their innumerable kindnesses. This book would have been impossible without their good counsel and the example of their scholarly practice. I first outlined the argument for this book in a conversation with the late W. Milne Holton and was encouraged by his keen interest in the project. Dr. Holton was an exacting and generous mentor. Would that I could thank him for his unfailing support.

Studies in American Fiction has kindly given me permission to reprint in chapter four a revision of my essay that appeared in the journal in 1994. I would like to thank the Interlibrary Loan Department at the M. D. Anderson Library of the University of Houston for its remarkable efficiency in meeting my every request. The University of Houston supported my research with a Faculty Development Leave, which was critical in helping me to initiate this study. I am very grateful to Sandy Crooms of The Ohio State University Press for her enthusiasm for this project. The anonymous readers at The Ohio State University Press contributed greatly to this book, and they have my sincere thanks.

My personal debts are too numerous to list. May it suffice to say that I live more ably and fully because of the goodwill and generosity of many wonderful people who daily show me the splendor and joy of this world. Foremost among them is Lawrence Baker. I would also like to acknowledge my daughter, Elizabeth Eve Baker, and my son, Daniel Abraham Baker, who are both *magnalia Dei* in my life.

Finally, this book is dedicated to the memory of Abraham Harris Baker, my husband's much-loved father, my children's wise and wonderful grandfather, and my great friend.

Dorothy Z. Baker
Houston, Texas
2007

Chapter 1

ເ3ີ່ຍ

Introduction

Providentialism was not born in Puritan America, but when seventeenth-century New England professed its belief in God's agency in the great and small, public and private events of their lives, this profession of faith took on uniquely American coloring. Moreover, it became a deep-seated and dominant notion in American culture. Belief in divine providence expressed itself in the national historical and aesthetic literature of the seventeenth and eighteenth centuries. Well into the nineteenth century, historians and literary authors continued to draw on the tropes of God's providential designs for his people. The language of this profound religious tenet also found its way into many of the nation's major political manifestos, such as those surrounding the Revolutionary War, Manifest Destiny, and the Abolition movement, and has continued in twentieth-century discourse concerning issues as diverse as John Kennedy's pronouncements on the U.S. government's involvement in foreign affairs and the religious right's claims regarding the AIDS epidemic. Religious imagery, scriptural allusion, and even religious doctrinal assertion form powerful components of American political and historical writing, the philosophical underpinning of which is a belief in divine providence. More specifically, national political and historical documents regularly suggest God's hand in the lives of individual Americans and the policies and practices of the nation.

Belief in divine providence is the basis of a narrative form that is the staple of Puritan letters. The providence tale in early America is a formulaic narrative that testifies to the omniscience and omnipotence of God, and especially to the belief that God exhibits these qualities in his active presence in the daily lives of his people in New England.[1] That the power

1. My understanding of providentialism in Calvinist New England is based largely on the work of the following critics. David D. Hall offers a thorough and insightful history of the

and will of God is exhibited in this world was a commonplace for colonial Puritans. The order and beauty of nature itself bespoke God's majesty. The Puritans also understood that unpredictable displays of nature and exceptional occurrences in the life of men and women were also signs of divine providence and represented God's special message to his people. Moreover, they sought to explicate and understand God's voice in the exceptional and remarkable events they saw around them, and they did so through the providence tale.

Each providence tale recounts an extraordinary occurrence, such as an eerie, prophetic dream, a remarkable religious conversion, a dramatic gallows confession, a miraculous deliverance from shipwreck, the exposé of sinful wrongdoing, or a deathwatch vision. Despite its brevity, the tale offers a measure of character development and dialogue, most frequently ejaculatory prayers. The plot of the providence tale relies on great suspense—what will become of the sailors lost at sea, will the young wife survive Indian captivity, will the bereaved parents recover from the death of their baby? Finally, within the author's narrative construction, the dénouement of the tale clearly illustrates not only the divine hand in the lives of his people, but divine judgment—God sends a bird to feed the one virtuous sailor aboard the shipwrecked vessel, punishes the blasphemer with the inability to speak, and causes the murder victim to cry out from the grave to reveal the name of his killer. Closure inevitably sets the anecdote within the framework of Puritan theology, and thereby articulates its significance and ensures its importance. The message is unchanging—God maintains an active presence in the world and in the lives of his people. He blesses and

---

European origins of the providence tale as well as the New English expression of providence in colonial wonderbooks in *Worlds of Wonder, Days of Judgment: Popular Religious Belief in New England* (Cambridge: Harvard University Press, 1990), and Michael P. Winship's *Seers of God: Puritan Providentialism in the Restoration and Early Enlightenment* (Baltimore: Johns Hopkins University Press, 1996) offers a detailed discussion of the theological support for providentialism as well as an excellent treatment of the cultural and religious forces that altered belief in divine providence in seventeenth-century New England. For a sketch of the varied approaches to providential historiography in seventeenth- and eighteenth-century New England, see Bernd Engler and Oliver Scheiding, "Re-Visioning the Past: The Historical Imagination in American Historiography and Short Fiction," in *Re-Visioning the Past: Historical Self-Reflexivity in American Short Fiction* (Trier: Wissenschaftlicher Verlag Trier, 1998), 1–27. Stephen Carl Arch's excellent treatment of providence tales as historical narrative in early New England is found in *Authorizing the Past: The Rhetoric of History in Seventeenth-Century New England* (DeKalb: Northern Illinois University Press, 1994). See especially 56–87, 124–28. See also James D. Hartman, *Providence Tales and the Birth of American Literature* (Baltimore and London: Johns Hopkins University Press, 1999), 1–14 and Perry Miller, *The New England Mind: The Seventeenth Century* (Cambridge and London: Harvard University Press, 1939), 228–31, 360.

preserves his elect while he brings public, definitive, and symbolic punishment to those who sin.

The providence tale is now recognized as an early expression of the short story and a fiction form that fascinated readers well into the nineteenth century.[2] Such tales are regularly found as embedded narratives in Puritan sermons. They are also found in collected form, most notably in Increase Mather's *Illustrious Providences* (1684), and then in book six of Cotton Mather's *Magnalia Christi Americana* (1702). Both works offer a full compendium of tales recounting extraordinary occurrences, such as exceptional medical cures, incidents of witchcraft, gallows confessions, and tales of depraved behavior, among other sensational topics. More than any other collection of New England's "remarkable occurrences," Cotton Mather's *Magnalia Christi Americana* captured the imagination of its audience. Peter Gay recounts that the book was "valuable enough to be stolen: in 1720, a burglar ransacking Jonathan Belcher's well-stocked warehouse included in his booty 'a Book Entituled, Magnalia Christi Americana.'"[3] Book six of *Magnalia* documents the "wonder-workings" of God among the common people of New England, and, like the earlier volumes of Mather's history, they underscore Mather's rationale for his extensive history of New England— to revive his readers' and his congregants' devotion to the Puritan commonwealth. Gay describes the book as "tribal history, expressing Puritan sentiments, feeding Puritan anxieties, and sustaining Puritan pride" (77). This was its social function in the early eighteenth century and served the same role well into the nineteenth century, where it continued to hold the attention of American readers.

---

2. For an exploration of this subgenre of Puritan literature, see Jane Donahue Eberwein, "'Indistinct Lustre': Biographical Miniatures in the *Magnalia Christi Americana,*" *Biography: An Interdisciplinary Quarterly* 4.3 (1981): 195–207; James D. Hartman's *Providence Tales;* Parker H. Johnson, "Humiliation Followed by Deliverance: Metaphor and Plot in Cotton Mather's *Magnalia,*" *Early American Literature* 15.3 (1980/81): 237–46; and Alfred Weber, "Die Anfänge des Kurzen Erzählens in Amerika des 17. und 18. Jahrhunderts: Die 'Providences' der Amerikanischen Puritaner," *Mythos und Aufklärung in der Amerikanischen Literatur,* ed. Dieter Meindl and Friedrich W. Horlacher (Erlangen: Erlanger Forschungen, 1985), 55–70. Although John F. Berens, *Providence and Patriotism in Early America 1640–1815* (Charlottesville: University Press of Virginia, 1978), focuses on the Puritan providence as a historical phenomenon and as a method of articulating social unity, his thorough study also investigates rhetorical features of this literary form. See especially 14–31.

3. *A Loss of Mastery: Puritan Historians in Colonial America* (Berkeley and Los Angeles: University of California Press, 1966), 71. Here and throughout the book, I neither alter the spelling, grammar, and punctuation of early texts to conform to current standards nor signal in any way that the language does not meet current prose standards.

The early volumes of *Magnalia* recount the great deeds of great public figures in seventeenth-century Puritan America. Included in these books are the biographies of early civic leaders, the ecclesiastical history of the New English colonies, an account of the early years of Harvard College, and the history of war with the native Americans, among other subjects of political, economic, and religious history. Mather's goal for these accounts is to educate and also to inspire. Thus, the early biographical miniatures of the Puritan forefathers resemble hagiography, designed to create culture heroes of the most prominent of the early settlers for subsequent generations of New English colonists, and Mather hoped that such accounts would remind them of the lofty vision and the sacrifices of the men who founded Plymouth and Massachusetts.

Book six of Mather's *Magnalia* is distinct from the preceding books in that it offers a compendium of providence tales about the common folk of New England. The book is divided into seven chapters, the first relating tales of remarkable rescues at sea and the second recounting extraordinary rescues from death. In chapter three, Mather investigates the phenomenon of thunder, which he understands to be the voice of God speaking to man. The fourth chapter describes dramatic religious conversions, while the following chapter, the longest in book six, documents the hand of God in disclosing the evil deeds of sinners and punishing those sinners. Chapter six recounts conversions and crimes among the native Americans, and the final chapter documents the work of demons and witches among the people of New England. Finally, an appendix to book six offers several anecdotes about exceptional conversions among young children, tales which Mather hopes will "encourage [. . .] piety in other children."[4]

Despite its broad range of subject matter, book six of *Magnalia Christi Americana* is not a random collection of strange stories. Accounts of wonderworking in early seventeenth-century America mix with contemporary tales to signal the continuity of experience of God's people in America. Further, in appending the epic tale of the Puritan forefathers found in the early books with personal, contemporary accounts in book six, Mather elides the political, religious, and social history of early New England with that of his current readers to further convince eighteenth-century colonists of their affinity to the spiritual origins of the New England colonies. His message is clear: God has a special abiding relationship with the people of New England and continues to work wonders among them.

4. *Magnalia Christi Americana; or, The Ecclesiastical History of New-England; From its First Planting, in the Year 1620, unto the Year of Our Lord 1689.* 1702 (New York: Russell and Russell, 1967), 2:480.

Later, this message was not lost on the nineteenth-century reader. In her semi-autobiographical novel, *Poganuc People,* Harriet Beecher Stowe wrote

> It was a happy hour when [father] brought home and set up in his book-case Cotton Mather's "Magnalia," in a new edition of two volumes. What wonderful stories these! and stories, too, about her own country, stories that made her feel that the very ground she trod on was consecrated by some special dealing of God's providence.[5]

Stowe was both convinced of the theory that divine providence guided her national history and attracted by the notion that being a descendant of the Puritan saints afforded her special grace.

"Remarkables of the Divine Providence Among the People of New-England," book six of Mather's *Magnalia,* provided many later authors and readers with examples of the early American literary type of the providence tale, which is now recognized as the beginning of the American short narrative. In a general introduction to his *Magnalia,* Cotton Mather asserts that he is mindful of his sacred charge as author of the history of the Puritan people in New England, and clearly states that his text is written with "all historical fidelity and simplicity" (1:25). Yet, Jane Donahue Eberwein observes that although the work was intended as history, "the imaginative ordering and interpretation of events . . . seem mythopoetic rather than scholarly" (195). The author's command of both rhetoric and narrative strategy is evident throughout *Magnalia.* As Larzer Ziff has noted, "on the eve of the novel's birth, his was the stuff of novelists."[6]

Indeed, more than a century after the initial publication of Cotton Mather's *Magnalia Christi Americana,* American authors continue to respond to the message and the narrative form of his providence tales. This book investigates the ways in which Edgar Allan Poe, Harriet Beecher Stowe, Nathaniel Hawthorne, Catharine Maria Sedgwick, and Edith Wharton rely on Mather's providence tales at critical moments in their work. These diverse authors, who are rarely grouped in literary studies, have radically divergent responses to Mather's theology, historiography,

5. *The Writings of Harriet Beecher Stowe,* 16 vols. (New York: AMS, 1967), 11:122–23. All subsequent reference to the novels and short fiction of Stowe are from this edition, and will be cited parenthetically in the text.

6. *Puritanism in America: New Culture in a New World* (New York: Viking, 1973), 217. For a discussion of Magnalia as a self-conscious literary text, see Susan Cherry Bell, "History and Artistry in Cotton Mather's *Magnalia Christi Americana*" (diss., SUNY Binghamton, 1991).

and literary forms. However, each takes up Mather's themes and forms and, in distinct ways, comments on the providence tales in *Magnalia Christi Americana* and interrogates these tales as foundational statements about American history, American identity, and God's providential designs for America and Americans. More interestingly, each author—regardless of his or her individual theological and religious position—subverts Mather's providence tales for his or her own narrative objectives.

One of the most provocative aspects of the nineteenth- and twentieth-century appropriation of Mather's providence tales is the later authors' concern with authorial ethos. While these authors interrogate the concept of God's providential design for America, their underlying anxiety centers on the role of the historian or narrator itself. Their questions are many: Who is entitled to speak on behalf of the American people? Who is in a position to conceptualize the events of the past? When we examine a historiographic framework based on God's providential design, who is charged with speaking for God? Mather's text is clear on this point. The minister is uniquely positioned to serve as historian. In divergent ways, the authors discussed in this book challenge this stance. Each draws the reader into a reconsideration of social authority and narrative authority. Each destabilizes the position of the teller of tales and cautions the reader to be ever alert to the authority and influence of the teller as well as the tale.

The writings of Cotton Mather had come under attack before these authors investigated and appropriated his *Magnalia Christi Americana.* In the eighteenth century, Benjamin Franklin, who had met Mather on occasion, was decidedly antipathetic to the rigid Calvinist orthodoxy that Cotton Mather had come to represent, and rejected the ways in which Puritanism had insinuated itself into scientific knowledge and judicial practice. Franklin parodied Cotton Mather's tales of witchcraft in a newspaper article, "A Witch Trial at Mount Holly," which appeared in *The Pennsylvania Gazette* in 1730.[7] The article was a hoax that reported on a witch trial in which neither the accused nor the accusers pass the purportedly scientific tests that were devised to prove the accused innocent of the charge of witchcraft. Likewise, critics have noted that Franklin's satiric "Silence Dogood" essays respond to Mather's prescriptive statements on how to live a Christian life.[8] The very name, Silence Dogood, echoes two

7. *The Pennsylvania Gazette* (No. 101, October 22, 1730).

8. See especially Gordon S. Wood, *The Americanization of Benjamin Franklin* (New York: Penguin, 2004), 19, 21, and Daniel Royot, "Franklin as Founding Father of American Humor," in *Reappraising Benjamin Franklin: A Bicentennial Perspective,* ed. J. A. Leo Lemay (Newark: University of Delaware Press, 1993), 390–91. For a comparison of Mather's and Franklin's

of Mather's publications, *Silentiarius: A brief essay on the holy silence and godly patience* and *Bonifacius: An essay upon the good*. Later, in his *Autobiography*, Benjamin Franklin refers directly to Cotton Mather, again for ironic purpose.[9] Franklin appears to boast of his heritage when he identifies his maternal grandfather, Peter Folger, as "one of the first Settlers of New England, of whom honourable mention is made by Cotton Mather, in his Church History of that Country, (entitled Magnalia Christi Americana) as a *godly learned Englishman*."[10] Yet, he notes that Folger's contribution to the colonies was his writing "in favor of Liberty of Conscience, and in behalf of the Baptists, Quakers, and other Sectaries, that had been under Persecution," positions that Franklin was well aware as being contrary to those of Mather (5–6). In exposing Cotton Mather's praise of an individual who advocates principles antithetical to Mather's, Franklin is able to undercut both Mather's religious and political positions as well as his credibility as an author.[11]

Donald Ringe rightly notes that Franklin's enlightenment principles enable him to "dismiss ghosts, goblins, and witches as the relics of a more credulous age and [he was] proud of the fact that American society had been formed when such phenomena were no longer credited and tales of superstition had been relegated to the nursery."[12] However, Franklin must have been sufficiently anxious about the legacy of Cotton Mather's remarkable providences to compel him to disparage Mather in newsprint and in books throughout his career. According to Mather's biographer, Kenneth Silverman, "by 1710 [Cotton Mather] may well have become the best-known man in America."[13] It was clear that he was the most prolific

---

ethics, see John C. Van Horne, "Collective Benevolence and the Common Good in Franklin's Philosophy" in *Reappraising Benjamin Franklin: A Bicentennial Perspective,* ed. J. A. Leo Lemay (Newark: University of Delaware Press, 1993), 427–29.

9. Viewing Franklin's *Autobiography* from a different perspective, Sacvan Bercovitch also links the text to Mather's biographical miniatures in *Magnalia* and finds that these texts provide the "form and outlook" for Franklin's work as well as for later rags to riches narratives. See Bercovitch's "'Delightful Examples of Surprising Prosperity': Cotton Mather and the American Success Story," *English Studies* 51.1 (1970): 40–43.

10. *The Autobiography of Benjamin Franklin: A Genetic Text,* ed. J. A. Leo Lemay and P. M. Zall (Knoxville: University of Tennessee Press, 1981), 5.

11. Michael T. Gilmore explores Franklin's rejection of the Puritan religious identity that he replaces with a "secular gospel" in *The Middle Way: Puritanism and Ideology in American Romantic Fiction* (New Brunswick: Rutgers University Press, 1977), 47–55.

12. *American Gothic: Imagination and Reason in Nineteenth-Century Fiction* (Lexington: University Press of Kentucky, 1982), 2–3.

13. *The Life and Times of Cotton Mather* (New York: Columbia University Press, 1985), 198.

published author in America with almost 400 separate titles to his name. Silverman reports: "it is imaginable that numerous people overseas, many people in the colonies, most people in New England, and nearly everyone in Boston owned some of his works" (198). Stephen Carl Arch notes that "Benjamin Franklin's connection to Cotton Mather is not just through one of Mather's books; it is through Mather's example as America's first public man of letters" (183). For Franklin and other contemporary writers, his was the voice to reckon with.

Later, Washington Irving joins Franklin in undercutting Mather's reputation. Irving does so through the character of Ichabod Crane, who is introduced as "a perfect master of Cotton Mather's history of New England Witchcraft, in which, by the way, he most firmly and potently believed."[14] The dénouement of Irving's tale reveals that the schoolmaster who persists in believing the superstitious tales of America's Puritan past is out of place in the new America. Both infantilized and feminized, his authority is limited to the schoolroom, and his appeal is limited to old women. The young men of his generation ridicule him, and the young girl he courts ends up in the arms of another man. More brutally, the Yankee is revealed as a shallow fortune-seeker, and, in this way, his Puritan values are linked to his avarice.

In addition, when Ichabod Crane, the teller of Mather's tales, counters Brom Bones, the teller of tales that issue from the Hudson Valley, the contest is almost one-sided. Brom Bones's story of the headless horseman not only entertains, but it has potency and immediate agency. It alters lives and fortunes. Ichabod Crane tries to banish Bones's tale from his mind by singing psalms, but in Irving's story, even the word of God cannot drown out the native legend. Crane's reprisal of Mather's antiquated tale is bested by Bones's folk tale, and Mather's authority is supplanted by that of a native Dutch farmer whose lack of erudition and refinement is more than compensated by ample honor and good humor. Speaking to Irving's central

---

14. *The Sketch Book of Geoffrey Crayon, Gent.* Ed. Haskell Springer (Boston: Twayne, 1978), 276. Irving was well read in the work of Cotton Mather, and while he was preparing his *Sketch Book* refers to Mather in his journal. See *Journals and Notebooks,* Vol. II: 1807–1822. Ed. Walter A. Reichart and Lillian Schlissel (Boston: Twayne, 1981), 179.

Speaking of another of Irving's characters, John Greenleaf Whittier wrote in his 1847 publication, *The Supernaturalism of New England,* "Modern skepticism and philosophy have not yet eradicated the belief of supernatural visitation from the New England mind. Here and there—oftenest in our still, fixed, valley-sheltered, unvisited nooks and villages—the Rip Van Winkles of a progressive and restless population—may be still found devout believers worthy of the days of the two Mathers." See Whittier (1847), *Supernaturalism,* ed. Edward Wagenknecht (Norman, University of Oklahoma Press, 1969), 40.

concern about the philosophical battle waged under the guise of Bones and Crane, Jeffrey Rubin-Dorsky concludes that "the farmer rightfully ousts the pedant from a world whose values he does not share."[15] The rational, utilitarian posture of Bones triumphs over superstitious, Puritan religious thought, with Bones using the devices of his rival—a supernatural tale—to defeat him.

In the case of Washington Irving's "The Legend of Sleepy Hollow," the eerie tales of Cotton Mather are countered and conquered by a gothic account of a purportedly historical event. As the legacy of Cotton Mather continues in the nineteenth century, with later authors invoking the person and his works, these authors revisit Mather's providence tales and revise them as gothic stories. In distinct ways, Edgar Allan Poe, Harriet Beecher Stowe, Nathaniel Hawthorne, Catharine Maria Sedgwick, and Edith Wharton rely on the gothic mode to resist Cotton Mather's historical narrative of the people of New England.

Scholarship surrounding the gothic mode in the American literary tradition is vast and varied. While early studies marginalized the gothic as regional and largely southern literature, or trivialized gothic texts as popular and overwrought, Teresa Goddu argues for the centrality of the gothic mode in American letters.[16] Goddu observes that gothic texts cannot be fully understood apart from their social and historical context precisely because gothic literature serves to "expose the cultural contradictions of national myth" (10)[17] Texts written in the gothic mode challenge

15. *Adrift in the Old World: The Psychological Pilgrimage of Washington Irving* (Chicago and London: University of Chicago Press, 1988), 109.

16. Goddu makes this argument in *Gothic America: Narrative, History, and Nation* (New York: Columbia University Press, 1997), 10. Leslie Fiedler was one of the earliest critics to identify the gothic as a mode of Southern literature. See *Love and Death in the American Novel,* 1960 (New York: Stein and Day, 1982), 397. For a thorough discussion of the ways in which the gothic is linked to popular literature, see David Reynolds, *Beneath the American Renaissance: The Subversive Imagination in the Age of Emerson and Melville* (Cambridge: Harvard University Press, 1989), 80–84, 199.

17. I concur with Louis S. Gross who writes, "The American Gothic narrative is primarily concerned with exploring personal identity through the roles played in both family and national history," but disagree that gothic fiction in the eighteenth and nineteenth centuries "reveals a kind of demonic history text, an alternative vision of American experience that reminds us of those marginal groups responsible for the guarding of the Gothic flame." My study insists that the gothic fiction of established and well-received authors such as Poe, Stowe, Hawthorne, Sedgwick, and Wharton uncovers the flawed historical narratives written by equally established and well-received authors in the past. See Gross, *Redefining the American Gothic from* Wieland *to* Day of the Dead (Ann Arbor and London: UMI Research Press, 1989), 2.

Additionally, the work of Lawrence Buell and Cathy Davidson on gothic literature is based on a historical understanding of this literary mode. See especially Buell, *New England*

the fictions of American identity that have been codified as foundational historical documents. Positioning themselves as a palimpsest upon earlier idealized histories, gothic texts "disrupt the dream world of national myth" (10). Extending her argument to the erratic structure that is characteristic of gothic literature, Goddu also explains that "in its narrative incoherence, the gothic discloses the instability of America's self-representations; its highly wrought form exposes the artificial foundations of national identity" (10).

Leslie Fiedler was one of the earliest critics to identify the psychological trauma expressed in American gothic literature from the perspective of the nation's religious culture, and he speaks of the gothic as "a Calvinist exposé of natural human corruption" (160). However, Lawrence Buell takes a different approach to Fiedler's observation and argues that "in New England gothic, the most distinctive thematic ingredient is the perception of Puritan culture as inherently grotesque" (359). Extending Buell's argument, this study asserts that the New England gothic is frequently an exposé of Calvinist historical accounts of America and Americans. Moreover, in the process of exposing the flawed and unstable narratives that construct an artificial and uncomfortable identity for the nation, nineteenth-century gothic literature frequently proposes alternate versions of America, its history, its citizens, and its historians.

It is not surprising that when the five nineteenth- and twentieth-century authors discussed in this book address American historical narratives they all look to the work of Cotton Mather. His *Magnalia Christi Americana* was a prominent and dominant history of early New England.[18] In his own time Mather had a large personality, and well into the nineteenth century he had an equally large reputation as a stiff and stern Puritan whom James Russell Lowell would later call a "conceited old pedant."[19] Furthermore, Mather was notoriously associated with the Salem witch trials of 1692, having served as secretary to the tribunal, after which he authored *The Wonders of the Invisible World,* a work that compiled many of the anecdotes of witchcraft that he heard throughout the trials. At the same time, Mather was not easily dismissed as a mere pedant or witch hunter from the distant past precisely

---

Literary Culture from Revolution through Renaissance (Cambridge: Cambridge University Press, 1986), 359–60 and 368–70, and Davidson, *Revolution and the Word: The Rise of the Novel in America* (New York and Oxford: Oxford University Press, 1986), 217–18.

18. In *New England Literary Culture: From Revolution through Renaissance,* Lawrence Buell discusses what he terms the "politics of historiography" concerning the reception of Cotton Mather in antebellum America. See especially 214–38.

19. "Reviews and Literary Notices," *The Atlantic Monthly* 6.37 (1860), 639.

because he was an acclaimed and compelling author. In the nineteenth century and well into the twentieth century, thinkers and writers continued to recognize Mather as a brilliant rhetorician and artful writer. Despite his irreverent description of the author, James Russell Lowell admits that "with all his faults, that conceited old pedant contrived to make one of the most entertaining books ever written on this side of the water" (639).

Chapter two of this book accounts for the entertaining quality of book six of *Magnalia Christi Americana* by documenting the origins of the Puritan providence tale and exploring the novel ways in which Cotton Mather adapts the earlier literary forms for a contemporary audience. This chapter also ties the dramatic and sometimes flamboyant stylistic features of *Magnalia* to the book's function in eighteenth-century New England. Subsequent chapters turn to the fiction of Edgar Allan Poe, Harriet Beecher Stowe, Nathaniel Hawthorne, Catharine Maria Sedgwick, and Edith Wharton and contend that these authors recognize the importance of Mather's work in codifying our understanding of American identity and shaping literary forms in the new nation, two distinct but related projects. Chapter three examines the work of Poe, whose "William Wilson," "The Black Cat," and *The Narrative of Arthur Gordon Pym* form the mirror image of Mather's providence tales. That is, they reflect Mather's plots, characters, and even his language, but invert them to express Poe's gothic view of providential design. The following chapter takes up Harriet Beecher Stowe's New England novels and tales. Because of her conservative evangelical upbringing and her personal religious orientation, Harriet Beecher Stowe is much more sympathetic than Poe to the theological underpinnings of Cotton Mather's writings, and her fiction gives evidence of her taste for the providence tales in *Magnalia*. Yet, Stowe's work also reveals the uncanny ways in which she departs from Mather's notion of religious leadership and narrative authority, just as she also refines aspects of Mather's theology. Chapter five speaks to Nathaniel Hawthorne's intellectual concerns regarding American providential historiography, which he identifies, to dramatic effect, with the person of Cotton Mather. Like Stowe, Hawthorne has a decidedly modern understanding of narrative authority. Further, he experiments with various fictional forms to express his discontent with earlier and contemporary historical tracts, and explores narrative voices and alternate modes of emplotment that are antithetical to those of Mather's providence tales. The book concludes with two distinct perspectives on historical narrative. The final chapter begins with a consideration of Catharine Maria Sedgwick's *Hope Leslie,* a novel that centers on a reconsideration of early American history and historians. *Hope Leslie* reflects the author's early training in providential literature, which she questions in her fiction and supplements with multiple and seemingly contradictory approaches to historical narrative. In this way, the novel's diffuse and even manic plot responds to the singular and definitive plots found in Mather's *Magnalia*. Like Sedgwick's *Hope Leslie*, Edith Wharton's New England tales contest the ownership of our national history. However, where Sedgwick gives voice to a multiplicity of historians who speak freely about their community, Wharton's historians are few, and they struggle to understand themselves and others and then to articulate their limited perceptions about their society. In distinct ways, each of the authors discussed in this book resists Mather's model for the historian and historical narrative.

This book does not claim that among the many novelists of nineteenth-century America only Nathaniel Hawthorne, Edgar Allan Poe, Catharine Maria Sedgwick, and Harriet Beecher Stowe respond to the words of Cotton Mather in their fiction and examine his work as a central feature of their own literary projects. To the contrary. Yet, because historical fiction in general was exceptionally popular in antebellum America, it is to be anticipated that authors of such novels and short stories would look to the work of one of the nation's earliest and most prominent historians.[20] Many critics have discovered that Herman Melville, for example, both incorporates Cotton Mather's literary forms and challenges his religious tenets in his fiction.[21] One can also identify authorial response to the themes, if not

20. Stephen Carl Arch demonstrates the importance of this mode of fiction in "Romancing the Puritans: American Historical Fiction in the 1820s," *ESQ: A Journal of the American Renaissance* 39.2 (1993): 107–32. See also Buell, 193–97, 239–60.

21. In a consideration of Melville's *Moby-Dick,* Jane Donahue Eberwein documents the similarities between Mather's sermons to fishermen and Father Mapple's sermon, and finds that Mather's statement in *The Religious Mariner* (Boston, 1700), "Sirs, That pitch't Box of Oak, in which you *Sail,* what is it, but a larger sort of *Coffin?*" anticipates the larger plot of Melville's novel. See "Fishers of Metaphor: Mather and Melville on the Whale," *American Transcendental Quarterly* 26 (1975): 30–31. Attending to the scriptural and religious language in *Moby-Dick,* Philip F. Gura explores the varying religious and philosophical "grammars" of the *Pequod*'s crew. See *The Wisdom of Words: Language, Theology, and Literature in the New England Renaissance* (Middletown: Wesleyan University Press, 1981), 159–70. Although T. Walter Herbert's *Moby-Dick and Calvinism: A World Dismantled* (New Brunswick: Rutgers University Press, 1977) does not take up Melville's relationship to Mather, it is an important study of the author's response to Calvinist doctrine.

Oliver Scheiding's essay, "Subversions of Providential Historiography in Herman Melville's 'Benito Cereno'" in *Re-Visioning the Past: Historical Self-Reflexivity in American Short Fiction,* ed. Bernd Engler and Oliver Scheiding (Trier: Wissenschaftlicher Verlag Trier, 1998), 121–40 examines Melville's use of Cotton Mather in works other than *Moby-Dick.* Michael

the specific language and literary devices, of Cotton Mather in such works as Lydia Maria Child's *Hobomok*, John Neal's *Rachel Dyer*, John Greenleaf Whittier's *Legends of New England*, and Henry David Thoreau's *A Week on the Concord and Merrimack Rivers*.[22] Indeed, the legacy of Mather's providence tales continues into the twentieth century in the work of Edith Wharton and many others.[23] Since the publication of *Magnalia Christi Americana* in 1702, Cotton Mather has been recognized as the foremost author in the tradition of the providence tale and a champion of providential historiography. Likewise, more than the works of his celebrated father or any number of his contemporaries, the providential literature of Cotton Mather captured the imagination of his contemporary readers and continued to fascinate, puzzle, and disturb readers and writers long afterward.

T. Gilmore identified the influence of *Magnalia* in Melville's "Lightning-Rod Man" (9). Frank Davidson explores Melville's commentary on Calvinism in "The Apple-Tree Table" in which one character, irresolute in his religious faith, is shaken by reading *Magnalia* late into the night. His essay, "Melville, Thoreau, and 'The Apple-Tree Table'" appeared in *American Literature* 25.4 (1954): 479–89. See also Marvin Fisher's "Bug and Humbug in Melville's 'Apple-Tree Table,'" *Studies in Short Fiction* 8.3 (1971): 459–66.

Looking to other works by Cotton Mather, Michael Clark's "Witches and Wall Street: Possession is Nine-Tenths of the Law" in *Texas Studies in Literature and Language* 25.1 (1983): 55–76 finds that dialogue in "Bartleby, the Scrivener" parallels the examination of Susannah Martin in Mather's *The Wonders of the Invisible World*.

22. These historical novels of Child and Neal are set in seventeenth-century New England and rely heavily on Mather's accounts of the characters and events the authors depict in their fiction. In addition to borrowing from *Magnalia*, in writing *Rachel Dyer*, Neal draws from Mather's *Wonders of the Invisible World*.

George Carey was early to identify John Greenleaf Whittier's use of Mather's tales in his essay, "John Greenleaf Whittier and Folklore: The Search for a Traditional American Past," *New York Folklore Quarterly* 27.1 (1971): 113–29. Ann-Marie Weis examines Whittier's relationship with Cotton Mather in her essay on the authors' treatment of Hannah Duston's captivity in "The Murderous Mother and the Solicitous Father: Violence, Jacksonian Family Values, and Hannah Duston's Captivity," *American Studies International* 36.1 (1998): 46–65. Additionally, Whittier's position on Cotton Mather is apparent in his sketch "The Double-Headed Snake of Newberry" in which he uses the man to comic effect.

Robert D. Arner explores Thoreau's revision of Mather's historical material in "The Story of Hannah Duston: Cotton Mather to Thoreau," *American Transcendental Quarterly* 18.1 (1973): 19–23. See also Marvin Fisher's "Seeing New Englandly: Anthropology, Ecology, and Theology in Thoreau's *A Week on the Concord and Merrimack Rivers*," *Centennial Review* 34.3 (1990): 390–92.

23. Although contemporary literature is outside the framework of this book, scholars have noted the continuing influence of the providence tale in Paul Auchter's *New York Trilogy*, Angela Carter's "Our Lady of the Massacre," and Bharati Mukherjee's *The Holder of the World*, among other late twentieth-century works of fiction.

Chapter 2

ദ്ധ

"We have seen Strange things to Day"

THE HISTORY AND ARTISTRY OF
COTTON MATHER'S REMARKABLES[1]

When Cotton Mather set about the task of compiling and writing his
"Remarkables of the Divine Providence Among the People of New
England," book six of *Magnalia Christi Americana,* he found no shortage
of models for this curious type of publication. Books of wondertales were
printed and reprinted in the late seventeenth century largely because there
was a substantial and enthusiastic readership for compendia of the world's
curiosities that Cotton Mather would later term "remarkable providences"
or simply "remarkables." In 1646 Samuel Clarke published *A mirrour or
looking-glass both for saints and sinners,* an enormous volume of over 700
pages of wonder stories; with five editions in twenty-three years, this book
enjoyed considerable popularity. The wonder stories in this book take
place in ancient, medieval, and early modern Europe, but similarly curious
events in the New English colonies were the subject of *Mr. James Janeway's
Legacy to his Friends,* a 1674 publication that offered uncanny accounts of
maritime disasters and rescues at sea.

Both Increase and Cotton Mather were readers of Clarke and Janeway,
and other similar popular books. When Increase Mather published his
own *Essay for the Recording of Illustrious Providences* in 1684, he acknowledged both Clarke and Janeway, among other authors, as the source of
several of his providence tales. Likewise, when Cotton Mather wrote the
sixth book of *Magnalia Christi Americana,* he borrowed directly from
Clarke, Janeway, Edward Johnson's *The Wonder-working Providence of*

1. "We have seen Strange things to Day" (Luke 5:26) is quoted by Cotton Mather in Article
I of *Parentator: Memoirs of Remarkables in the Life and the Death of the Ever-Memorable Dr.
Increase Mather Who Expired, August 23, 1723.* In *Two Mather Biographies* Life & Death *and*
Parentator, ed. William J. Scheick (Bethlehem, PA: Lehigh University Press, 1989), 87.

Sions Saviour (1654), and his father's book. He also reprinted material that he had published earlier in such works as *Memorable Providences, Relating to Witchcrafts and Possessions* (1689), *The Wonderful Works of God* (1690), *Terribilia Dei* (1697), and *Pillars of Salt* (1699).[2]

However redundant these publication projects may seem, the remarkable providences recorded in the sixth book of *Magnalia* assume different coloring for the reader precisely because these tales are found in *Magnalia*. Placed near the close of his epic history of New England, Mather's providence tales are read against the backdrop of the biographies of the early Puritan leaders, the history of Harvard College, the annals of the early New England Church, and the accounts of wars with the native Americans. Within the context of political, economic, religious, and military history, the sixth book of "Remarkables" emerges as social history; that is, it is less a catalogue of curiosities than a historical narrative of the people of New England. This is not to say that the earlier texts of Janeway and Increase Mather are in any way less than sober, but the same tale reprinted in the sixth book of Mather's epic history takes on weight and import by virtue of its context and the implicit equivalence of the *magnalia dei* on behalf of a William Bradford or a John Winthrop with those *magnalia dei* on behalf of seaman Philip Hungare or young Abigail Eliot, who are otherwise common folk. Correspondingly, God metes out his *terribilia* or terrible judgment upon the servant Mary Martin just as he did on the earlier Goodwife Anne Hutchinson.

Indeed, prior to the publication of *Magnalia Christi Americana*, historical books written in New England only rarely included narratives of the private lives of private men and women alongside accounts of the public events of public individuals. Edward Johnson's *History of New England* (1654), more familiarly known by its subtitle, *The Wonder-working Providence of Sions Saviour in New England,* focuses primarily on the installation of civic leaders and the establishment of churches throughout the New English colonies, including wondertales concerning public figures, while William Hubbard's *The Present State of New-England* (1677) chronicles economic and military encounters with the native Americans. Nathaniel Morton's *New Englands memoriall* (1669), like William Bradford's *Of Plymouth Plantation*, includes limited material concerning private lives, Morton recounting such events as James Pierce's death by lightning and Mrs. Mary Dyer's "monstrous birth."[3]

2. While book six of *Magnalia* is, in many ways, a culminating statement of Mather's persistent inquiry into "remarkables," it is not his final publication of providence tales. For example, his *Mirabilia Dei* appeared in 1719.

3. The tale of Mary Dyer (or alternately, Dier) is also found in Clarke, 259; Winthrop,

However, what we now consider social history represents a minor portion of the entire historical tract. To this extent, Cotton Mather's *Magnalia* departs from the model of historical texts in the seventeenth and early eighteenth centuries in America in that he incorporates the extraordinary occurrences in the lives of common men and women into his history of the political, religious, and economic leadership of New England. Indeed, he devotes an entire book of *Magnalia Christi Americana* to *magnalia dei* and *terribilia dei* of private individuals.[4] Recognizing that this is an exceptional shift in historical writing, Mather notes in his "General Introduction,"

> And into the midst of these Actions, I interpose an entire Book, wherein there is, with all possible veracity, a Collection made of Memorable Occurrences, and amazing Judgments and Mercies befalling many particular persons among the people of New-England.
>
> Let my readers expect all that I have promised them, in this *Bill of Fare;* and it may be they will find themselves entertained with yet many other passages, above and beyond their expectation, deserving likewise a room in History. (1:25)

Thus, at the outset of *Magnalia,* Mather acknowledges that his subject matter will include elements of social history as well as the accounts of the great deeds of great public figures, and argues that the exceptional narratives concerning private individuals constitute history. In this way, he is able to fuse two seemingly disparate modes of writing: recounting wonder-tales and accounting for more traditional historical events.[5]

Furthermore, the earlier wonderbooks and many of the earlier historical tracts cannot be considered true histories to the extent of Mather's

---

2:266; and Mather, *Magnalia* 2:519.

4. In part, book seven of *Magnalia* shares this narrative orientation. The volume announces that it documents the activities of "adversaries" of the church, and could be understood as part of Mather's ecclesiastical history. However, Mather elides ecclesiastical history and social history when he focuses on the actions of private individuals, such as Quakers, Separatists, Familialists, accused witches, and native Americans.

5. In this respect, Mather may have found a model for the authorship of *Magnalia* in the *oeuvre* of Samuel Clarke, who during his career wrote biographical narratives of such figures as Herod, Alexander the Great, Elizabeth I, and Charles the Great, as well as theological tracts (*A demonstration of the being and attributes of God and other writings* and *A discourse concerning the connexion of the prophecies in the Old Testament, and the application of this to Christ,* for example), religious conduct books (such as *Whole duty of a Christian* and *A Warning-piece to all drunkards and health-drinkers*), in addition to his magnum opus, *A mirrour or looking-glasse.* While Mather writes in each of these disparate veins in individual publications, he fuses his interest in political, historical, religious, and social argument within a single work, *Magnalia.*

accounts of often the same events. The collections authored by Clarke, Janeway, and Johnson—and one could include in this category Morton's *Memoriall,* the second book of William Bradford's *Of Plymouth Plantation,* and the journals of John Winthrop—should be more appropriately understood as chronicles rather than histories. Indeed, David Hall terms the works of Bradford and Winthrop "journal histories" (90), a journal relating a chronological sequence of events without the unifying structure that subsequent reflection and revision might supply. According to Hayden White, a chronicle or "journal history" may narrate a sequence of historical events, but a history creates a rhetorical framework that supports an argument surrounding those same events. Given that the building blocks of historical narrative are discrete details that can be readily organized in terms of chronology, when the historian asserts other than chronological relationships among otherwise discrete details, that historian fills in the logical gaps that the organizing principle of chronology cannot itself accomplish. That is, a historian not only recounts and thus represents events but also creates a narrative structure that points to the relative value of sets of historical detail, and then associates one element of the narrative to another by positing causation and ultimate significance. In this way, a historian emplots the events in a narrative that argues his or her coherent vision of those details.[6]

In addition, Hayden White insists that "historical events are value-neutral" (*Tropics,* 84). A set of events takes on value by virtue of the way in which a historian emplots these events.

> The same set of events can serve as components of a story that is tragic *or* comic, as the case may be, depending on the historian's choice of the plot structure that he considers most appropriate for ordering events of that kind so as to make them into a comprehensible story. (*Tropics,* 84)

White also finds that the plot and form of a historical narrative give evidence of the culture's values. To be sure, White goes considerably further in his analysis of the relationship between ascribing value to a historical detail and emplotting historical events. He asserts that

6. My understanding of the distinction between the historical texts of these authors is informed by Hayden White's theory of annals, chronicles, and histories; for a full exploration of his argument, see *The Content of the Form: Narrative Discourse and Historical Representation* (Baltimore and London: Johns Hopkins University Press, 1987), especially 1–25, and *Tropics of Discourse: Essays in Cultural Criticism* (Baltimore and London: Johns Hopkins University Press, 1978), 51–63.

narrativity, certainly in factual storytelling and probably in fictional storytelling as well, is intimately related to, if not a function of, the impulse
to moralize reality, that is, to identify it with the social system that is the
source of any morality that we can imagine. (*Content*, 14)

To that end, a historian's ability to create closure in his or her narrative, and
to build a coherent plot that works toward that resolution, is a direct result
of his fusing his chronicle of events with an ideology that is otherwise
extrinsic to those events. This fusion creates meaning and argument, and,
thus, fully realized historical narrative.

For example, *Of Plymouth Plantation*, which, next to Mather's *Magnalia*,
has attracted the most critical commentary of the above-mentioned
histories, has been problematic to critics because it lacks the fully articulated rhetorical unity of historical narrative. Stephen Carl Arch finds that
Bradford's book one is "integrated and carefully ordered," going so far as
to characterize the work as "mythic." At the same time, he determines
that book two "spirals down" and is the work of a "frustrated historian"
(*Authorizing*, 5). Walter Wenska is less convinced of the structure of the
first book and asserts that "our view of the history as a whole and of the
second book in particular remains partial, sometimes confused, and often
contradictory,"[7] while Robert Daly characterizes Bradford's second book
as "a tedious account of unsorted administrative details . . . in which all
coherence and confidence seem gone."[8] The diffuse and episodic construction of Bradford's text marks it, in White's terms, as a chronicle rather
than a fully realized history. One need only look to the two final entries in
Bradford's second book as evidence of his inability to construct historical
narrative. The author lists anno 1647 and anno 1648, but these are empty
entries, which, according to Bernd Engler and Oliver Scheiding, "seem to
document the historiographer's failure to order secular history along the
lines of an overruling master-narrative."[9] Closure, an essential element of
argument, is impossible for Bradford, which bespeaks his inability to construct a fully articulated history of the events of Plymouth Plantation.[10]

7. Walter P. Wenska, "Bradford's Two Histories: Pattern and Paradigm in *Of Plymouth
Plantation*," *Early American Literature* 13.2 (1978), 152.

8. Robert Daly, "William Bradford's Vision of History," *American Literature* 44.4 (1973),
557.

9. "Re-Visioning the Past: The Historical Imagination in American Historiography and
Short Fiction" in *Re-Visioning the Past: Historical Self-Reflexivity in American Short Fiction*
(Trier: Wissenschaftlicher Verlag Trier, 1998), 15.

10. For important statements on Bradford's historiography, see also Sacvan Bercovitch, *The
Puritan Origins of the American Self* (New Haven: Yale University Press, 1975), 45 and David

However, in the case of Cotton Mather's remarkables in book six of *Magnalia Christi Americana,* it is clear that the author makes sense and makes story of enigmatic events within his community by configuring them according to the imperatives of his culture's religious belief. Specifically, Mather creates history surrounding his wonder stories consistent with his belief in the agency of God in every event of man's life, divine providence.[11] That is, Cotton Mather creates a history by investing every element of his narrative with argument toward the agency of God. We see this at every level of narrative construction beginning with the title, *Magnalia Christi Americana.* From the title page onward, let no one be misled as to Mather's mission. The opening paragraph of his "General Introduction" to *Magnalia* supports the title in asserting his thesis:

> I WRITE the WONDERS of the CHRISTIAN RELIGION, flying from the depravations of Europe, to the American Strand; and, assisted by the Holy Author of that Religion, I do with all conscience of Truth, required therein by Him, who is the Truth itself, report the wonderful displays of His infinite Power, Wisdom, Goodness, and Faithfulness, wherewith His Divine Providence hath irradiated an Indian Wilderness. (1:25)

The historian has set as his objective the recording of evidence that God shaped the Puritan colonial venture in America and continues to shape the public and private ventures of his people. Mather's central argument is restated regularly throughout his text, and in the title of the sixth book, the reader is again returned to the import of his history, "Thaumaturgus. The Sixth Book of the New-English History: Wherein Very Many Illustrious Discoveries and Demonstrations of The Divine Providence in Remarkable Mercies and Judgments on Many Particular Persons Among the People of New-England, Are Observed, Collected, and Related" (2:339). The title

---

Levin, "William Bradford: The Value of Puritan Historiography" in *Major Writers of Early American Literature,* ed. Everett Emerson (Madison: University of Wisconsin Press, 1972), 26.

11. Cotton Mather's impulse to create fully realized historical narrative is not exclusively a feature of his public posture as a minister; his understanding of his private life is also informed by his faith in divine providence. As we see in his diary, many entries exhibit similar plotting and conclusion. See, for example, his account of the March 1693 death of his infant daughter due to immature development of the rectum. He yokes this tragedy to an earlier event when a witch frightened his pregnant wife, causing her temporary bowel dysfunction and promising much worse for the unborn child. Mather concludes his narrative with the moral that he "submitt unto the Will of my Heavenly Father without which, *Not a Sparrow falls unto the Ground*" which is an expression of his faith in God's continual intervention in the life of man. See *Diary of Cotton Mather 1681–1709,* 2 vols. (New York: Frederick Ungar, 1957), 1:164.

of each chapter and each subsection within the chapter as well as the introduction to each set of narratives issue an identical refrain. However tedious and unsophisticated this practice may seem to the modern reader, these assertions and reassertions are central to Mather's production of history as argument.

The motivation of book six of *Magnalia* is not exclusively that of asserting God's providence. This theological tenet is the underpinning of his larger design for the work. In the manner of Edward Johnson and Increase Mather, earlier writers whose work he emulated and at times borrowed from, Cotton Mather's primary goal for his *Magnalia* was to revive a waning commitment to Calvinist orthodoxy in New England.[12] In 1679 Increase Mather lamented that "there is doleful degeneracy appearing in the face of this generation, and no man can say but that the body of the present generation will perish both temporally and eternally."[13] In the opening pages of *Magnalia Christi Americana,* Cotton Mather echoes his father's words and confesses to being "smitten with a just fear of incroaching and ill-bodied *degeneracies*" in New England (1:40). To thwart the loss of Calvinist community in the colonies, Mather offers his *Magnalia.*

> [C]ertainly one good way to save that *loss,* would be to do something that the memory of the *great things done for us by our God,* may not be *lost,* and that the story of the circumstances attending the *foundation* and *formation* of this country, and of its *preservation* hitherto, may be impartially handed unto posterity. THIS is the undertaking whereto I now address myself. (1:40)

Thus, Cotton Mather's intention is to display the providential design for New England in order to inspire the present generation with the sacred role of their Puritan ancestors. To emphasize the relationship between those exalted ancestors and his contemporary readers, Mather speaks of the *"great things done for us by our God,"* and, in this way, he asserts that the sacred role and lofty mission of the early New English Puritans are also those of the present colonists.

---

12. Stephen Carl Arch details the specific challenges to the church and religious culture in New England that Mather wished to counter by publishing his *Magnalia.* See especially *Authorizing the Past,* 138–59. Arch also identifies the earlier challenges of the 1640s and 1650s to which Edward Johnson responds in *History of New England,* and those of the 1670s and 1680s that Increase Mather addresses in his historical writing. See *Authorizing the Past,* 59–87 and 92–135, respectively.

13. *A Call from Heaven To the Present and Succeeding Generations* (Boston, 1679), 19.

When Mather turns to social history in the sixth book of *Magnalia Christi Americana,* his "Remarkables of the Divine Providence Among the People of New England," he expands this claim. Not only has God worked wonders on behalf of the exalted public figures among us, but he also acts on behalf of private individuals.[14] Just as Mather laments the loss of awareness of New England's past glories in his preface to *Magnalia,* in his introduction to book six, he speaks to his contemporaries' loss of awareness of the wonderful works of divine providence in their daily lives.

> Unaccountable therefore and inexcusable is the *sleepiness,* even upon the most of good men throughout the world, which indisposes them to *observe* and much more to *preserve* the remarkable dispensations of Divine Providence towards themselves or others. (2:341)

Calling his readers to recognize their exceptional relationship to God, Mather also elides the history of the Puritan greats with the stories of his contemporaries to further assert the continuity of the Puritan errand in the new world. However, the *magnalia dei* on behalf of God's people is only one manifestation of God's providence. God also visits *terribilia dei* on New England, and book six documents many such testaments to God's wrath. For those readers who will not be called to religious vigilance by inspirational accounts of God's marvelous blessings, in chapter six of book six Mather speaks to the wisdom of fearing the Lord, and offers accounts of sinners and their inevitable discovery and punishment.

Additionally, in book six of *Magnalia,* Mather responds to current interest in scientific inquiry, chapter three being devoted to "Brontologia Sacra: The Voice of the Glorious God in the Thunder." Mather, who authored many scientific documents and was elected to the Royal Society in 1713 for his contributions in the field of natural history, acknowledges "the common laws of matter and motion" that describe this natural phenomenon. Yet, he immediately counters this assertion with a series of rhetorical questions: "But, still, who is the author of those laws, according whereunto things are thus moved into thunder? yea, who is the *first mover* of them?" For Cotton Mather, the answer is obvious. "Christians,

---

14. Mather's fusion of political, ecclesiastical, and military history with social history is another example of what Jan Stievermann has identified as Cotton Mather's project of *copia.* As Mather's "authoritative voice integrat[es] and transcend[s] all other voices," it also integrates and transcends disciplines—theology, politics, social history, and science, among them. See "Writing 'To Conquer All Things': Cotton Mather's *Magnalia Christi Americana* and the Quandary of *Copia,*" *Early American Literature* 39.2 (2004): 270.

'tis our glorious God" (2:366). Trumping the scientific truths held by his contemporaries with the wisdom that is the exclusive purview of the minister, Mather then attempts to decode God's message in the thunder. Mather wishes to ensure that contemporary science does not encroach on theology, so he subsumes science under the great umbrella of religion and asserts that all seemingly new knowledge simply manifests Christian theology and Calvinist religious practice.[15] In this way, Mather again is able to bind the experience of his contemporaries with the experience of the earliest Puritans in New England. Moreover, once he establishes the authority of theology over that of science, he is able to disquiet those readers who found solace in a materialist explanation of the natural phenomenon of thunder. Mather has reclaimed the mystery of thunder, and uses it to both exemplify God's providential design and encourage fear of the Lord, two of his objectives for *Magnalia Christi Americana*.[16]

As prelude to his work, Mather asserts the special authority of the minister to serve as the historian of Puritan society. In Mather's judgment, there is no one better suited to interpret God's meaning for man and woman as He operates in the daily events of their lives. Throughout the *Magnalia*, and at the opening of the sixth book, Mather stakes his claim: "To *regard* the illustrious displays of that PROVIDENCE wherewith our Lord Christ governs the world, is a work, than which there is none more *needful* or *useful* for a Christian: to *record* them is a work, than which, none more proper for a minister" (2:341). The laity is exhorted to marvel at the works of God, but a minister, such as Cotton Mather, is privileged to "record" those works, that is, to invest them with meaning within his historical narrative. Mather's assertion of the ethos of the minister *cum* historian is consistent with Hayden White's theory of the imperative of the historical narrator's pretense to moral authority. Indeed, White asks, "Has any historical narrative ever been written that was not informed not only by moral awareness but specifically by the moral authority of the narrator?" (*Content*, 21). Finally, at the center of Cotton Mather's argument is the axiom that all meaning is inherently religious, and thereby the exclusive purview of the minister. For Mather, there is meaning in worldly, temporal events only in their relationship to the divine and the eternal. Any earthly event is personally significant only as it speaks to one's spirituality, the condition of one's soul, and the prospect of one's eternal salvation

15. Winship speaks to the ways in which both Increase and Cotton Mather respond to scientific rationalism. See especially 93–110.

16. See also David D. Hall's discussion of Mather's attempt to wrest interpretation of natural phenomena from secular writers (109–15).

or damnation. More pointedly, a worldly event—be it a *magnalia dei* or a *terribilia dei*—has import in that it offers an unambiguous statement regarding the condition of one's soul.

As a means of compelling his readers with God's message in the events of New England, Cotton Mather's prose in *Magnalia Christi Americana* is marked by rhetorical flourishes that are rarely found in his father's more dispassionate narratives.[17] Where his father is concerned with precise historical detail—dates, the number of survivors, the cargo and tonnage of the ship, the direction in which the devil hurled the bricks at the house—Cotton Mather's accounts in *Magnalia Christi Americana* argue their case both by a surfeit of historical detail and by the tenor and structure of the prose. In a general introduction to *Magnalia,* Cotton Mather is mindful of his sacred charge as author of the ecclesiastical history of American Puritanism, and clearly states that his text is written with "all historical fidelity and simplicity" (1:25). Yet, Kenneth Silverman describes his prose as "distinctively showmanlike" (*Cotton Mather,* 159).[18]

Although Cotton Mather fashions himself as an "impartial historian" (1:29), he also acknowledges that readers may fault his writing for exhibiting "too much of *ornament*" (1:31). Even more important to the Calvinist minister, he worried that God would fault his prose style. Mather's biographer, Kenneth Silverman, reports that Mather was concerned that his passion for "plush language" should be met with God's retribution by making him stutter (*Cotton Mather,* 48–49). Indeed, the prose of *Magnalia Christi Americana* is replete with allusion not only to scripture, but also to the imaginative literature of the Greeks and Romans.[19] Compared to

17. This is consistent with William J. Scheick's observation concerning Cotton's Mather's *Parentator,* his biography of Increase Mather, as compared to Increase Mather's biography of his father, Richard Mather. Scheick describes *Parentator* as "more full-bodied [than his father's text], including glimpses of Increase as a person, details about his setting, and even transcripts of some of his dialogue with others" (*Two Mather Biographies,* 22). That is, Cotton Mather employs the devices of fiction—characterization, setting, and dialogue—that were not part of the earlier model of the genre of religious biography. In his discussion of the disparity of their prose styles, Michael Winship places weight on Increase Mather's interest in adhering to the standards of writing objective natural history, which were set by Robert Boyle (64–67).

18. David Levin issues a more moderate statement about the variety of Mather's prose styles in *Magnalia,* explaining that it varies widely depending upon the specific chapter, and he concludes that "the prose of the *Magnalia* is both baroque and plain." See *Cotton Mather: The Young Life of the Lord's Remembrancer, 1663–1703* (Cambridge and London: Harvard University Press, 1978), 266. See also Arch, 155–59. I would add that the prose of Mather's book six, which is the focus of this study, is more often artistic—even to the point of baroque—than otherwise.

19. See Gustaaf Van Cromphout's 1977 essay that explores the rhetoric of *Magnalia* as the work of a "Renaissance humanist."

Increase Mather's *Essay for the Recording of Illustrious Providences*, book six of *Magnalia* is marked by its emphatic prose. Although Cotton Mather takes several of his narratives in *Magnalia* directly from his father's text, he makes substantive stylistic changes in the narrative. He regularly inserts an adjective where there had been none, and where there is one adjective, Cotton Mather adds yet another. The drama of tricolons and exclamatory phrasings inject life into Cotton Mather's tales, as do the active voice constructions, the extended dialogue, and the directive voice of the narrator, these features being new to Cotton Mather's version. These rhetorical flourishes invite the reader's emotional involvement with the text, they continually return the reader to the argument of the text, and they invest the argument with urgency.

Austin Warren was one of the earliest scholars to identify Cotton Mather as a literary stylist, and exclaims that "the gust—the taste—of the *Magnalia* runs the range of the Puritan Baroque."[20] Likewise, Larzer Ziff identifies Mather's "lavish allusion, tireless unreeling of convoluted syntax, and insistent display of polylingualism" as elements of his pyrotechnical literary style.[21] At the same time, Ziff connects this feature of Mather's historical narrative to Mather's ethos as a historian and a teller of tales:

> . . . *Magnalia Christi Americana* starts with the epic convention of the writer as an oral transmitter of all known history, from the moment when the divinity created the natural world through the election of a special people with a special history; and throughout his book Mather relies heavily on anecdote, folklore, and hearsay to inform his work. He does not use evidence to construct a rationale for New England; rather, that rationale is a given, and he goes to the record of writings and the oral tradition to demonstrate that the given has been fulfilled. (303)

Ziff suggests that Mather's use of literary devices is not limited to his prose style. He situates his work within the tradition of fiction by drawing on earlier fictional material, as is a convention of imaginative letters. Likewise, his authorial ethos is consonant with that of epic literature.

Consistent with Hayden White's theory of historical narrative, Cotton Mather's use of literary devices allows him to make history of his father's chronicles. White observes that the historian employs prose techniques

20. "Grandfather Mather and His Wonder Book," *Sewanee Review* 72.1 (1964), 112.
21. "Upon What Pretext? The Book and Literary History," *Publications of the American Antiquarian Society* 95.2 (1985): 303.

that are traditionally considered literary—characterization, varied strategies of description, figurative language, repetition of motifs, dialogue, and so forth—because the process of creating historical narrative is so closely related to the strategies to create literary narrative. Beginning with features such as point of view and emplotment, which are characteristic of the development of fully realized history, Hayden White argues the "essentially *literary* nature of historical classics" (*Tropics*, 89). The literary features of the historical text serve the rhetorical goals of the historian by foregrounding a complex set of symbols by which the reader understands how and why events unfold. As White puts it, the historical narrative

> *describe[s]* events in the historical record in such a way as to inform the reader *what to take as an icon* of the events so as to render them 'familiar' to him. The historical narrative thus mediates between the events reported in it on the one side and the pregeneric plot structures conventionally used in our culture to endow unfamiliar events and situations with meanings on the other. (*Tropics*, 88)

According to White, that this is the goal of both the fiction and the nonfiction writer does not compromise the authority or integrity of the nonfiction writer; it simply explains the function and the tools of the historian.

An important structural element of Mather's artistic narrative is his foregrounding the context of his tales, without which they might appear to be a mere *omnium gatherum* of curiosities. The opening paragraph of "Christus Super Aquas," the first chapter of the sixth book, which is a collection of remarkable sea deliverances, provides an example of the importance of Mather's emphasis on contextualizing his work for the reader.

> They "that go down into the sea in ships, these do see the works of the Lord, and his wonders in the deep." And what if our collection of remarkable providences do begin with a relation of the wonderful works which have been done for them that "go down into the sea in ships," by that great Lord "whose is the sea, for he made it?" I will carry my reader upon the huge Atlantick, and, without so much as the danger of being made seasick, he shall see "wonders in the deep." (2:343)

Mather first offers his reader an assertion that in his time was a theological commonplace: God made the sea; thus they who observe the sea are privy to the wonderful works of God. He thus puts the reader on notice that the subsequent tales will serve as testimony to this theological statement. Secondly, the author addresses the reader directly, and predicts that through these tales, the reader will be metaphorically transported "upon the huge Atlantick," such will be the emotional impact of the experience of reading. Finally, through his use of the metaphorical expression, "I will carry my reader," Mather suggests an intimacy and a trusting relationship between author and reader, each device employed in the interest of securing his theological claim on his historical material.

In other passages, Mather's language reveals that the author is aware of his artistry and even relishes his writerly flourishes. Whereas he fashions the native Americans in stereotypical metonymical terms as "tawnies," and as allegorical "black Satans" and "*devils in flesh,*" he also uses more inventive, metaphorical expressions, such as "perfidious caitiffs," "Scythian *wolves* of our wilderness," "dragons," and "adders in the path." Attracted to clever phrasings, Mather appears to sneer at native Americans who were struggling to cross a muddy river bed, "if *mud* could add *blackness* to such miscreants." Similarly, he concludes an anecdote about a profligate, yet intriguingly unidentified, young man by appealing, "God make this young man our *warner;* his name was WARNER." Mather also attempts humor, as in his assertion that Quakers preach "Quackerism" (2:565, 665, 666, 637, 617, 396, 646). The author who makes a claim for the "simplicity" of his prose nonetheless makes ample use of linguistic and literary devices to motivate and secure the case for orthodox Calvinism.

Many critics have underscored Mather's frequent claims that he wishes to entertain as well as edify the reader of *Magnalia*. The selection of his material and the artistry of his narratives suggest that his goal is even more radical. Cotton Mather sought to popularize religious history, and the savvy author was acutely aware of the interests and tastes of his readership. As Michael T. Gilmore concludes, "Mather's entire career can be seen as an effort to breathe fresh life into the religion he inherited from his ancestors" (35). Extravagant and bizarre tales written in a witty and dramatic style would attract and retain an audience whose ear was dulled to Puritan sermonizers. Moreover, by the late seventeenth century, religious tracts that announce and explicate wonder-workings of God had heavy competition from secular, sensational publications on the same topic, works that Mather descried as "wretched books" (1:205).[22] The author's abiding reputation as an "old pedant" has somewhat obscured

22. See David D. Hall, 55 and 112–14.

current critical recognition that Cotton Mather knew his audience and his competition for that audience, and was more than willing to appeal to the contemporary taste by shaping his texts for his readers. Daniel Cohen has identified Mather's genius for capturing the attention of his readership by sensationalism in the design and language of the title pages of his broadsides, in addition to the elaborate and extravagant literary devices of his providence tales.[23] In the language of Daniel Cohen, "one man's providence is another's sensation" (10).

Cotton Mather's account in *Magnalia* of Mary Martin's infanticide illustrates how Mather uses artistry in the service of a fully articulated history. This tale also exhibits how the historian *cum* minister manipulates historical elements to construct a narrative of this event toward the larger goal of illustrating a religious principle.[24] Mather writes,

It hath been thought, that the *dying speeches* of such as have been executed among us, might be of singular use to correct and reform the crimes wherein too many do live: and it has been wish'd that at least some fragments of those dying speeches might be preserv'd and publish'd. Upon this advice from some good persons, I have stollen an hour or two, wherein I have collected some accounts of several ill persons, which have been cut off by the sword of *civil justice* in this land; and this collection I suffer to go abroad, in hopes that, among many other essays to suppress *growing vice,* it may signifie something with the blessing of Heaven thereupon, to let the vicious understand what have been the cries of our miserables when passing into another world. Behold, an history of criminals, whom the terrible judgments of God has *thunder-strook* into *pillars of salt.*

About the year 1646, here was one Mary Martin, whose father going from hence to England, left her in the house of a marry'd man, who yet became so enamour'd on her that he attempted her chastity.

Such was her weakness and folly, that she yielded unto the temptations of that miserable man; but yet with such horrible regret of mind, that begging of God for deliverance from her temptations, her plea was, "That if ever she were overtaken again, she would leave herself unto his justice, to be made a publick example."

---

23. *Pillars of Salt, Monuments of Grace: New England Crime Literature and the Origins of American Popular Culture, 1674–1860* (New York and Oxford: Oxford University Press, 1993), 7–11.

24. Mather first used the story of this crime as an embedded narrative in a sermon and then published his account in his 1697 *Terribilia Dei* (44–45) before reprinting this material in *Magnalia.*

Heaven will convince the sinful children of men, that the vows which they make, relying on the stability and resolution of their own hearts, are of no significancy. A chain of hell was upon her, and the forfeited grace of Heaven was with-held from her; she fell a *third* time into the sin against which her vows had been utter'd.

Afterwards going to service in Boston, she found herself to have conceiv'd; but she lived with a favourable mistress, who would admit and allow no suspicion of her dishonesty.

A question (like that convincing one of our Saviour's unto the woman of Samaria) was once oddly put unto her: "Mary, where is thy husband?" And one said also, "Did I not think thou wert an honest and sincere creature, I should verily think thou wert with child!" These passages, which were warnings from God unto her guilty soul, did serve only to strike her with amazement—not with any true repentance.

She conceal'd her crime till the time of her delivery; and then being deliver'd alone by her self in a dark room, she murdered the harmless and helpless infant; hiding it in a chest from the eyes of all but the jealous GOD.

The blood of the child cried, when the cry of the child it self was thus cruelly stifled. Some circumstance quickly occurr'd which oblig'd her friends to charge her with an unlawful birth. She deny'd it impudently. A further search confuted her denial. She then said, the child was dead born, and she had burn'd it to ashes. With an hypocritical tear, she added, "Oh that it were true, that the poor babe were any where to be seen!" At last it was found in her chest; and when she touch'd the face of it before the jury, the blood came fresh unto it. So she confessed the whole truth concerning it.

Great endeavours were used that she might be brought unto a true faith in the blood of the Lord Jesus Christ for the pardon of her blood-guiltiness; and, it may be, none endeavour'd it more than that reverend man, old Mr. Wilson, who wrote several sheets of pathetical instructions to her while she was in prison. That renown'd man, old Mr. Cotton also, did his part in endeavouring that she might be renew'd by repentance; and preach'd a sermon on Ezek. xvi. 20, 21: "Is this of thy whoredoms a small matter, that thou hast slain my children?" Whereof great notice was taken. It was hoped that these endeavours were not lost: her carriage in her imprisonment and at her execution was very penitent. But there was this remarkable at her execution: she acknowledged her *twice* essaying to kill her child before she could make an end of it: and now, through the unskillfulness of the executioner, she was turned off the ladder twice before she died. (2:404–5)

Mather's account of Mary Martin's crime is thick with pathos and high moralizing, and, as such, it strikes a different tenor from that of John Winthrop, who also recounts these same events in his *Journal:*

There fell out at this time a very sad occasion. A merchant of Plymouth in England, (whose father had been mayor there,) called [*blank*] Martin, being fallen into decay, came to Casco Bay, and after some time, having occasion to return into England, he left behind him two daughters, (very proper maidens and of modest behavior,) but took not that course for their safe bestowing in his absence, as the care and wisdom of a father should have done, so as the eldest of them, called Mary, twenty-two years of age, being in [the] house with one Mr. Mitton, a married man of Casco, within one quarter of a year, he was taken with her, and soliciting her chastity, obtained his desire, and having divers times committed sin with her, in the space of three months, she then removed to Boston, and put herself in service to Mrs. Bourne; and finding herself to be with child, and not able to bear the shame of it, she concealed it, and though divers did suspect it, and some told her mistress their fears, yet her behavior was so modest, and so faithful she was in her service, as her mistress would not give ear to any such report, but blamed such as told her of it. But, her time being come, she was delivered of a woman child in the back room by herself upon the 13 (10) (*December* 13) in the night, and the child was born alive, but she kneeled upon the head of it, till she thought it had been dead, and having laid it by, the child, being strong, recovered, and cried again. Then she took it again, and used violence to it till it was quite dead. Then she put it into her chest, and having cleansed the room, she went to bed, and arose again the next day about noon, and went about her business, and so continued till the nineteenth day, that her master and mistress went on shipboard to go for England. They being gone, and she removed to another house, a midwife in the town, having formerly suspected her, and now coming to her again, found she had been delivered of a child, which, upon examination, she confessed, but said it was still-born, and so she put it into the fire. But, search being made, it was found in her chest, and when she was brought before the jury, they caused her to touch the face of it, whereupon the blood came fresh into it. Whereupon she confessed the whole truth, and a surgeon, being called to search the body of the child, found a fracture in the skull. Before she was condemned, she confessed, that she had prostituted her body to another also, one Sears. She behaved herself very penitently while she was in prison, and at her death, 18 (1,) (March 18) complaining much of the hardness of her heart. She confessed, that the first and second time she committed fornication, she prayed for pardon, and promised to commit it no more; and the third time she prayed God, that if she did fall into it again, he would make her an example, and therein she justified God, as she did in the rest. Yet all the comfort God would afford her, was only trust (as she said) in his mercy through Christ. After she was turned off and had hung a space, she spake, and asked what they did mean to do. Then some stepped up, and turned the knot of the rope backward, and then she soon died.[25]

It would be foolish to suggest that Mather's and Winthrop's accounts could or should be identical. Yet, because the authors had access to approximately the same information concerning Mary Martin's infanticide, it is nonetheless instructive to note the differing selection and presentation of the events in the two narratives. First, Winthrop introduces this event as a "very sad occasion"—not an example of "growing vice," as Mather's didactic account would have it—and in this way, sets the tone and creates a context for a divergent narrative. While Winthrop calls on the reader's quiet reflection on a random occurrence that "fell out" in the community, Mather immediately enjoins the reader to recognize his or her own sinfulness and "correct and reform" personal wrongdoing.

Although more abbreviated than Mather's account, Winthrop's tale delivers more detailed information concerning Mary Martin's situation and her eventual crime; one might argue that the additional information serves to soften our stance regarding Mary Martin as murderess. For example, we learn from Winthrop that her grandfather was an English mayor and her father a merchant, which suggests that she comes from solid stock, a point that would have carried weight for the seventeenth-century reader. Further, she and her sister were both "very proper maidens and of modest behavior." Thus, in Winthrop's version, the ethos of the young woman is initially above reproach. Furthermore, when her father was obliged to return to England, "*he* took not that course for their safe bestowing in his absence, as the care and wisdom of a father *should* have done" (my emphasis). The married man, too, is an active agent in her ruin because Winthrop writes that he was "taken with her," "solicit[ed] her chastity," "obtained his

    25. *Winthrop's Journal 1630–1649*, ed. James Kendall Hosmer (New York: Barnes and Noble, 1959), 2:317–18.

desire," and "committed sin with her" "divers times." Writing the events large and valuing these details, John Winthrop demonstrates to the reader the shared responsibility for Mary Martin's virtue.

Yet, Mather suppresses those elements because they are inconsistent with his desire to present Mary Martin as a "pillar of salt," an "ill person" as opposed to a good person. Consequently, he does not give us the context of her situation and the context of her fall, and asks her to shoulder all responsibility for her misdeed. Mather's reader is led to believe that her father placed her wisely in a good home. The unnamed married man was merely "enamour'd on her," although she alone was weak and foolish. When she "falls" once, twice, and a third time, there is no longer mention of the man who simply disappears from the narrative because it is a history of the woman's sin. Mather omits other details that Winthrop includes because they would compromise the coherence of his history: the fact that she had a female child, that she cleaned the room after the delivery—details that many readers could easily invest with significance—and that the executioner needed to adjust the knot of the noose so that the slack end would pull tight.

Cotton Mather makes much of the fact that Mary Martin did not die immediately at the gallows; he tips his hat to physics by stating that "through the unskillfulness of the executioner, she was turned off the ladder twice before she died." However, he values providence over physics because he then insists that she suffered a double execution because she had attempted twice to murder her own child, symbolic retribution being a remarkable sign of God's hand.

Hayden White finds that "the demand for closure in a historical story is a demand . . . for moral meaning, a demand that sequences of real events be assessed as to their significance as elements of a moral drama" (*Content*, 21). For Mather, an awareness of divine providence, symbolic retribution, and *terribilia Dei* are the narrative mortar to the bricks of his history of Mary Martin, and consequently are evoked in summation. However, Winthrop's account has no real closure other than the end to the chronological events: "She soon died." Likewise, it has little coherence other than the sequencing of historical detail. Mather's account, on the other hand, achieves its unity—or what we might now call overemplotment—by what Hayden White describes as "a tailoring of the 'facts' to the requirements of the story form" (*Tropics*, 91). According to the information that is currently available, Mather does not falsify his facts; he merely tailors them to his argument and, in this way, creates a coherent history.[26]

---

26. Bernd Engler offers an excellent analysis of the implications of narrative coherence in

Because John Winthrop's chronicle is not attached to a given argument, he is free to provide a full range of historical information surrounding the infanticide. Indeed, Winthrop offers the reader difficult and graphic detail that might prejudice the reader against Mary Martin, if the author were burdened by this rhetorical claim on the material. Winthrop reveals that Mary knelt on her child's head to kill her, then "used violence to it." Given the range of available options, she chose a somewhat vicious method of murder; that is, she employed no tool to separate herself from the child in the act of murder, and chose instead to use her body to kill her baby's body. Likewise, the reader is told of Mary's subsequent sexual relationship with another man, which the seventeenth-century Puritan would understand as damning evidence of the woman's corruption. Indeed, the reader might be confused by Winthrop's seemingly conflicted stance toward Mary Martin. While he appears to implicate others in her crime, and thus mitigate our harsh response to the woman, he offers further evidence of her questionable character and ill deeds. One could perhaps account for Winthrop's broad and seemingly unprejudiced interest in the case of Mary Martin by citing his training as a lawyer and his position as a civic leader.[27] Detailed description of the crime and the crime scene would be important to Winthrop, as would the motivation of the criminal before the act, the defendant's prior and subsequent criminal offenses, and signs of remorse following the act. Responsible for governing the community, Winthrop might well be concerned about the social context of this crime, and thus might focus on those details that concern the familial and communal situation that would foster or otherwise contribute to criminal activity.

Likewise, Mather's pointed interest in the case is related to his training and position as a minister of the Church of Christ. In eighteenth-century New England, the good Puritan fully expected depravity from one's fellow man, and indeed from one's self. Such is the legacy of Adam's fall. However unworthy in the eyes of God, the Puritan lived and worshiped in hope of free grace of God that would ensure salvation in the afterlife. As a minister, Cotton Mather understood that his congregants faced their creator as individuals, not as a community, and thus spoke

American historical and historiographic texts in "The Dismemberment of Clio: Fictionality, Narrativity, and the Construction of Historical Reality in Historiographic Metafiction" in *Historiographic Metafiction in Modern American and Canadian Literature,* ed. Bernd Engler and Kurt Müller (Paderborn: Ferdinand Schöningh, 1994), 13–34.

27. I am grateful for a conversation with Reiner Smolinski that led me to consider the divergent education and profession of John Winthrop and Cotton Mather in chronicling the story of Mary Martin's infanticide.

to individuals in terms of saving souls one by one. In his casting the tale of Mary Martin as an illustration of the sinful woman, Mather's history describes an individual who alone is accountable to God for the murder of her child.

The subjects of most providence tales in book six are the common men and women who either show themselves as visible saints or pillars of salt as they respond in exceptional ways to extreme situations. Dramatic narratives of the seafarer compelled early New English readers because theirs was a seafaring culture. Not surprisingly, then, tales of remarkable sea deliverances became a staple of wonderbooks. James Janeway, Increase Mather, and Cotton Mather all published many such stories, and all three authored an account of the events surrounding Philip Hungare's shipwreck and rescue at sea. As in the varying accounts of Mary Martin's infanticide, the differences in their narratives are telling. The basic plot of their accounts—typical of many of the remarkable sea deliverances—is similar. A group of sailors is forced into a lifeboat when their ship is in danger. They manage to stow a few provisions in the craft, but when they find themselves without food, flying fish jump into the boat for their consumption. Then they catch a shark, and drink his blood to quench their thirst. Ultimately, they see land, come ashore in the West Indies, and live to tell of their miraculous deliverance.

Janeway's version of this tale is a brief account of less than three hundred words, but rich in detail, descriptive elements, and authorial observations. Five times in the narrative, Janeway interjects into the narrative a statement about the providential nature of the developing plot, noting, for example, that when the fish flies into the boat, "God's Providence now prov[es] the Caterer."[28] With a full complement of interjections such as "alas" and "at last," he embellishes his account with emotional descriptions, such as the raw fish providing nourishment "more acceptable than the greatest rarities and dainties at another time" (17). Nonetheless, the author also emerges as a careful historian in that he offers precision in the exact size of the original vessel, the number of seamen who gain a seat in the lifeboat, the number of leagues they sail, and the number of weeks they are adrift. His attention to factual accuracy extends to his dénouement, although the close of his narrative introduces ambiguity. Janeway recounts that God's gifts of food and drink gave the sailors hope of rescue, but then reveals that "alas, they were so weak, that when they came ashore, one or

---

28. *Mr. James Janeway's Legacy to his Friends: Containing Twenty Seven Famous Instances of Gods Providences in and about Sea-Dangers and Deliverances* (London, 1674), 17.

two of them dyed." Finally, although "most of them lived to declare the works of the Lord," others among them were since lost at sea, including his informant (17). If Janeway's purpose in writing the story of Philip Hungare were to extol God's miracles on behalf of his faithful, he compromises his argument repeatedly in the process of chronicling the tale. In particular, the tragic close of his narrative casts a shadow on the otherwise felicitous plot that he works toward constructing.

Increase Mather reprinted this material in abbreviated form in *Illustrious Providences,* his version excising most of the figurative or emphatic language of Janeway's account. In this fashion, Increase Mather's narrative may initially appear more objective or authoritive than his source material. Increase Mather's close to his tale, like that of Janeway's account, provides little conclusion to the events; rather they merely offer the final element in the chronology: "Some of them were so weak as that they soon died; but most of them lived to declare the works of the Lord."[29] For lack of resolution, his account shies away from definitive argument, and refuses final authority over the material.

Modern readers do not know the actual details of this Philip Hungare's shipwreck; we rely on the earliest extant account, that of Janeway. But because we know that James Janeway's and Increase Mather's accounts provide the source material for Cotton Mather's version, Mather's departure from his sources reveals the goals of his text. In *Magnalia Christi Americana,* Mather clearly shapes his history as a statement regarding God's judgment of the sailors. To this end, he omits details of the earlier chronicles that do not contribute evidence of his thesis, and would otherwise blur the objective of his history. He also returns to the emotional appeal of the Janeway version, injecting figurative language in his prose and drama in his plot. As in the earlier tales, God first sends fish to the sailors for food, then sends a larger fish whose blood quenches their thirst. Although both early tales indicate that these gifts are providential, Janeway and Increase Mather treat the fish merely as food and drink, sustenance for the physical body in anticipation of their safe return to shore. Janeway notes that the fish gave the sailors "hopes to release them out of this insupportable misery," but the narrative does not suggest that the "misery" is other than physical. However, Cotton Mather describes the first providential offering of flying fish as a "strange relief," inviting the reader to contemplate in what sense the gift of food is "strange" in its ability to sustain man. He later resolves

29. *Remarkable Providences Illustrative of the Earlier Days of American Colonisation,* 1684 (London, 1890), 13.

this tension in his account when he metaphorically describes the blood that quenches the thirst of the sailors as "cool waters to their thirsty souls" (1:347). Mather's figurative language from Proverbs 25:25—not found in the earlier versions—conflates physical sustenance with spiritual salvation. The argument of Cotton Mather's history, which is less prominent if indeed existent in Janeway's or Increase Mather's tales, is that Philip Hungare's rescue at sea bespeaks his salvation. When God offers these sailors food to sustain them throughout their trials, he reveals his gift of free grace to these men.

Consonant with his thesis, Mather concludes his narrative with their safe arrival in the West Indies. His historical account suppresses the death of several among them, because to include such material would compromise his singular, definitive religious statement regarding divine providence. Mather would not want his reader to query why God would save a man simply to dispose of him immediately thereafter with no clear explication of the meaning of this death for the people of New England. Thus, Mather tailors his narrative as befits the rhetorically self-conscious historian.

Tales of remarkable sea deliverances were compelling to the people of New England in the seventeenth and eighteenth centuries because they depended so strongly on the sea and were acutely aware of its dangers. More importantly, though, readers of such tales would apprehend the symbolic value of this genre. All of God's creatures are metaphorically at sea in this insecure world, so fraught with spiritual hazard. Yet, when God offers man food to eat and blood to drink, motifs that suggest the sacrament of communion, he is extending a gift of free grace, man's only true security. Hayden White observes that a certain form of historical representation

> consists of nothing but plot; its story elements exist only as manifestations, epiphenomena of the plot structure, in the service of which its discourse is disposed. Here reality wears a face of such regularity, order, and coherence that it leaves no room for human agency, presenting an aspect of such wholeness and completeness that it intimidates rather than invites imaginative identification. (*Content,* 21)

Indeed, Cotton Mather asserts a universe which "leaves no room for human agency" and, to the contrary, insists that faith in an omniscient and omnipotent God as creator of the world and judge of man implies belief that, in the words of his father, Increase Mather, "the providence of

God is extended to the least and most inconsiderable things that happen in the world."[30] The resolution of the plot of each tale—whether the tale recounts a rescue at sea, a Satanic possession, an extraordinary conversion, an Indian captivity, a medical cure, or a death—serves to make only one statement: God illustrates his power over man and his judgment of man in the events of the world. *Terribilia dei* with their tragic plots are instructive of the tragic condition of one man's soul, while the comic plots of *magnalia dei* are indicative of the felicitous state of another man's soul. Virtue is rewarded, and vice punished. Cotton Mather's remarkables are, then, somewhat ironic in that the goal of his compendia of exceptional events is the argument that there is, finally, nothing truly exceptional in this world; all is subject to divine "regularity, order, and coherence." Even disorder is part of the divine scheme.

The sole truly dramatic element in the tales of remarkable occurrences is the specific and often symbolic character of God's reward or punishment toward his saints and sinners. It remains only for the minister to explicate—in a definitive and moralistic conclusion—the significance of divine judgment. Mrs. William Dyer, who was notorious for holding "about *thirty* monstrous opinions" on theological matters, delivered of "about *thirty* monstrous births at once" (2:519). Drunken men perish by tumbling into the fire in advance of their falling into the eternal flames (2:395). Those who issue false oaths often suffer from their rash statements, such as Wollery who was blinded when he swore that if he were guilty of a certain crime, then the devil might put out his eyes (2:393). Likewise, when one of God's faithful servants is mindful to pray—however briefly—in a moment of trial, God answers his prayer. When the "honest carpenter" lost control of his lumber, which was positioned immediately over the heads of his eight children, he asked God to redirect its fall, a feat that, according to Mather, God performed in recognition of the carpenter's righteousness (2:356). Throughout *Magnalia Christi Americana,* when God speaks to man through symbolic events, Cotton Mather argues that he is privileged to discern the voice of God because of his clerical wisdom. As such, the sixth book of *Magnalia* codifies the social history of seventeenth-century New England according to the divine order and will that Mather perceives in their world, and does so in an imaginative way that enlightens and engages its readership.

---

30. *A doctrine of divine providence open and applied* (Boston, 1684), 11.

Chapter 3

ॐ

"A Wilderness of Error"

EDGAR ALLAN POE'S
REVISION OF PROVIDENTIAL TROPES

When Larzer Ziff observed that Cotton Mather's providence tales in book six of *Magnalia Christi Americana* was "the stuff of novelists," he was speaking generally of the artful construction, the inventive language, and the enormous appeal of these strange tales. However, he could have been speaking also of the ways in which later American fiction writers have found the *Stoff* of literature—as well as tropes, characters, and even dialogue—in Mather's tales. Edgar Allan Poe not only was a master of the short story, but was a master of adapting the plots of earlier fiction to his own use. Many critics have looked to the works of European authors as source material for Poe's fictive invention, and it is clear that Poe read broadly and borrowed liberally from European Medieval and Renaissance literature as he approached his own writing projects.[1] Yet, it is also true that Poe looked to his own literary heritage, the legacy of early American authors, as source material for his fiction. In particular, his work exhibits the influence of the motifs and narrative form of the early American providence tale, such as those in the sixth book of Cotton Mather's *Magnalia Christi Americana*.

While it is abundantly clear that the adult Edgar Allan Poe did not adhere to a specific religious creed—Christian or otherwise—it is equally clear that he was more than conversant with scripture and the many issues of Christian theology and religious practice that commanded the attention of his contemporaries. Like his character William Wilson, Poe attended religious services while he was a student in England, and subsequently

---

1. This aspect of Poe's career is well documented in Burton R. Pollin's *Discoveries in Poe* (Notre Dame and London: University of Notre Dame Press, 1970).

he was required to attend religious exercises at West Point.[2] William Mentzel Forrest's comprehensive documentation of biblical allusions in Poe's fiction and poetry attests to the author's thorough education in scripture.[3] Moreover, Jules Zanger has identified Poe's boyhood exposure to the conservative evangelical movement in his family's Richmond congregation.[4] Bishop Richard Channing Moore, minister of the Protestant Episcopal Monumental Church where the Allan family had a pew, was an impassioned evangelical preacher in the tradition of Jonathan Edwards, and impressed the young Poe to the extent that he would mention him a decade later in his review of Francis L. Hawk's *Contributions to the Ecclesiastical History of the United States—Virginia* in the *Southern Literary Messenger*.[5] Poe's attendance at Moore's services notwithstanding, Zanger argues that the author "grew up in a culture in which the principles of religious revivalism developed and rationalized by Jonathan Edwards in the eighteenth century continued to operate in a widespread and pervasive fashion" (99).

Central to this study is Edgar Allan Poe's familiarity with providential history. Poe's 1836 review of Hawks's *Contributions to the Ecclesiastical History of the United States* demonstrates his knowledge of the goals and conventions of this historiographical mode by way of his persistent reference to George Bancroft's 1834 *History of the United States*. Bancroft, one of the most celebrated early nineteenth-century historians, was dedicated to perpetuating the early Puritan understanding of the national history as part of God's design for his chosen people.[6] George Bancroft was not alone in embracing the theory of providential history in nineteenth-century America. Indeed, many historians and authors of diverse literary works subscribed to this belief. The same issue of the *Southern Literary Messenger* in which Poe's review appeared carried an essay on "Manual Labor Schools," advocating an educational policy based on God's plan for

2. That Poe's dismissal from the military academy was based in part on his absence from church services in January 1831 suggests that this was a requirement of West Point cadets. See Kenneth Silverman, *Edgar A. Poe: Mournful and Never-Ending Remembrance* (New York: HarperCollins, 1991), 66–67.

3. See *Biblical Allusions in Poe* (New York: Macmillan, 1928).

4. See "Poe's 'The Pit and the Pendulum' and American Revivalism," *Religion in Life* 49 (1980), 99–101. Zanger uses this biographical information to support his interesting and convincing thesis that Jonathan Edwards's Enfield sermon "Sinners in the Hands of an Angry God" is a source text for Poe's "The Pit and the Pendulum."

5. *Southern Literary Messenger* 2.4 (1836), 282–86.

6. See pages 90–91 for a fuller exposition of Bancroft's historiographical objective and that of other antebellum historians.

the bodies and minds of young men and God's special disposition toward the young men of this nation.[7] Similarly, the lead piece in the following issue was Benjamin Franklin's "A Lecture on the Providence of God in the Government of the World" in which Franklin debates aspects of eighteenth-century thinking on divine will, yet concludes that God directs the daily life of his people through his providence.[8] Although it is difficult to believe that Edgar Allan Poe did not read Cotton Mather's *Magnalia Christi Americana* when it was reprinted to such acclaim in 1820, he would, nevertheless, have been steeped in the language and the literary forms of providential history and the providence tale. Such notions were not only in the air: they were pervasive in his culture, and he circulated them as editor of the *Southern Literary Messenger*.

Within his creative work, Poe appropriates the generic conventions of Puritan providence tales in the form of early American gallows confessions, remarkable sea deliverances, and accounts of "self-murder" in such stories such as "The Black Cat," "MS. Found in a Bottle" and "William Wilson," and in the novella *The Narrative of Arthur Gordon Pym*. However, Edgar Allan Poe is no Puritan. His fiction mirrors the structure and language of these providence tales, yet rejects the premise of the genre. When Poe evokes Cotton Mather's topoi, he creates readerly anticipation of its themes of epiphany, regeneration, and salvation—themes that he ultimately refuses to realize. Contrary to Mather's accounts, Poe's tales give voice to the man who will not confess and the sailor whom God will not save, and Poe does so to establish ironic distance between the early eighteenth-century spiritual fictions of American belief and the nineteenth-century dark romantic fictions of the self.

More specifically, Poe's short fiction expresses his rejection of the theory of divine providence that enabled authors such as Cotton Mather to create history and story from events that occurred in colonial New England. In the absence of a belief in divine order and divine intervention, Poe is, correspondingly, unable to achieve the coherence of plot and the tight, definitive closure of the earlier providence tales. When Hayden White asks, "Could we ever narrativize without moralizing?" (*Content*, 25), the reader of Mather's tales must affirm that this author is able to construct coherent narrative only because of the moral structure that imposes itself on the emplotted events. However, when Poe takes up the tropes, plots, and

---

7. Rev. E. F. Stanton, "Manual Labor Schools," *Southern Literary Messenger* 2.4 (1836), 244–52.

8. "Mss. of Benjamin Franklin: A Lecture on the Providence of God in the Government of the World," *Southern Literary Messenger* 2.5 (1836), 293–95.

even the dialogue of the Puritan providence tale, yet refuses to subscribe to the theological underpinning of this genre, his narratives exhibit the stress of working in counterpurpose. His plots are often ruptured, his narrators assume limited authority, and his closures are aborted or ambiguous. As Poe dismantles Mather's plots by simultaneously invoking and undermining their reliance on providential history, his characters are thus removed from Mather's neatly ordered, theocentric world, and are relegated to a modern "wilderness of error," as he puts it in "William Wilson."[9]

The implications of Poe's appropriation of providence tales are both numerous and important. By breaking with the fundamental notion of divine providence as a national precept and an ordering principle for our community's narratives, the nineteenth-century author is asking his reader to envision another mode of emplotment for the private narratives of the self and for our public accounts. The new plot must either discover alternate comic plots to express our personal and public optimism, or the plot may indeed be tragic. That Mather's providence tales bear the weight of historical documents puts additional pressure on the writer who endeavors to recraft their plots.

Additionally, Poe's reconfiguration of providential literature offers a key to the nature of the gothic mode in American literature, and suggests that gothic literature's insecure narrative authority, fractured plotting, and ephemeral closure reveal its rejection of the ideology that it invokes. Consequently, the instability of its generic conventions bespeaks the author's insecurity in the philosophical and religious beliefs supporting the historical narrative that it seeks to disrupt. Teresa Goddu has argued that American gothic literature does not seek to escape its historical moment, as critics have previously assumed, but instead "challenges the critical narratives of American literary history." Speaking to the relationship between the gothic mode's darker themes and its structural difficulties, she notes that "in its narrative incoherence, the gothic discloses the instability of America's self-representations; its highly wrought form exposes the artificial foundations of national identity" (10).

One might also see Poe's attempt to undercut the narratives that establish national identity—such as those framed by Mather, one of the earliest, most prominent, and longstanding pillars of New England—as part of his rivalry with contemporary New England writers. As Kenneth Silverman observes, Poe

9. In *Tales and Sketches,* ed. Thomas Ollive Mabbott (Urbana and Chicago: University of Illinois Press, 2000), 427. All quotations from Poe's short fiction are from this edition.

had been rankled by what he and others considered the smugness of many New England writers and their claim to social, moral, and literary superiority over other regions of the country. He planned in the "Stylus," he said, to "make war to the knife against the New-England assumption of 'all the decency and all the talent.'" (*Poe*, 200)

Counterplotting the popular providence tales of Cotton Mather would allow Poe to attack the core of conservative New England's social establishment, religious community, and literary circles with one blow.

Irrespective of authorial motivation, much of Poe's fiction provides valuable evidence for Goddu's thesis regarding the construction of gothic fiction. Cotton Mather's providence tales, like those of Increase Mather, James Janeway, and others, rely on several key structural elements—the omniscient ministerial narrator, an assertion of the historicity of the account, and a firm sense of divine causation leading to a singular conclusion that affirms God's judgment of the events. Every comic plot celebrates the miracles that God effects on behalf of his faithful, whereas every tragic plot warns the reader of God's terrible punishment of man's sin. At the same time, this genre of narrative also argues for the divine approbation of the mythic errand into the wilderness and the divine presence in founding the New English colonies in North America. However, Poe's narratives that mirror providence tales defy each of these structural elements, as they also challenge the pieties inherent to the genre.

First, Poe's fiction challenges Mather's statements concerning authorship by replacing the omniscient, ministerial narrator with a self-proclaimed unreliable narrator. The minister who alone can decode God's message for man in the events of the world is thus replaced by an otherwise common man who in "The Tell-Tale Heart" is "very, very dreadfully nervous" or "dizzy" in the case of "A Descent into the Maelstrom," or who problematically protests being called mad in both "Eleonora" and "The Black Cat" (792, 578, 638, 849). The ethos of Poe's narrators is not that of the wise bard or the community historian, rather that of the drunkard, the convicted murderer, the card shark, and the womanizer. To confront directly the issue of narrative reliability, in the opening sentence of "The Black Cat" and in the final sentence of "A Descent into the Maelstrom," the narrator indeed tells his reader that he does not expect to be believed. The narrative voice of "The Black Cat" insists that he does not seek the reader's confidence, while that of "A Descent into the Maelstrom" suggests that those who believe his account are foolishly gullible. Contrary to Mather's

impulse to monitor the reader's interpretation of his narratives by layer-
ing his accounts with authorial explication of each detail of each event,
Poe insists that his reader rely on his own wits to decode the ambiguous and often contradictory information that the text displays. Cotton
Mather's readers are obliged to subordinate their personal observations
of their seventeenth-century and eighteenth-century world and its texts
to the didactic, religious interpretation of the minister. Yet, Poe's readers
are virtually abandoned for lack of narrative authority to puzzle their way
through their complex and often chaotic nineteenth-century world and its
texts. Much like Poe's characters, his readers are forced to wander a "wilderness of error." The author demands that his audience read the text as
he or she reads the world. If the text of the world is enigmatic, the author's
text that purports to interpret the world only adds an additional layer of
insecurity.

Where Poe's narrators advertise their accounts as unreliable and
implausible, the plot itself often defies the normal standards of causation
that contribute to verisimilitude. Critics can only postulate why Ligeia dies,
and surely cannot say with any certainty why she returns. When William
Wilson murders William Wilson, who kills whom and why? Poe's narrators address this issue by asserting that a quest for causation within the
tale—providential causation or otherwise—is a "weakness" ("The Black
Cat," 853). With limited adherence to statements of causation, Poe's narrators naturally struggle to reach conclusion, and, in many cases, simply
close their accounts with a final chronological element independent of any
culminating observation or evaluation. In lieu of resolution, the Prefect in
"The Murders in the Rue Morgue" can explain only what did not happen,
and the narrator of "The Gold Bug" throws up his hands to exclaim, "Who
shall tell?" (568, 844) Hayden White has argued that "the demand for closure in the historical story is a demand . . . for moral meaning, a demand
that sequences of real events be assessed as to their significance as elements
of a moral drama" (*Content*, 21). He pushes this argument further by the
claim that

> if every fully realized story, however we define that familiar but concept-
> ually elusive entity, is a kind of allegory, points to a moral, or endows
> events, whether real or imaginary, with a significance that they do not
> possess as a mere sequence, then it seems possible to conclude that
> every historical narrative has as its latent or manifest purpose the desire
> to moralize the events of which it treats. Where there is ambiguity or

ambivalence regarding the status of the legal system, which is the form in
which the subject encounters most immediately the social system in which
he is enjoined to achieve a full humanity, the ground on which any closure
of a story one might wish to tell about a past, whether it be a public or a
private past, is lacking. (*Content*, 14)

Thus, to express his distrust of the Calvinist underpinnings of the providential narrative, Poe rejects not only the principle of causation, divine or
otherwise, but also the formulaic, singular closure that is essential to the
genre. By dismantling the structural conventions of the providence tale,
Poe sets his fiction in ironic relationship with the grander ambitions of the
early American works he evokes.

Significant, too, is Poe's attempt to blur the distinction between fiction
and nonfiction prose. At times he makes direct claims to writing within the
framework of historical or journalistic genres as in "The Mystery of Marie
Roget" and *The Narrative of Arthur Gordon Pym*. Frequently, he relies on
detailed information of date, place, names, ships, cargo, and tonnage to
secure the guise of historicity in his fiction. Invoking the conventions of
historical tracts, Poe's seafaring tales mirror the popular Renaissance travel
narratives of Richard Hakluyt and Samuel Purchas as well as the seven-
teenth- and eighteenth-century wondertales of remarkable sea deliverances
of James Janeway, Increase Mather, and Cotton Mather. In addition, Poe's
tales of intemperance and crime are composed in the vein of the gallows
confessions popularized by any number of early New English ministers,
Cotton Mather among them. Hayden White would not be surprised by
the generic affinity between Poe's fiction and the larger culture of nonfiction, White's analysis of historical writing centering on the use of literary
device to construct historical narrative. Indeed, Poe anticipates White's
theoretical stance. In his 1836 review of Francis L. Hawks's *Contributions
to the Ecclesiastical History of the United States of America*, Poe draws a distinction between "naked facts" and a crafted historical narrative of those
facts. He further acknowledges that the facts documented in *Ecclesiastical
History* are "arranged" and "shaped" by the historiographer, a position that
Hayden White would later theorize (282).

There is considerable evidence within American literary history to
support White's thesis regarding the symbiotic relationship between fiction
and nonfiction genres. Daniel Cohen has studied the close relationship
between seventeenth- and eighteenth-century accounts of serious crimes
and resultant gallows sermons and nineteenth-century crime fiction.

David S. Reynolds, too, has identified the roots of eighteenth- and nineteenth-century literature in the period's sensational and sometimes sordid journalism and other nonfiction accounts of social ills. Execution sermons were the primary form of criminal literature until the 1730s, but were immediately followed by equally popular, but surely worldlier, crime fiction, which was modeled after the earlier religious genre. As Cohen observes, "one man's providence is another's sensation" (10). Subsequently, in the antebellum period, many authors—Poe, Melville, and Hawthorne among them—looked to popular journalism to nourish their literary imagination.[10] This medium included not only the major newspapers, but also what Reynolds terms the "seamy social texts" of penny papers, trial reports, and crime pamphlets (171).

Daniel Cohen also looks to the material text as evidence for the symbiotic relationship between these nonfiction and fiction genres in early American texts, and notes the historical development of the title pages of these books and broadsides.[11] Cohen offers the example of a gallows sermon published by Increase Mather in 1675 that advertises itself in large font and boldface type as "A Sermon" with the title page including two scriptural quotations and two moralistic commonplaces. The title page also identifies the author as "Teacher of a Church of Christ." By contrast, in the smallest font of the page, the reader learns the briefest details of the crime: two men had murdered their master. The language and composition of this title page advertise the text primarily as a religious document, and only secondarily as reportage of a current event. However, the language and composition of later examples of gallows sermons illustrate the marked shift in this genre. Cotton Mather's *Pillars of Salt,* published only some twenty years later in 1699, advertises itself most prominently as "An History" of "Capital Crimes" as well as "Speeches" by the criminals, these three phrases in boldface with the largest font. A single quotation from scripture is included in small font. In a subordinate position, under the announcement of the history, the crimes, and the speeches, is appended the following note: "Whereto is added, For the better Improvement of this History, A Brief Discourse abut the Dreadful *Justice* of God, in Punishing of SIN, with SIN." The implication of the language and the visual presentation of this statement is that the religious admonition is secondary to the sensational crime story. Finally, Cotton Mather's 1713 gallows sermon

10. See Reynolds, *Beneath the American Renaissance,* especially 171–81.

11. See Cohen 7–11. Daniel E. Williams also explores the increasing sensationalism in such tracts in his introduction to *Pillars of Salt: An Anthology of Early American Criminal Narratives* (Madison, WI: Madison House, 1993), 58–63.

entitled *The Sad Effects of Sin* highlights the single word "Murder" on the title page. Missing is the biblical quotation that was requisite for the title page of the genre ten years earlier, although foregrounded is the lurid account of crime.

Clearly, Cotton Mather was aware of his readers' appetite for the story of crime that gave occasion to his sermonizing, and was eager to take full advantage of their worldly interests in order to inculcate his audience with his religious principles. Later authors, such as Poe, were also alert to the value of these texts at the level of fiction, and finally relish making a statement regarding the fictive element in nonfiction writing. Poe replaces the definitive, coherent assertions of our national visions and our national vices with ambiguous and often incoherent statements in order to problematize our American mythologies of self and society. As White has shown, historical narratives lend the comfort of completeness and coherence to otherwise frightening and disorderly events; Poe's gothic revision of historical narrative unmasks the nonfiction, reveals it as fiction, and displays its terror and incoherence.

Poe's Remarkable Sea Deliverances

The tale of sea deliverance is a staple of providential literature. James Janeway's *Legacy* is devoted exclusively to such accounts, and Cotton Mather dedicates the opening chapter of book six of *Magnalia Christi Americana* to testimonies of miracles during shipwrecks. Edgar Allan Poe reprises the formulaic accounts of remarkable sea deliverances in a number of his works whose drama centers on distress at sea and whose plot and language parallel those of the earlier remarkables. The earlier narratives were, of course, both written and read as nonfiction, although the modern reader easily recognizes the dramatic and even melodramatic plotting and phrasing of such texts. However, Poe's tales of disasters at sea develop a contrary strategy: the author offers many signals that his tales are based on reality, but undermines the verisimilitude throughout the narratives.[12]

In the 1831 tale "MS. Found in a Bottle," Poe's narrator initially identifies himself as a methodical, diligent man, and claims that "no person could be less liable than myself to be led away from the severe precincts of

---

12. Pollin speaks to this very issue: "In the *Baltimore Saturday Visiter* of October 12, 1843, Poe had published the first of his tales of sea horror, 'MS. Found in a Bottle,' conceived entirely in the spirit of the hoax. Similar was *The Narrative of Arthur Gordon Pym of Nantucket*, which was issued as a book, in 1838, 'edited' by Poe" (168).

truth by the *ignes fatui* of superstition" (135). An exclusively rational man, he also derides "moralists" and actually delights in discovering the inevitable errors in their arguments. However, once in peril at sea, this unlikely believer acknowledges that his shipwreck places him "on the brink of eternity," and his deliverance is not only a "miracle" but a "miracle of miracles" (143). The shift in language signaling a shift in creed, Poe's narrator undergoes a form of conversion. Echoing Mather's accounts where the sea deliverance is occasion for regeneration or a sign of salvation, Poe's narrator confesses that with the extraordinary events at sea "a new sense—a new entity is added to my soul" (141). Indeed, the man examines his "very soul" and "ponder[s] upon [his] destiny"; he feels ashamed, trembles, and expresses both hope and despair as he approaches "the blackness of eternal night" (145, 146). The narrator's sentiments and the language used to express these sentiments are precisely those of a conversion narrative.

Yet, Poe's object in this tale is not to bear witness to God's mercy. He invokes the topoi of the Puritan providence tale for the purpose of subverting the spiritual motivation of this fiction form. Poe's narrator is not the man whom God will save from the ship's wreckage. In fact, he drowns, and does so even as he invokes the name of God. As such, Poe's story gives voice to the man whom God will not save. Thus, in this tale, Poe writes an alternate history of the American seafarer that stands in opposition to the history that Cotton Mather fashioned to exhibit the wonders of Christ in the new world.

There is no fully articulated dénouement to Poe's tale, only the final chronological element in the man's life: he died. Within the framework of Hayden White's analysis of historical narrative, the resistance to resolution other than chronological conclusion signals a resistance to disclose meaning in the narrative. However, that this tale is framed as a "MS. Found in a Bottle" begs the reader to speculate on the message that the narrator wished to communicate. Poe's message, however, is ambiguous. We are led to surmise that, contrary to the belief in providential history, God does not always protect his faithful or perhaps God never participates in the events of this world. The narrator may wish the reader to understand that the shipwreck conversions or deathbed conversions of Calvinist tracts are a sham, and part of the narrator's terror is his realization that he has not received God's grace. The possibilities are surely multiple, and in this respect, defy the convention of the singular, definitive, and moralizing closure of the genre of providential literature. The sole terrifying message of this flagon tossed to sea is that the critical questions that probe our understanding of ourselves, our life in this world, and our life in the next can never be answered with any security. We will struggle with these questions in terror and agony, and the answers will be denied us until our struggle is ended, and it is too late. Ultimately, the chance of our attaining great wisdom is as probable as our receiving a message in a sea-borne bottle. In Poe's words, such knowledge is a "never-to-be-imparted secret, whose attainment is destruction" (145). Likewise, the probability of imparting great wisdom to our fellow man is as likely as posting it to him in a bottle at sea.

Studies of *The Narrative of Arthur Gordon Pym,* an enigmatic text that is often compared to "MS. Found in a Bottle," frequently center on problems of narrative coherence of this novella. J. Gerald Kennedy speaks of the text as "patch-work narrative," and Paul Rosenzweig laments that the work is "frustratingly protean in form."[13] However, Curtis Fukuchi finds that Pym's faith in providential design informs the narrative, and argues convincingly that this religious conviction both motivates and unifies the text.[14] A cursory reading of the text will indeed confirm the persistent reference to divine intercession on behalf of Pym and his fellow sailors. Yet, when *Pym* is approached not only as statement concerning divine providence, but also as a statement concerning the literature of divine providence, the text changes color.[15] Despite Pym's claim of confidence in his voyage, which is fueled in part by his confidence in the special mercy of God toward him, Poe's invocation and subsequent defiance of the conventions of early American literature of divine providence cast doubt on Pym's faith.

13. J. Gerald Kennedy, The Narrative of Arthur Gordon Pym *and the Abyss of Interpretation* (New York: Twayne, 1995), 38, and Paul Rosenzweig, "'Dust Within the Rock': The Phantasm of Meaning in *The Narrative of Arthur Gordon Pym*" in *Studies in the Novel* 14.2 (1982): 137. See also J. V. Ridgely's essay, "Tragical-Mythical-Satirical-Hoaxical: Problems of Genre in *Pym*" in *American Transcendental Quarterly* 24.1 (1974): 4–9, which surveys the scholarship that attempts to attach *Pym* to generic conventions.

14. See Curtis Fukuchi, "Poe's Providential *Narrative of Arthur Gordon Pym*" in *Emerson Society Quarterly* 27.3 (1981): 148–56. Fukuchi argues that "the human plots and counterplots in the narrative are played out against this divine plot, and their repeated collapse suggests the inadequacy of materialistic quests and reinforces the increasingly disinterested motives that Pym displays in his providential survival and return" (148). Fukuchi also describes *Pym* as a "prophetic text" in that his study is predicated on his reading of a felicitous resolution to the work (155). Like Paul John Eaken in "Poe's Sense of an Ending," *American Literature* 45.1 (1973): 1–22, Fukuchi believes that Pym survives his voyage and gains access to divine knowledge; yet Poe withholds this wisdom from the reader.

15. J. Gerald Kennedy's reading of *Pym* speaks to the reference to divine providence and, somewhat generally, to conventions of the "providential novel." See The Narrative of Arthur Gordon Pym *and the Abyss of Interpretation,* 38–40, 81–83.

Read against the backdrop of such early texts, *The Narrative of Arthur Gordon Pym* emerges as a complex variant of the providential deliverance at sea. The novella chronicles the sea voyage of Pym and Augustus, two young men given to intemperance and willfulness. Within the context of Mather's sea adventures, one might anticipate the conversion of one or both men as they mature intellectually and spiritually during their voyage, especially when confronted with extreme circumstances that almost appear to be designed by God to test their souls. However, neither young man finds salvation through earthly trials; Augustus does not survive the voyage and Pym survives for a time, but reveals neither the culminating experiences aboard the *Jane Guy* nor the meaning of the voyage.[16] Although Poe invokes the language of divine providence throughout the text, the author simultaneously undermines the conventions of the providence tale. Consequently, it appears that the unity of the narrative issues from its negative posture. *The Narrative of Arthur Gordon Pym* delivers a seemingly endless series of blows at the conventions that are characteristic of providence literature with the object of challenging the theory of providential intercession and the narrative forms that are predicated on a belief in divine providence.

The most obvious feature of Mather's tales, whether they are captivity narratives, conversion accounts, or sea deliverances, is the appeal to the deity in all confidence that God both hears his people and acts on their behalf. Much like Mather's visible saints, Pym regularly invokes the name of God. He recommends himself to God, recognizes the mercy of God, and attributes his good fortune to the special intercession of Providence.[17] However pious his prayers, Pym also speaks otherwise. And on the many occasions when Pym looks to the heavens, Poe chooses a variety of ways to compromise his heavenly gaze, which J. Gerald Kennedy describes as the character's "confusion." "Pym's earliest invocation of providence in chapter one hints at his confusion: his rescue from the *Ariel* occurs, he remarks, *either* through 'good fortune' or through the 'special interference' of a providential power" (82, 3). Not the confident assertion of a man of faith, Pym's assessment vacillates between a worldly and spiritual understanding of the events of his life.

---

16. My reading of the text, unlike that of either Fukuchi or Eaken, is consonant with the more traditional interpretations of *Pym* as a failed quest. I concur with Joel Porte who concludes that *Pym* "is an American *Pilgrim's Progress* which leads not to eternal salvation but to eternal terror." See *The Romance in America: Studies in Cooper, Poe, Hawthorne, Melville, and James* (Middletown, CT: Wesleyan University Press, 1969), 84.

17. *Collected Writings of Edgar Allan Poe, Vol I: The Imaginary Voyages*, ed. Burton R. Pollin (Boston: Twayne, 1981), 60, 117, 96.

In later chapters, Pym's invocation of the deity is less confused than it is strategic. When in desperate straits aboard the *Grampus*, Pym characteristically seeks his Maker: "Throwing ourselves on our knees to God, we implored his aid in the many dangers which beset us" (122). However, lest the reader believe that he subscribes fully to a belief in the providential design for his life, Pym immediately adds, "[we] arose with renewed hope and vigour to think what could yet be done *by mortal means* towards accomplishing our deliverance" (122, emphasis mine). His profession of faith in the agency of God is trumped by his recommendation of human efforts. In another instance, the presumption of divine intercession is quickly contradicted by earthly reality. Sighting an approaching brig, Pym instinctively praises God for the rescue: "We poured out our whole souls in shouts and thanksgiving to God for the complete, unexpected, and glorious deliverance that was so palpably at hand" (124). However, the sailors soon recognize that the crew of their blessed rescue ship has been stricken with disease and the deck is littered with decaying bodies. Much short of divine, the ship is described as emitting a "hellish" odor of putrefying flesh (124). Yet another providential intercession proves otherwise when Pym and Peters search for provisions on the *Grampus*, and discover a bottle of port wine. Pym immediately "giv[es] thanks to God for this timely and cheering assistance" (127), but just as quickly, the sailors drink a good bit of the wine, are quickly inebriated, and act the fool until they are reduced to despair. Thus, in an ironic turn, the gift from the heavens becomes the most grievous of the seven deadly sins, despair.

Again, Poe both invokes and undermines a belief in divine providence when Pym attributes the discovery of a tortoise aboard the *Grampus* to divine loving-kindness. Poe uses this opportunity to revisit Cotton Mather's fusion of disparate disciplines—history, natural science, and theology. Pym's claim that the tortoise is a gift from God is problematic because it immediately follows Pym's thorough explanation of the provenance of the tortoise. Captain Barnard had taken the animal on board earlier in the Galapagos Islands because that species of tortoise provides excellent food and a store of water in a membrane at the base of its neck. Pym details the appearance, weight, and distinguishing characteristics of this animal, even explaining the Spanish derivation of its name. We learn where it was stored on the ship, and how Augustus and Peters lifted it from below the deck. Pym spares us no detail. We are also apprised that the nutritious meat of the Galapagos tortoise has "no doubt, been the means of preserving the lives of thousands of seamen" (138). On the heels of this elaborate explanation and celebration of the turtle, Pym's abrupt "thanks to

God for so seasonable a relief" seems disingenuous in that he has already revealed that the provenance of the turtle was not divine providence (138).

Characteristic of Mather's providential accounts, the god-fearing individual may be visited by an apparition of a distant, much-loved relative, the spirit of a dead man, or even God himself for the purpose of encouraging the faithful or provoking the conscience of the depraved.[18] In the hands of Poe, this motif becomes the object of parody. When Peters and Pym suspect a man of poisoning his fellow sailors one by one, they contrive one such apparition, and do so with "the idea of working upon the superstitious terrors and guilty conscience of the mate" (107). Recognizing that such events are a sham, but that nonetheless they have currency among the common man, Pym disguises himself as Hartman Rogers, the most recent victim, and makes his appearance among the mutineers and murderers. True to form, these hardened men are susceptible to the remarkable occurrences found in religious folklore. In a dramatic flourish that is the equal of those crafted by Cotton Mather, the murderer rises from his seat when he sees the "ghost" of Rogers and falls dead, his body rolling off the ship into the sea. However, unlike Mather's accounts, this remarkable does not give rise to sober statements about the hand of God that metes out punishment among the depraved because Pym never believes that God will act on his behalf. He must then save himself, and merely appropriates the strategies of a religious past for this purpose.

At the close of this scene, there is yet another dramatic moment when Augustus is within seconds of death at the hands of the three remaining mutineers, and the combined efforts of Pym and Peters are ineffective to save him. There is no one to aid them. Cotton Mather would use this precise moment to introduce the intercession of God in such a situation, but Poe forgoes the *deus ex machina* in favor of a dog *ex machina*. Pym's dog, Tiger, enters the scene, pins one man, and pierces his throat with his sharp teeth, allowing Pym and Peters to "beat out the brains" of one sailor and strangle another. In a complete reversal of the tropes of providential literature, a sham apparition and a dog *ex machina* facilitate the bloody slaughter of men of low character by men of questionable character. There are no heroes in this novella; they are no visible saints; and whereas Pym speaks of a God, there is no God.

---

18. See, for example, Cotton Mather's "A Man Strangely Preserved on the Keel of a Boat at Sea" (2:345) and "the story of Mr. Joseph Beacon" (2:468–69).

The plot of chapter twelve directly responds to a classic element of early American tales of sea deliverance—the temptation of cannibalism. In Cotton Mather's "The Wonderful Story of Major Gibbons," for example, when men at sea prove desperate for sustenance, they look to the heavens, then look to themselves and decide to draw lots to determine whom they will eat. They debate the decision, identify their victim, and pause for prayer before selecting an executioner to kill the fated man. At this very moment, God answers their prayers by sending a large fish into their boat. They are gratified, but once again fall into the same condition of extreme hunger, and once again enact their lottery. God responds a second time with a large bird to nourish them, and a third time with a friendly ship to rescue them, God proving to be their "friend in adversity" (2:346).[19]

The Narrative of Arthur Gordon Pym mirrors this plot element of providential literature when the sailors aboard the *Grampus* find themselves in a similar state of want. They, too, debate the issue of cannibalism, and then draw lots to select a victim. No divine intercession occurring in Poe's narrative, the murder is consummated, and the body is consumed. At the end of the four-day's provisions, Pym's crew, like that of Major Gibbons, is again reduced to want. However, in an ironic turn, Pym finally discovers how to avoid repeating their cannibalism. He remembers that he has an axe that will allow the crew to gain access to the lower deck storeroom that holds ample provisions. Oblivious to the tragic timing of his recollection, Pym simply informs the reader that the axe "was hailed with the most ecstatic joy and triumph, and the ease with which it had been obtained was regarded as an omen of our ultimate preservation" (136). Within the context of the events, one hardly believes that his axe was obtained with "ease" as it came as an aftermath to cannibalism. In addition, within the larger context of the formulae of remarkable sea deliverances, the religious tenor of the language of "omens" of "ultimate preservation" appears to be misapplied in reference to murderous dimwits who resort unnecessarily to cannibalism because they simply forget that they are literally sitting on a storehouse of food and drink.

To complete the tale of divine providence, three days later a large fish leaps into the *Grampus*.[20] Unlike Major Gibbons's divine gift, Poe's fish

19. The motif of the fish as manna is also found in Mather's tale of William Laiton (2:349–50) and his "Mantissa" concerning Mr. William Trowbridge (2:354).

20. Naoki Onishi argues convincingly that Herman Melville also draws on Mather's "The Wonderful Story of Major Gibbons" in *Moby-Dick*. He finds that the image of Tashtego and the bird at the moment of the *Pequod*'s sinking mirrors the appearance of the providential bird in Mather's tale, and he asserts the "revealing contrast" between "the credulity expressed in

strikes Peters violently with his great tail, and jumps back into the water. When we read this passage through the filter of its analogue in Cotton Mather, the trope of the fish as the sailors' manna is rendered ironic. If Pym had any faith in God's supplying him with sustenance from the sea, which he surely does not, this fish would have quickly discouraged him in his faith. For Mather's characters, survival is a sign of salvation. However, Poe's survivors are painted as fools and cannibals.

The above scenes occur in the *Grampus* chapters of *Pym*, after which the tenor of the narrative changes dramatically. The *Jane Guy* sequence is less a challenge to the conventions of providential literature than an attempt to discern meaning by an alternate faith in empirical inquiry. Pym changes his strategy of survival in these chapters, and relies on rational, and sometimes scientific, analysis—whether consulting the ship's navigational log, investigating historical accounts of similar sea voyages, or dispassionately examining the natural phenomena he encounters. However, this is not to assert that Pym finds his salvation or even his rescue at sea by virtue of scientific knowledge. In J. Gerald Kennedy's evaluation,

> geographic and scientific information appear to validate the truthfulness of the narrative as it demonstrates the intelligibility of physical reality. Yet the young narrator repeatedly makes faulty inferences by misreading visual signs. . . . Experience disconfirms Pym's assumptions so persistently that the very possibility of arriving at "truth" becomes doubtful and problematic. (12)

All efforts to decode the world of the Tsalal or to understand the physical challenges to the *Jane Guy* are futile. Thus, Poe undermines man's faith in the ability of rational inquiry to unlock the truths of the physical world, just as he earlier demythologizes man's faith in divine providence to reveal truth. Where in the early chapters Poe dismantles the seventeenth- and eighteenth-century man's faith in the ability of God to know and to act on His knowledge, in the later chapters Poe critiques the nineteenth-century man's faith in his own ability to know and to act on his knowledge. Neither comprises an authoritative basis for narrative.

Consistent with Poe's "MS. Found in a Bottle," *The Narrative of Arthur Gordon Pym* reveals no spiritual or worldly truth. To the contrary, it testifies to the inability to lay claim to wisdom, and further expresses distrust of

---

Mather's story and the pessimistic catastrophe of *Moby-Dick*." See "Melville's *Moby-Dick*" in *Explicator* 50.3 (1992): 14–50.

man's ability to communicate truth, even if he were to acquire such. While Paul Rosenzweig admits that *Pym* encourages "movement toward meaning," he concludes that the text refuses meaning. "Nothing is certain in the world of the *Narrative of Arthur Gordon Pym,* not even the certainty that nothing is" (137, 149). If the details of the plot of both the *Grampus* and the *Jane Guy* chapters did not convince the reader of the impossibility of securing truth through divine or human efforts, then Poe appends a "note" to this effect. The note, like Mather's many "Mantissa," simply reprises the author's argument, but in a different way. Following this narrative on the challenge to create meaning, the note informs the reader that Pym's manuscript is inaccurate, incomplete, and incoherent. It is not to be believed, if it were ever understood.

J. Gerald Kennedy observes that "Pym's situation often mirrors our own predicament as well—that of imperfect readers of signs, determined to find coherence or meaning or intelligibility in the texts we confront" (39). The reader of *Pym* should look to the image of Pym as reader for an analogue of "our own predicament." Locked in the hold of the *Grampus,* Pym attempts to read a fragment of a note written in blood. Although he sheds what little light he has on the paper, and although he reads with "caution," he is unable to decode the message. In this particular situation, Pym is literally and metaphorically delirious and in the dark. Syllables are "vague" and words are "disjointed" (80). As such, he is prompted to a wildly imaginative and inaccurate reading of his text.[21] However, his greater mistake is assuming that he is able to read his world once he emerges from the hold. Pym's challenge and our challenge as readers is that we are always delirious and in the dark, and that we always hold a fragmented text, however urgently written in blood.

Ultimately, *Pym* is a self-reflexive evaluation of man's urge to create meaning of his life in terms larger than his singular experience might suggest. In Kennedy's words,

> *Pym* unfolds a powerful fable of the human need to interpret life-shaping events in relation to a transcendent meaning or purpose. The narrator's craving for certitude and his persistent efforts to construe his experience as fortune or misfortune reveal a seemingly naive faith in providence. (*Abyss of Interpretation,* 12–13)

---

21. J. Gerald Kennedy's *Poe, Death, and the Life of Writing* (New Haven: Yale University Press, 1987) offers an insightful deconstructive analysis of the acts of reading and writing in this scene (152–54).

Thus, in *The Narrative of Arthur Gordon Pym*, Poe seeks a form of emplotting that is distinct from the classic binary of comic and tragic modes. Such is the limited narrative vision of a Cotton Mather who forces each event in man's life into a plot that discloses God's approval or disapproval of that man. Moreover, God's judgment becomes the singular, definitive conclusion of the narrative. For the providence tale in *Magnalia*, there is no alternate plot or conclusion. When *Pym* denies its reader coherent emplotting of events and proffers implausible narrative threads and plural, inconclusive conclusions, it strikes out at man's belief in his ability to emplot his' life, while it acknowledges man's tremendous desire to do so. In his analysis of *Pym*'s refusal to conclude, Paul John Eaken speaks to the psychology of endings: "We want to believe that we could know all, but the urgency of our wanting is directly proportionate to our conviction of the impossibility of our knowing" (21). Poe's *Pym* points to the instability of man's knowledge, and, by extension, the instability of all narrative.

Pym's prefatory statement to his narrative rehearses Poe's rationale for publishing the account "*under the garb of fiction.*" According to the putative author, that the history appeared as fiction is a "*ruse*" (56). In reality, the ruse is the assertion that history is other than fiction.

The Gallows Confession

Several scholars have identified newspaper articles appearing in the 1830s and 1840s that relate events that are uncanny in their similarity to the plot of Poe's "The Black Cat." Their studies argue convincingly that such journalistic pieces provide source material for Poe's composition of this tale.[22] Stephen Rachman looks to literary source material and cites a chapter in Charles Dickens' *The Old Curiosity Shop* as Poe's inspiration for "The Black Cat."[23] Yet, read against the backdrop of book six of *Magnalia*, "The Black Cat" emerges as a composite of many of Mather's providence tales, prin-

---

22. I refer here to E. Kate Stewart's discovery of a story entitled "The Black Cat" by "T.H.S." in an 1836 issue of the *Baltimore Monument* and John E. Reilly's identification of a news item in the *Philadelphia Ledger* in 1842, both pieces bearing substantive resemblance to Poe's "The Black Cat." See Stewart's "Another Source for 'The Black Cat,'" in *Poe Studies* 18.2 (1985):25, and Reilly, "A Source for the Immuration in 'The Black Cat,'" in *Nineteenth-Century Literature* 48.1 (1993): 93–95.

23. "'Es lässt sich nicht schreiben': Plagiarism and 'The Man of the Crowd'" in *The American Face of Edgar Allan Poe,* ed. Shawn Rosenheim and Stephen Rachman (Baltimore and London: Johns Hopkins University Press, 1995), 86.

cipally the temperance tale and the gallows confession.[24] Much like Poe's reprisal of Mather's tales of maritime disasters and deliverances, "The Black Cat" offers an ironic revision of a variety of accounts from *Magnalia*.

The opening words of "The Black Cat" identify the tale as a "most wild, yet most homely narrative" (849). As such, the fusion of two opposing currents in this account mirrors the focus of Mather's book six, which showcases extraordinary events in the lives of ordinary people. However, while Mather insists that his reader have complete faith in his explanation of the commingling of the demonic and the domestic, Poe's narrator "neither expect[s] nor solicit[s] belief" (849). He is a murderer who is sentenced to die the following day. For the modern reader, the narrator's persona as a criminal might automatically compromise his authority, but within the context of Mather's tales, this would not necessarily be true. *Magnalia* contains numerous accounts of gallows confessions in which a criminal, after much prayer and consultation with the minister, confesses his sinful life, exhibits great remorse, at times admonishes others to avoid his example, and ultimately prepares to meet his maker. The ethical appeal of the otherwise criminal narrator springs from various elements: his intimate association with a minister whose remarks often preface those of the criminal, his conversion, and the exceptional moment of his discourse, minutes from death and eternity. Likewise, Poe's narrator claims that one of his motivations for recounting his crime is to "unburthen [his] soul" (849). By mirroring the language of the earlier narrative form, Poe fashions his account within the tradition of the gallows confession.

Similarly, "The Black Cat" invokes the form and language of *Magnalia*'s testimonials concerning the fate of the drunken man. Rarely offering an extended narrative, Mather's brief anecdotes simply recount the spiritual and social disgrace of the intemperate and assert his damnation. In the most general of terms, these individuals are described as "debased," "diseased," and "open unto the worst of all temptations of the devil." However, two specific motifs emerge consistently in Mather's accounts. First, he describes the drinking man as satanic: "We have seen them turn *beasts*—yea, turn *devils!*" (2:394). Secondly, he recounts that the fiery beverage causes men (and women) to stumble and fall into the fire of their domestic

---

24. See Mather's tale of James Morgan (2:409–12) for an example of an eighteenth-century tale of intemperance, which is also a gallows confession and a conversion narrative, these being intersecting genres in their early appearance.

Many scholars have studied Poe's use of the nineteenth-century temperance tale, which has its origins in Puritan sermonic literature. Regarding "The Black Cat," David S. Reynolds concludes that the story "exploits" the popular genre of the temperance tale, while "avoiding didactic statement" implicit in the genre (*Beneath the American Renaissance*, 68–70).

hearth, as such anticipating their fall into the eternal fires of hell (2:394–5). These are the same motifs that David Reynolds identifies in the popular temperance tale of the nineteenth century, a fiction form with its roots in *Magnalia* and other temperance tracts by Cotton Mather (65–73).[25]

"The Black Cat" also duplicates the language of moral outrage and self-recrimination often found in the earlier Puritan texts. Poe's narrator begins his account by speaking of himself as "mere *Man*," and as such invokes the doctrine of innate depravity, which is implicit in the providence tale (850).[26] Recognizing that he is "fashioned in the image of the High God," the narrator repeatedly refers to his soul just as the spiritually introspective Puritan gauges the state of his soul in hopes of a sign of regeneration (856). Poe's narrator in "The Black Cat," like the intemperate sinners of *Magnalia*, describes himself as satanic. When he is intoxicated, he reports that "the fury of a demon" possesses him, and he seems to lose his soul (851).

However, these motifs, like those of the gallows confession, serve Poe only as a foil for the larger purpose of his fiction. When Poe appropriates the conventions of the Calvinist narratives, he simultaneously strips them of their moralistic import. In "The Black Cat," the narrator admits being under the influence of the "Fiend Intemperance," his soul expressing a "fiendish malevolence," but he nonetheless concludes that his cat is the "Arch-Fiend" (851, 858). In doing so, he externalizes his guilt and transfers his satanic identity to the cat, a posture that would have been inconceivable in the earlier tales of intemperance. Although the reader is not obliged to accept this concluding statement from the mad drunkard, the dénouement of his account cannot invoke the themes of contrition and regeneration that the tale might have otherwise offered.

Thus, the gallows confession that Poe sets in motion ultimately contains no confession. Neither does it offer conversion. In Poe, we see little evidence of remorse or fine moralizing. Throughout his drunkenness, and his

25. T. J. Matheson's insightful essay, "Poe's 'The Black Cat' as a Critique of Temperance Literature," *Mosaic* 19.3 (1986): 69–80, places this tale against the backdrop of nineteenth-century temperance fiction, in terms of both language and motifs. His argument is the analogue of the one presented here in that Matheson concludes that in this story "Poe is both rebutting and criticizing certain aspects of temperance literature" (80), just as I assert that in appropriating the language and motifs of providential literature, Poe is rebutting the religious principles underlying this literature.

26. The typesetting of "The Black Cat" evokes the format of the eighteenth-century religious tract. Emphasis is denoted by italics (such as "this infathomable longing of the soul to *vex itself*" and "incumbent eternally upon my *heart*"), key terms that begin with an uppercase letter (such as "Law," "Man," "Humanity," and "Horror"), and the two words that stand completely in uppercase letters, "PERVERSENESS" and "GALLOWS," as if to mark their critical importance for this text.

subsequent violence, Poe's narrator finds no sign of conversion. His heart and his fancy are moved, but "the soul remained untouched" (851). At the close of the tale, the narrator—unlike the gallows confessor—assumes no responsibility for his deeds. In lieu of spiritual regeneration, the narrator is spiritually dead. He persists in identifying the cat as "the monster" and the "Arch-Fiend," his language revealing his unwavering belief that he was a victim of the cat "whose craft had seduced [him] into murder" (859). Moreover, despite the narrator's invocations to the deity—"But may God shield and deliver me from the fangs of the Arch-Fiend!"—there is no God in "The Black Cat" (858). There is merely a fictive framework of providential intervention, rendered ironic because of the absence of a deity that is at the center of the narrative genre that Poe both invokes and inverts in this tale.

Additional conventions from various accounts of criminal action in *Magnalia* reappear in Poe's "The Black Cat." Like Poe, Cotton Mather was interested in the ways in which crime is detected within a community. Mather observed of early New England that "many people have sinned horribly, upon a presumption that they sinned secretly: but the judgments of God have been wondrously and prodigiously and stupendously display'd in the discovering of secret sinners among us" (2:400). He further exclaims, "But, Oh, how strangely have the sins of men found them out!" and recounts any number of tales in which murder, adultery, bestiality, fraud, and excessive profiteering have come to light in unusual and often symbolic fashion. This is the very premise of Poe's "The Black Cat."

In this respect, Poe's story bears remarkable similarity to Mather's tale of Mary Martin, a gallows narrative in which a young woman confesses to hiding the body of her murdered child in a chest, thus concealing her crime "from the eyes of all but the jealous GOD" (2:404, 5). Like Mary Martin, the narrator in "The Black Cat" takes extraordinary steps to hide his victim's corpse, and, in doing so, claims that "no eye could detect any thing suspicious" (857). In each case, despite repeated denials, the murderous act is revealed only when there is a cry from behind Poe's wall and inside Martin's chest.[27] In her confession, Mary Martin reveals that she attempted twice to kill her child much as Poe's murderer twice violates his cat. In the closure to his account, Mather makes much of the symbolic retribution meted against the murderess. He insinuates that Martin must step from the gallows platform twice to complete her execution because she

---

27. It is interesting to note that Poe initially describes the cat's cry in human terms, "at first muffled and broken, like the sobbing of a child" (859).

twice attempted to murder her child before she was successful. In Mather's eyes, God's judgment speaks through this remarkable occurrence, this evaluation serving as the text's proper closure. In Poe's tale, however, there is no moralistic evaluation. Indeed, there is no reach toward consequence, when causation itself is understood as folly. Moreover, there is no logical conclusion. The reader is merely informed of a detail that he already surmised: the cat was secreted in the wall, and serves to alert the authorities of the mad narrator's crime.

Were Poe's story to reflect a belief in divine providence, the animal's cry would have become a symbol of God's omniscience and unrelenting vigilance in delivering punishment for man's sin. However, for true consonance with providential literature, the animal would not have been a cat, for, in Mather's accounts, the cat is often a harbinger of evil, not of divine righteousness. It is also true, however, that in Mather's narratives cats are frequently associated with women. Daniel Hoffman has observed that Poe invokes the "old superstition" of identifying odd or difficult women as cats, Hoffman's logical expression of this motif being "wife = witch. Ergo, black cat = wife."[28]

In the American folk tradition, the fusion and confusion of women and cats was a feature of tales about Salem in the late seventeenth century. As secretary to the witch trials, Cotton Mather was the actual "author" of such accounts.[29] In book six of *Magnalia,* he offers further examples of the satanic transformation of women into cats for the purpose of afflicting men, and thus further promulgates this eerie equation. In fairness, Cotton Mather also rejects the conclusion that all complaints of feline mischief should be attributed to female misrule. In *Magnalia,* he argues that this common misconception "proceeded from some mistaken principles: as that Satan cannot assume the shape of an innocent person" (2:478). He even insists that many such complaints result from *post hoc ergo propter hoc* argumentation, and must be subject to additional proof to establish witchcraft. Nonetheless, his recounting the fantastic tales that dramatize a woman's transformation into a monstrous cat serves to plant in the minds of men and women the very principles that he questions.

28. *Poe Poe Poe Poe Poe,* 1972 (New York: Paragon House, 1990), 231.

29. See, for example, Cotton Mather's recording of Robert Downer's testimony that the night after Susanna Martin threatened him with evil purpose, a cat jumped through his bedroom window, attacked him on the throat, and almost killed him in *Wonders of the Invisible World. Being an Account of the Tryals of Several Witches Lately Executed in New England. To Which is Added, A Further Account of the Tryals of the New England Witches, by Increase Mather* (Boston, 1693), 142–43.

In "The Black Cat," the wife and her cats are confused in the mind of the narrator. Indeed, in the opening paragraphs of the story, he refers to his wife's superstitious belief that "all black cats [are] witches in disguise" (850). Although he immediately makes multiple attempts to distance himself from the belief, the narrator, like Mather, has already promulgated this notion if only by attributing it to another speaker. Poe secures this superstition with the closing image of the tale, that of the cat sitting on the head of the wife's corpse, the cat squalling its accusations at the narrator. In this way, Poe successfully invokes and undermines the earlier trope of providential literature. The innocent women is compromised by dint of identification with the black cat, especially because of her supposed belief that "all black cats [are] witches in disguise," although this statement is uttered only by her husband, not by herself. Ultimately, when the crime is disclosed, the informant is also the black cat, now associated with the satanic voice. What would have been in Mather a glorious moment in which God's hand is able to effect the triumph of the godly woman and the destruction of the evil man is otherwise in Poe. The righteous woman is a grotesque corpse, the murderer disavows his crime, and the informant literally and metaphorically stands with the grotesque. The dénouement of Poe's tale defies the earlier belief in absolute good and absolute evil, and is eager to confuse both these concepts and the symbolic representations of these concepts.

Poe further elides the identities of the wife and the cat in sacrificing the life of the woman for the animal. In the death of the young wife, he also reverses the providential belief that God preserves the righteous individual. *Magnalia Christi Americana* offers several narratives in which God-fearing men and women suffer exceptional physical trauma, and are restored by the hand of their God. "The Black Cat" mirrors and subverts this motif of Puritan providential literature as well. In particular, Poe's final disposition of the narrator's wife parallels Mather's account of Abigail Eliot who was struck on the head with an iron, and lost brain matter in the accident. Nonetheless, Abigail's "intellectuals" were not diminished by her misfortune, and she "liv'd to be a mother of several children" (2:356). In Mather's felicitous plot, God rewards the good wife with health, fertility, intelligence, and longevity. Yet, in Poe's story, God does not spare the narrator's wife when he plants his axe in her skull. Unlike the faithful in *Magnalia,* this patient and long suffering spouse does not live to testify to God's power and mercy in restoring her to health. As such, Poe's story is the shell of Mather's providence tale, but without the hand of God.

Poe's lack of larger commentary on the wife's murder is also telling, especially in contradistinction to the closure of providential literature.

Whereas Mather concludes that Abigail Eliot's return to health is a sign of God's loving-kindness, Poe avoids any culminating statement whatsoever. He reverts to the limited narrative structure of the chronicle, and simply announces that "she fell dead upon the spot, without a groan" (856). As he suggested earlier, he eschews full narrative and is merely "detailing a chain of facts" (853). As a result, for Poe, this event calls for no larger statement because his account does not serve any overarching philosophical or religious concerns, as does Mather's. There is no absolute good or evil, and physical occurrences are unremarkable and ultimately symbolic of nothing.

Indeed, the goals of Poe's narration run counter to those of Cotton Mather. Where Mather extrapolates greater moral and social truths from his accounts, Poe calls in his opening paragraph for a more logical and sober mind to "reduce" his tale to an "ordinary succession of very natural causes and effects" (850). That is, he seeks the truth of the story in "very natural" exposition of the facts, rather than in supernatural explication. Of course, questions of interpretation—especially those of causation—are at the center of "The Black Cat," and they defy exposition by either narrator or reader. In their stead, Poe adheres to his stated goal of "plac[ing] before the world, plainly, succinctly, and without comment, a series of mere household events" (849), but ultimately renders his events meaningless by pushing his claim of veracity and objectivity to its logical extreme. This authorial posture strikes a blow at that of Cotton Mather who insists that the ministry assume responsibility for exposing the "evident operations of the Almighty God" in the events of life. Yet when Poe eschews his interpretive role, he invites the reader to establish causation, thus placing this critical responsibility in the hands of the random reader. Or, as he later suggests, an attempt at determining motive and reason is pointless. Following his first mutilation of the cat and the subsequent fire, Poe speaks again to the issue of causation: "I am above the weakness of seeking to establish a sequence of cause and effect, between the disaster and the atrocity. But I am detailing a chain of facts" (853), the narrator states. Understanding an author's search for causation—providential or otherwise—to be a "weakness," Poe places his goals for "The Black Cat" at odds with the grander ambitions of early providential literature. Because Poe's story mirrors the structure of the providence tale, yet rejects the premise of the genre, "The Black Cat" asserts that nineteenth-century America can no longer assent to the belief in providential intervention in the lives of men and women. Neither can they identify an ordering principle for their lives that will stand in place of divine providence for antebellum America.

Where Mather sees design, Poe casts the events of one's life as a "series" or a "chain," as bald chronicle rather than interpretive history.

Poe's "William Wilson," too, takes on the framework of Mather's gallows narratives. Yet, once again, the criminal confessor will not accept responsibility for his crimes, claiming instead to be a "victim" and a "slave of circumstances beyond human control" (427). Neither will he disclose the full record of his evil deeds. Nor will he even reveal his true name. However, the narrator wills himself a name. Although he suggests that his life has been ordained by other than his free will, he exercises that will to choose a name that symbolizes his human agency, William Wilson. Wilson opens the tale with the language of moralistic self-remonstration that is characteristic of Mather's sinners and criminals. In Mather, a confession of the abject condition of one's soul—whether on the gallows or in the privacy of one's prayer closet—is prefatory to conversion and ultimately, one hopes, to salvation. Yet, in Poe's ironic revision of the Puritan topoi, the narrator's self-recrimination anticipates only an exposition of the crime that leaves Wilson "*dead to the World, to Heaven, and to Hope!*" (448). Further playing with Mather's language, Poe takes up the early author's term for suicide, which is "self-murder" because when William Wilson murders his double, he murders himself. And, where Mather looks to man's innate depravity that "dogg[s]" a man to self-murder (2:467), William Wilson looks to the rival outside himself when he threatens his double/his self, "you *shall not* dog me unto death!" (447).

The goal of "William Wilson" is not merely a rejection of Calvinist literary convention, but a challenge to the religious underpinnings of that literature. Wilson characterizes his early religious education as "Draconian," every hour marked by the "deep hollow note of the church-bell" and every transgression measured by the minister's ferule (429, 428). The passage from the religious school of Reverend Bransby to Eton, then to Oxford, and finally to foreign sites signals a passage from a theocentric early American identity to an increasingly liberal, humanist self-fashioning. In each venue, however, the voice if not the person of the earlier "companion" and "rival," William Wilson, cautions the narrator and exposes his vice. Finally, when Wilson murders Wilson, he hopes to rid himself of the moralistic principles that he attempted to leave behind in the physical site of Bransby's church and school.

Because the story is a retrospective of William Wilson's life, Poe exposes the consequence of Wilson's philosophical maneuvering in his initial depiction of the character. In the opening paragraph, Wilson is fashioned as Cain. He is the "outcast of all outcasts most abandoned" whose ill repute is known throughout the world (426). Although he does not fully renounce his lifelong turpitude, he acknowledges that his understanding of his life lacks a guiding principle other than his personal whim or self-gratification. Indeed, he asks his fellow man to "seek out for me, in the details I am about to give, some little oasis of *fatality* amid a wilderness of error" (427). As such, he is asking for man to restore a set of foundational principles that might replace those that he rejected throughout his life. No longer convinced of the validity of his amoral wilderness, he at last seeks an element of fate—a God or gods—to order his life. Having rejected his religious past and devoid of its replacement, he is dead to the world and holds no hope of attaining heaven.

The irony of the tale is that Wilson rejected the pieties of providential literature, but has yet to discover their replacement in the nineteenth century. Constructed without substitute foundational principles, Poe's nineteenth-century narrative lacks its own means of evaluation and interpretation. It does not recognize and value parallelism (the birth date and physical similarity of William Wilson and William Wilson) or repetition (ill doing and the discovery of ill doing); it identifies these elements of plot as "remarkable coincidence" and "remarkable fact," which unlike Mather's remarkables remain unmoored, without the potential to be analyzed or evaluated (432, 434). Whereas this material would have prompted Mather's definitive, moralistic statement celebrating the hand of God, these details render Poe's narrator mute. He is surprised, but incapable of interpretation.

In a self-reflexive moment in the text, Poe's narrator almost apologizes for the quality of his anecdotes. He characterizes his tale as "a few rambling details" that are "utterly trivial" and even "ridiculous" (428). Yet, he simultaneously seeks to make more of them.

> These [details], moreover, utterly trivial, and even ridiculous in themselves, assume, to my fancy, adventitious importance, as connected with a period and a locality when and where I recognize the first ambiguous monitions of the destiny which afterward so fully overshadowed me. Let me then remember. (428)

Poe's self-murderer yearns for narrative coherence for the events of his life, a coherence that would establish causation, and thus a plot expressive of the unity of his life. Although he guards against definitive statement of purpose, the narrator wants to make meaning of his life and see his life whole. This urge for integrity compels him to search the past, and permits the narrative—however diffuse and inconclusive—to unfold.

At the same time, however, the author ultimately does not permit William Wilson this wisdom, and suggests that such understanding is impossible. In other tales, Poe openly discloses his belief that the search for continuity and coherence in the events of one's life is an unfortunate human "weakness" (853). This is, of course, the primary "weakness" of historians who believe in providential design, and for whom both continuity and coherence are established by God. Thus, when Poe takes on the form of early American historical literature of divine providence and rejects its theological platform, he establishes ironic distance between the early spiritual fictions of the American self and the nineteenth-century dark romantic expressions of the self.

That Poe cloaks his fiction in the guise of a historical account makes his challenge to early American historical narratives even more pointed. Poe crafted his "MS. Found in a Bottle" to be read as a journalistic account of a sea deliverance. Because "MS. Found in a Bottle" was first published in the *Baltimore Sunday Visiter* of October 12, 1833, alongside reportage of current events, which the story largely resembles, and because the title of the story resembles a journalistic headline, it blurs the distinction between fiction and nonfiction, works of the imagination and historical accounts. Likewise, *The Narrative of Arthur Gordon Pym of Nantucket* was issued as a book, in 1838, purportedly "edited" by Poe. The style and the content of its title page resemble those of contemporary travel narratives. In addition, "The Black Cat" and "William Wilson" invoke the structure, language, and tone of the genre of the gallows sermon, yet another historical tract from early America. More than a tease or a hoax, Poe is calling into question his readers' notions of the stability of history. Additionally, Poe's fiction works toward eroding the authority of historical narrative. By his fictive guise as editor who openly discloses his sources, Poe mirrors the authorial position of Cotton Mather who chronicles the uncanny occurrences of New England, while taking care to note the source of each account.

Finally, in the process of undermining the providence tale by refashioning this material as gothic fiction, Edgar Allan Poe simply furthers the developing process of writing historical accounts that Cotton Mather put into motion in the late seventeenth century. Where Increase Mather published and marketed his gallows sermons as religious tracts, Cotton Mather amplified his sermons with sensational information about the crime and, perhaps even more dramatic, a statement from the criminal, these aspects designed to attract readership. Taking his cue from Cotton

Mather, Poe's narratives continue this trajectory. They retain the formula of the providence tale, but dispense entirely with the moralistic dénouement.

Moreover, they dispense with the voice of the minister as historian. Because Mather asserted the primacy of the minister as historian, he alone assumed authority to narrate and interpret the uncanny events of New England. Where he had no immediate knowledge of a "remarkable occurrence," he meticulously documented his source, which was most often a minister or multiple ministers. However, Poe eliminates the third-person narrator with claims of serving as dispassionate and disinterested interpreter, and seats authority in the man at the center of an extraordinary event. In this way, Poe gives his narrative over to the man who is passionately involved in the uncanny and even implicated in crime, and gives voice exclusively to the criminal or the man whom no God will save.

Chapter 4

ოჰე

Cotton Mather as the
"old New England grandmother"

HARRIET BEECHER STOWE
AND THE FEMALE HISTORIAN

In her semi-autobiographical novel, *Poganuc People,* Harriet Beecher
Stowe wrote,

> It was a happy hour when [father] brought home and set up in his book-
> case Cotton Mather's "Magnalia," in a new edition of two volumes. What
> wonderful stories these! and stories, too, about her own country, stories
> that made her feel that the very ground she trod on was consecrated by
> some special dealing of God's providence. (11:122–23)

Many literary historians have explored the Calvinist upbringing of Harriet
Beecher Stowe, and the profound influence of her father, Rev. Lyman
Beecher, on her life and her letters, and, for their part, literary critics have
examined Stowe's response to Calvinism in her fiction. Indeed, theology and religious practice are major thematic elements in novels such
as *Oldtown Folks, The Minister's Wooing, Poganuc People,* and *The Pearl
of Orr's Island,* each of these works testifying to Stowe's belief in divine
providence.[1]

1. For studies of Stowe's commentary on Calvinism within her fiction, see Lawrence Buell,
"Calvinism Romanticized: Harriet Beecher Stowe, Samuel Hopkins, and *The Minister's Wooing*,"
ESQ: A Journal of the American Renaissance 24 (1978): 119–32; Alice C. Crozier, *The Novels of
Harriet Beecher Stowe* (New York: Oxford University Press, 1969), especially 91–93; Joan D.
Hedrick, "'Peaceable Fruits': The Ministry of Harriet Beecher Stowe," *American Quarterly* 40.3
(1988): 307–22; Vernon Louis Parrington, "Harriet Beecher Stowe: A Daughter of Puritanism,"
in *Main Currents in American Thought,* 2 vols. (New York: Harcourt, Brace, Jovanovich, 1930),
1: 371–78; and especially Charles H. Foster, *The Rungless Ladder: Harriet Beecher Stowe and New
England Puritanism* (1954; New York: Cooper Square, 1970), an excellent analysis of theology
and religious practice in Stowe's novels.

An analysis at the structural level reveals that these novels also exhibit Stowe's reworking of topoi from early American religious literature. In particular, Harriet Beecher Stowe looks to the tales of Cotton Mather's *Magnalia Christi Americana* as generic models for her fiction. This book, she claimed, "proved a mine of wealth to her" (11:122). While Stowe acknowledges *Magnalia* as a historical document, she also recognizes its value at the level of narrative. In *Poganuc People,* she describes the collection as "wonderful stories" (11:122), and in *Oldtown Folks,* Stowe describes Mather as a "beloved gossip" and "delightful old New England grandmother" who wrote "nursery tales" of colonial America (9:195). The providence tales in book six of Mather's *Magnalia* not only influenced Stowe's religious and historical views, but also informed her approach to narrative construction and guided the characterization in several of her novels.

In addition, Stowe's fiction responds directly to Mather's assertions about the authority of the minister to document and explicate the history of a community. In her curious characterization of Reverend Mather as a "grandmother," Harriet Beecher Stowe offers a clue to the way she will reshape the persona of the historian. A conservative and profoundly religious author, Stowe nonetheless challenges Mather's position by installing female narrators and historians in her fiction, charging them with maintaining the history of their communities and authorizing them to interpret both the quotidian and exceptional events in the lives of men and women. Moreover, when she revises Mather's role of the historian and emplotment of history, she does so by appropriating and refashioning his providence tales of remarkable occurrences.

The Female Historian

We see Stowe's interest in the narrative strategies of the Puritan providence throughout her literary work—in *The Minister's Wooing, The Pink and White Tyranny, Poganuc People,* and *Sam Lawson's Oldtown Fireside Stories,* for example—but one of the most potent illustrations of Stowe's affinity with historical providence literature is *The Pearl of Orr's Island.* In this novel, providential occurrences motivate the plot, appear as tales within the main narrative, and provide thematic as well as structural unity to the novel. This novel also addresses Stowe's vision of the female historian.

The Pearl of Orr's Island opens with a shipwreck like many of those described in Mather's "Christus Super Aquas," the opening chapter of book six of *Magnalia.* In Stowe's novel, this tragedy is followed not by a deliverance at sea, but with the delivery of a baby, Mara, whose birth is pronounced a "providence" by those who immediately interpret this event in terms of God's plan for his people. This scene and its placement in the early pages of the text are critical to an understanding of the novel. First, this scene motivates the remainder of the text. Although Mara's father, Captain Lincoln, drowns at sea and her mother dies from the shock of witnessing her husband's shipwreck, their infant is literally delivered, or born, and metaphorically delivered, that is, spared from death. If one reads *The Pearl* as a providence modeled after those in *Magnalia,* one must assume that God delivered Mara Lincoln for good purpose. At her birth, the child exhibits her favor with the deity and will continue to exhibit her privilege. The arrival of Mara, her "wishful" gaze and "real New-Jerusalem look," her ministry to Moses Pennel and to the community at large, all key elements of the narrative, can be directly attributed or are centrally related to the providential circumstances of her birth (6:26, 295).

Second, from the very beginning of the novel, the reader is asked to submit to the belief that God charts the course of one's metaphorical ship. James Lincoln, an experienced shipmaster, dressed for his homecoming and steered his ship toward a port he knew well. He wisely sat out a gale at sea and would later take advantage of a leeward wind to bring him home. His wife, too, prepared to greet him. All bode well until a wind forced Lincoln's ship into a narrow channel where it was shattered upon the rocky shore. Thus, within the context of the fiction, we are asked to believe that man's finest efforts are fruitless in the face of the divine scheme for each man's life. The wind—here symbolic of the presence of the deity—illustrates its power over the fragile lives of men. *The Pearl of Orr's Island* does not allow for belief in fate, blind fortune, or coincidence. Rather, the novel echoes Mather's historiographic claim for his *Magnalia,* that "all the *rare occurrences* will be evident operations of the Almighty God" (2:343).

The narrative continues to rely on a series of rare occurrences that portend divine providence. Moses' miraculous deliverance at sea parallels those of "Christus Super Aquas," and also serves as the fulfillment of other providential events announced by nature. In chapter three of book six, "Ceraunius" ("The thunderer"), Cotton Mather counsels his reader to heed the voice of God in the thunder. Mather's scriptural reference for this lesson is from Psalm 29, "The voice of the Lord is upon the waters; the God of glory thundereth," which is the same verse that Zephaniah Pennel invokes on the stormy night of Moses' shipwreck (6:40). As the Pennel household meditates upon this psalm, and listens to the violent wind, they experience a "sense of a Divine presence," and, like Mather, assert that God truly speaks to his people through extraordinary displays of nature. On that same night, Mara Lincoln also hears the storm in her sleep, and, unlike the typical child, is comforted by the thunder and raging ocean. Because this young prophetess intuits the wisdom of the psalms, she senses that the storm is "her kind-tempered old grandfather singing her to sleep" (6:47). Within the framework of the novel, if we understand her grandfather in this case to be her ancient eternal father, God, she is entirely correct. Consequently, she is prepared to receive his message, or, in the words of Mather, the "brontologia sacra," the sacred lessons of the thunder (2:363).

God's message is communicated to Mara as a dream, a motif that recalls the apparitions and premonitions that Mather describes in "Thaumatographia Pneumatica" ("Wonders of the Spirit World"), chapter seven of his collection of providences. In this section, Mather narrates extraordinary events that were predicted in dreams or visions. Mara's vision is her introduction to Moses. A pale woman dressed in white approaches Mara at the cove near the Kittridge house, and offers her the boy's hand, saying, "Take him, Mara, he is a playmate for you" (6:48). When Mara wakes, she looks for her "pitty boy" because her dream, like those of Mather's characters, was so vivid and clear that she is convinced of its reality. Once again, Mara is correct because, in the context of the novel, the premonitions offered by God are every bit as real as physical reality. Furthermore, the vigilant Christian must attend to God's voice in dreams and visions. The very next morning, of course, Mara finds a woman in white on the beach, her dead body protecting a young boy, both of whom she recognizes from her dream. The full significance of this providence will become evident to Mara only as she matures in age and in spirituality. When Mara later speaks of her unique relationship with Moses, she says, "He sent you and gave you to me . . . to be mine in time and eternity" (6:322). Stowe adds that

> the words were spoken in a kind of enthusiasm so different from the usual reserve of Mara, that they seemed like a prophecy. That night, for the first time in her life, had she broken the reserve which was her very nature, and spoken of that which was the intimate and hidden history of her soul. (6:322)

This announcement assumes the tone of prophecy because this is, in effect, the nature of the providence. Mara's language, too, evinces the ecstasy of the Old Testament prophet in pronouncing the word of God.

The very character of Mara Lincoln appears to be an elaboration of those sketched in Mather's appendix to book six, which is subtitled "Some Examples of Children in whom the Fear of God was remarkably budding before they Died." In this section of *Magnalia* Mather offers five examples of children who, like Mara Lincoln, exhibit exceptional and precocious religious devotion, and die at a very early age. In each case, the child not only is resigned to death, but welcomes the reunion with Christ. Each child is prepared by a vision or a religious experience in which they find "joy unspeakable" in their imminent death (2:482). They chastise those who weep for them, and are impatient to see their "victory," eternal life. That Mara Lincoln also exhibits early religious fervor is indisputable. Furthermore, she gains resolve in her final days because of a dream-like vision of Jesus who approaches her on the shore of the Sea of Galilee and asks her to join him, this event and its effect on Mara mirroring Mather's examples of young people whom "God fill'd . . . with a marvellous assurance of his love" (2:482).

Moses' conversion through the agency of Mara Lincoln is yet another remarkable occurrence of *The Pearl of Orr's Island,* and an echo of *Magnalia* as well. Mrs. John Bailey in "Thaumatographia Pneumatica" effected her husband's salvation on her deathbed. Much like Mara, she received a vision of Christ, was filled with the peace of the Holy Ghost, but was eager to persuade Mr. Bailey to "give up all unto God" (2:470). Her husband was moved by her conviction, and she died with the knowledge that he had accepted the free grace of God. Mather explicates this providence for his reader: "'tis very certain that the good angels *continually,* without any defilement, fly about in our defiled atmosphere, to minister for the good of them that are to be the 'heirs of salvation'" (2:470). In Stowe's novel, Mara Lincoln is one such angel. Not only is she identified explicitly throughout the text as an angel; she is responsible for the salvation of Moses who, after much battle with despair, eventually accepts the peace of Christ. At the close of the novel, both Moses and Sally understand that they "have been trained in another life" at the hands of Mara Lincoln (6:401). Aunt Roxy, too, is assured by Mara that her great virtue will constitute beauty in the afterworld, and Zephaniah Pennel receives a vision that he finds everlasting life in Jesus through Mara, his pearl of great price.

In addition to extraordinary events that occur within the fiction of the narrative, tales told by the celebrated storytellers of Orr's Island relate anecdotes that are often analogues of *Magnalia*'s providence tales. For example, Miss Roxy's uncanny stories of simultaneous deaths and deathwatch specters mirror accounts in "Thaumatographia Pneumatica." In one tale, Roxy describes caring for Mrs. Titcomb, and recalls that the woman worried about dying alone, asking, "Oh, Aunt Roxy, . . . it's so dark, who will go with me?" (6:69). However, she brightened at the moment of death when she announced cryptically that her son John would accompany her. With characteristic efficiency, Roxy noted the exact time of Mrs. Titcomb's death, and later learned that John had, in fact, died on a ship in far away Archangel at that very hour. Roxy's eerie tale is an almost verbatim retelling of Mather's account of the death of Mrs. J. C.[2] According to Mather, the woman was

> last seiz'd with the pangs of death; in which being delireous, and asking divers time "who would go with her, whither she was going?" at length she said, "Well, my son Robert will go," and addressing her speech thereupon as unto him, she express'd her satisfaction that they should *go together.* This son of hers was at that time in Barbadoes; and his friends here have since learn'd that he also dy'd there, and this at the very *hour* when his mother here gave up the ghost; and (which is further odd) not *without* the like expressions concerning his mother, that his mother had concerning him. (2:469–70)

The two accounts are virtually identical in characterization, in dialogue, and in resolution. They are analogous with the exception of the narrative voice. Where Reverend Mather alone is the teller of tales in *Magnalia,* Harriet Beecher Stowe extends the privilege of recounting providence tales exclusively to one woman on Orr's Island.

When, in *Magnalia* and *The Pearl of Orr's Island,* one is asked to understand extraordinary events as evidence of God's active presence in the affairs of man, to whom is God's plan evident? Who among us is charged with documenting and interpreting the history of God's people? When Mather insists that "all the *rare occurrences* will be evident operations of the Almighty God," he himself, as minister and author, assumes the posture of God's earthly interpreter (2:343). In the introduction to book six, Mather asserts that "[t]o *regard* the illustrious displays of that PROVIDENCE wherewith our Lord Christ governs the world, is a work, than which there is none more *needful* or *useful* for a Christian: to *record* them is a work, than which, none more proper for a minister" (2:341). Mather also chastises the "sleepiness" and even "stupidity" of ministers who ignore providential events, or those who recognize the hand of providence but fail to

---

2. The similarity of these tales was first noted by Charles H. Foster, 262.

record it for posterity (2:341). In *The Pearl of Orr's Island*, Stowe explicitly identifies the characters who are able to recognize providence. Moreover, within the novel, Stowe's characters are valued to the extent that they are able to recall past providences and discern God's hand in the current providential occurrences on Orr's Island. This notion, too, can be found in Mather's introduction to book six: "[T]here have been raised up, now and then, those persons who have rendered themselves worthy of *everlasting remembrance*, by their *wakeful zeal* to have the memorable providences of God remembered through all generations" (2:341).

On Orr's Island, the ministerial role is most often assumed by Aunt Roxy, who "spoke generally as one having authority" (6:19). Her authority derives not from an official, public position, but from the community's recognition that she is a woman of "faculty" who shares her domestic skills with neighbors and friends. On Orr's Island, domestic skill is yoked with wisdom. In "Earthly Care A Heavenly Discipline," Stowe extols "the Christian that really believes in the agency of God in the smallest events of life" (15:199–200), and in her fiction the author invests spiritual authority in domestic women.

Everybody's "aunt," Roxy presides over mundane familial rituals of sewing new clothes and reworking the old, of canning and cooking, and of tending the sick; she likewise witnesses exceptional events, such as weddings, births, and deaths. As such, Roxy lays claim to the history of her community. She herself asserts her unique position: "folks don't tend the sick and dyin' bed year in and out, at all hours, day and night, and not see some remarkable things" (6:68). Roxy also indicates that the domestic sphere is the site of God's most exceptional workings in the lives of man. In this and other novels by Stowe, domestic activity is conflated with religious activity, and is valued because of its spiritual significance.[3] By dint of her position on Orr's Island, Roxy recognizes the significance of the singular events she witnesses. Because she is a spinster, not compromised

---

3. For discussions of the theme of the spirituality and domesticity in Stowe's novels, see Dorothy Berkson, "Millennial Politics and the Feminine Fiction of Harriet Beecher Stowe," *Critical Essays on Harriet Beecher Stowe*, ed. Elizabeth Ammons (Boston: G. K. Hall, 1980), 244–58; Joan Hedrick; Laurie Crumpacker, "Four Novels of Harriet Beecher Stowe: A Study in Nineteenth-Century Androgyny," *American Novelists Revisited: Essays in Feminist Criticism*, ed. Fritz Fleischmann (Boston: G. K. Hall, 1982); Mary Kelley, *Private Woman, Public Stage: Literary Domesticity in Nineteenth-Century America* (New York: Oxford University Press, 1984), especially 294. Stowe herself addresses these issues in a nonfiction work, *The American Woman's Home or, Principles of Domestic Science*, 1869 (Hartford, CT: The Stowe-Day Foundation, 1991) in which she and her co-author, Catherine Beecher, write, "The family state then, is the aptest earthly illustration of the heavenly kingdom, and in it woman is its chief minister" (19).

by allegiance to a family of her own, she has sufficient distance to interpret the events around her. Describing the character of Aunt Roxy, Stowe asks,

> Was she not a sort of priestess and sibyl in all the most awful straits and mysteries of life? How many births, and weddings, and deaths had come and gone under her jurisdiction! And amid weeping or rejoicing, was not Miss Roxy still the master-spirit,—consulted, referred to by all?—was not her word law and precedent? (6:19)

In this early passage, Stowe informs the reader that Roxy serves in a ministerial capacity. As such, she both conforms to Mather's notion that to recognize and record providence is "a work . . . none more proper for a minister" while subverting his authority by her gender and her profession (2:342). Yet, if Cotton Mather is cast as an "old New England grandmother," then Miss Roxy, an old wizened New England seamstress, assumes the position of the community's historian.

Indeed, Aunt Roxy announces the birth of Mara Lincoln as "a strange kind o' providence," using her authority to predict that the infant would grow to be an agent of God's plan for Orr's Island (6:20). Her wistful look, Roxy explains early in the novel, is a symbol of Mara's longing to return to her creator, and a sign of her early death. Later, when the entire community finds Mara glowing with the preparation for her wedding, only Roxy sees beyond the physical to assert,

> I hain't never had but jist one mind about Mara Lincoln's weddin',—it's to be,—but it won't be the way people think. I hain't nussed and watched and sot up nights sixty years for nothin'. I can see beyond what most folks can,—her weddin' garments is bought and paid for, and she'll wear 'em, but she won't be Moses Pennel's wife,—now you see. (6:338)

That is, in the enigmatic language of the spiritual Aunt Roxy, Mara will be buried in her wedding dress, her finest worldly moment being her call to eternity.

Roxy's tales are eerie accounts of supernatural working, but it would be a mistake to classify them as gothic tales, which destabilize the pieties of the community. At the same time, they take on the coloring of gothic tales because they are embedded in a work of fiction that is otherwise written in a sentimental mode. Furthermore, the tales cannot be divorced from their teller, and the character of Roxy as an old and strange spinster contributes to our coding her providential accounts as gothic. The gothic element of Roxy's stories is Roxy herself because her position as a female historian subverts the platform of Mather's authorship.

The gift of recognizing and explicating divine providence is accorded to very few of the residents of Orr's Island. Interestingly, this privilege is denied most men who serve in positions of authority on Orr's Island. The minister, for example, neither recounts nor interprets events of providential importance. His tales are largely limited to Roman history and are dismissed as extraneous to Christian life in New England. Stowe's critical evaluation echoes that of Mather who outlines the work of the many great historians of Greece and Rome, only to conclude that their collective writings do not equal either the gospel of Luke or the letters of Paul (1:27–29). Reverend Sewell also tells a story of his early romantic involvement, but it is a tale of decadence that has the flavor of romantic fiction, not a substantive account with moral import. Offering nothing to exemplify proper Christian life, Sewell's tragic story depicts the degenerate family life of Roman Catholics and reveals that his purported Calvinist moral superiority is rendered worthless by his lack of personal courage.

More significantly, when Mr. Sewell is confronted with evidence of divine providence, he equivocates, fails at recognition, or offers flawed explication. With the rescue of Moses from the sea, Sewell comments, "It may be a gracious deliverance, . . . who knows?" (6:92). He later muses, "Strange ways of God . . . that should send to my door this child, and should wash upon the beach the only sign by which he could be identified. To what end or purpose? Hath the Lord a will in this matter, and what is it?" (6:108). A cornerstone of Sewell's religious creed is the doctrine of providential history, and, as a minister, Sewell should never have questioned if God had "a will in this matter." Unlike Aunt Roxy and Mara Lincoln, the minister has little insight into the mysterious ways of the Lord. Echoing Mather's description of the believer who is "sleepy" in the face of providence, Sewell is, in Stowe's words, "a little dizzy and dreamy" (6:109). The Reverend Sewell's questioning regarding the providence of God parallels poetic lines by Claudian, cited in *Magnalia*:

Sæpe mihi dubiam traxit sententia mentem,
Curarent superi terras, an ullus inesset
Rector, an incerto fluerent mortalia cursu . . . (2:342)

(To doubts like these my thoughts are oft betrayed—
is God e'er mindful of the world He made?

Does Providence control our mortal state?
Or Chance direct our dark and wavering fate?)[4]

Mather's commentary on these heretical lines alerts his readers to the
danger of this inquiry: "But, reader, if any doubts like these of Claudian's,
about the *existence* and *providence* of God begin to poison thy soul, there
are six or seven chapters of history now before thee that may be thy anti-
dote" (2:343). Likewise, in the context of *The Pearl of Orr's Island,* the
reader would hardly be tempted to think as Sewell does because of the
compelling, contrary evidence of divine providence in the history of the
community.

Only at the close of the narrative does Moses Pennel recognize the role
of divine providence in his life. He is especially late to appreciate his deliverance into the good hands of Mara, and, at the time of her death, concedes
with faltering confidence, "It seemed if there was ever such a thing as God's
providence, which some folks believe in, it was in leading me to you, and
giving you to me. And now, to have all dashed—all destroyed—It makes
me feel as if all was blind chance; no guiding God" (6:390). In this respect,
the minister and the unregenerate young man are similar in their inability
to recognize and interpret God's intervention in their lives. Likewise, when
Moses attempts to reach an understanding of his exceptional relationship
with Mara, and to reconcile himself with her death, Stowe describes his
meditation as "musing and dreaming" (6:383). Like Mather's "sleepy"
Christians who remain oblivious of daily providence, Moses lies on the
beach, "hour after hour glid[ing] by," never confronting the central issue
of Mara's love as God's offering of eternal salvation (6:382).

Consonant with his spiritual struggles, throughout his childhood and
adolescence, Moses has little use for the eerie providence tales of the spinster sisters, yet is enthralled by stories of ancient warriors or contemporary
seafarers. Moses' personal accounts of his sea voyages, however, rarely
appear in the narrative, largely because they are not germane to the novel.
Judith Fetterley suggests that "although to Moses, his life is both story and
history, Stowe drops him from her text when he sets out to sea; his masculine adventures take place off a stage occupied instead by the women
who remain at home."[5] Not in the least providential, the otherwise exotic
adventures of Moses Pennel are peripheral, not central, to the social and

4. The translation of Claudian is by Lucius F. Robinson and is offered as a footnote in
Magnalia 2:342.
5. *Provisions: A Reader from 19th-Century American Women* (Bloomington: Indiana
University Press, 1985), 8.

religious history of Orr's Island. They serve as pale foils to the domestic stories that are critical to the individual's salvation and the social and religious health of the community. Paradoxically, in *The Pearl of Orr's Island*, the ordinary is extraordinary. Stowe has chosen to reverse the aesthetic of American literature and the mores of American society in her construction of the novel. Birth, death, sewing, courting, and childrearing are purposeful and therefore steeped in gravity, mystery, and infinite interest. Tales of ancient Rome, modern China, and wealthy Cuban plantations are not evocative in that they lack the importance of the ordinary for the good people of Orr's Island.

Likewise, Captain Kittridge spins yarns about his sea-faring adventures, many of which parallel those of Cotton Mather, but Kittridge fails to convince his community of their significance. Because his tales are exotic rather than domestic and speak to worldly interests but have no bearing on eternal life, they are devalued for his audience, just as his authority as narrator is devalued.[6] For these reasons, Kittridge is unable to assume the role of community historian. Consequently, although his witchcraft stories are reminiscent of those documented by Cotton Mather in "Thaumatographia," they, too, are received as outlandish. Later, when the Captain recognizes his mother's dreams and premonitions as "a sartin sign," his wife dismisses them as idle "levity" (6:129).

Mrs. Kittridge, too, is without the gift of interpreting providence. When Moses and his mother are found on the beach, Mrs. Kittridge recognizes this exceptional event as "a loud providence," but, unfortunately, she cannot hear what it says (6:57). She erroneously believes that it bears a message of untimely death for her unregenerate husband. In this, she is twice mistaken. First, Mrs. Kittridge fails to appreciate her husband's piety. Furthermore, she does not yet understand that the lesson of the providence

6. Captain Kittridge tells of polar bears aiding sailors lost at sea, his tale a parallel of Mather's story in which God sends dolphins to attend to stranded seafarers. In "Mantissa," Mather recounts the tale of Captain Trowbridge of New Haven whose ship, seventeen weeks from port, was devoid of provisions. Once the crew "cry'd unto the Lord," thereby exhibiting their piety, "he heard and sav'd them." God sent dolphins, who, according to Mather, "surrendred themselves" and allowed the sailors to catch one each day for nourishment, and two on Saturday so that they would not break their Sabbath by fishing (2:354). Kittridge's analogous tale details his trials at sea when his boat collided with an iceberg in the fog, but, miraculously, sustained no damage. By the Captain's account, nearby polar bears were "so hungry, that they stood there with the water jist runnin' out of their chops in a perfect stream," yet never harmed the men who lived to tell the tale (6:128). Because of his deliverance, Captain Kittridge assures Mara that the polar bears would care for Moses, who was lost at sea, just as the dolphins "surrendred themselves" for Mather's seafarers. Each passage offers narrative development similar to that of Mather, and concludes with a confident explication of a divine message offered the people of Orr's Island.

is not of death, but life. The extraordinary occurrence is not the death of the mother, but the miraculous deliverance of the child whose life brings the promise of salvation to Mara. No "cunning woman," Mrs. Kittridge busies herself with preparations for the funeral, and personally looks upon this providence merely as an opportunity to socialize. Although an orthodox Calvinist in her religious practice, Mrs. Kittridge is not a spiritual woman.

Ruey is sister and companion to the sage Roxy, yet does not share her ability to recognize providence. Ruey is a thoroughly sentimental, "pliant, cozy, easy-to-be-entreated personnage, plump and cushiony" (6:19). A devoutly religious woman, she quotes hymns rather than scripture, and thus incurs her sister's disapproval. In one telling scene, Ruey presumes to identify Moses Pennel's inheritance as "kind o' providential," mistaking as providential what is merely felicitous (6:340). Roxy deliberately chooses not to respond to her sister's pronouncement. The reader, who at this point is well initiated into the nature of divine providence, understands that Moses' financial gain is exclusively secular and without spiritual import. In fact, in the hands of Moses, this windfall has the potential to undermine his Christian upbringing.

The language of the providence tale is also the language of typology. In her use of early literary forms for *The Pearl of Orr's Island*, Stowe relies heavily upon Christian typology, which is one of the dominant rhetorical devices of Mather's *Magnalia*. According to the conventions of typology, as described by Sacvan Bercovitch, the figures and events of the Old Testament, which serve as prefigurations of the figures and events in the New Testament, are then continually repeated in the history of the Christian people following the death of Christ. Mather's use of typology allows him to situate the lives of New England's visible saints within the grander framework of scriptural history. In this way, he is able to conflate *allegoria* and *historia*.[7] Bercovitch also notes that Mather's Christian mythopoetic interpretation of New England history influences the American vision of self and society well into the nineteenth century, and cites the novels of Harriet Beecher Stowe for their expression of the sacred origins and future of the American society (87, 88).

In the sixth chapter of *The Pearl of Orr's Island*, Stowe identifies Orr's

---

7. In *The Puritan Origins of the American Self* (New Haven: Yale University Press, 1975), Sacvan Bercovitch puts forth a comprehensive analysis of *exemplum fidei, figura,* and typology in early American letters (35–50, 58–66). See also Mason I. Lowance, "Typology and the New England Way: Cotton Mather and the Exegesis of Biblical Types." *Early American Literature* 4.1 (1970): 15–37.

Island as an analogue of the Negev oasis, Kadesh-barnea, where Moses and the Israelites restored themselves before their final journey to the land of Israel.[8] "The wilderness of Kadesh, with its great cedars, was doubtless Orr's Island, where even now the goodly fellowship of black-winged trees were groaning and swaying, and creaking as the breath of the Lord passed over them" (6:40–41). The reader is asked to understand that Orr's Island, like the oasis of the Old Testament, is where the God of Exodus nourishes and blesses his people. One feels his presence in the motion of the trees and hears his voice in the wind. As corollary of this biblical type, the reader must expect that God will make his presence known in this community through miraculous and often strange works, just as he did for the ancient Hebrews. Ultimately, he will preserve them, and lead them to His promised land, which was, in the Old Testament, Israel, and is, in this novel, eternal life.[9]

Characterization in *The Pearl of Orr's Island* is also modeled after the typological mode of early American historical literature. Moses is easily identified as a type of his Old Testament namesake. Zephaniah suggests the boy be named Moses "because we drew him out of the water," to which Ruey issues her testimony to the validity of Christian typology, "Now, did I ever! . . . there's something in the Bible to fit everything, ain't there?" (6:79). Like the biblical Moses, the Pennel boy is characterized by his struggle with the divine call to responsibility and piety. Just as the Hebrew Moses is sometimes plagued by disbelief as he wanders in a foreign land, so too Stowe's Moses wrestles at home and abroad with God's design for his life. Ultimately, both men are privileged by their intimate relationship with their God, the Hebrew Moses through the burning bush and the tablets of the law, and Stowe's Moses through the person of Mara Lincoln. Roxy and Ruey, too, are first identified typologically "in the Old Testament language" as the "cunning women" (6:17). Even Mary and Zephaniah Pennel serve as types of Mary and Joseph, the patient parents of a child savior, who both is and is not their offspring. Critics have spoken of Mara both as a Christ figure and as an example of the nineteenth-century figure of the dying angel. Perhaps a more appropriate and richer interpretation can be found in the identification of Mara as a type of Miriam, both women closely associated with a Moses. Miriam, sister of the biblical Moses, is an artist,

8. The Hebrews' sojourn at Kadesh is recounted in Num 11–20:1.

9. Stowe reinforces this identification of Orr's Island as a type of Kadesh in many later references in the text, among them the narrator's commentary that "the state of society in some of the districts of Maine, in these days, much resembled in its spirit that which Moses labored to produce in ruder ages" (6:131).

the first poet of the Old Testament, who chants her praise of God immediately after deliverance from the Red Sea (Ex 16:20–21). Moreover, she is
recognized as God's prophet to her people (Mic 6:4), and is compelled to
chastise Moses for his questionable behavior (Num 12). Miriam, however,
is not privileged to enter the Promised Land with the Hebrew people; she
dies in the wilderness and is buried in Kadesh (Num 20:1). Like the rescue
of the Hebrew people from the sea, which Miriam celebrates in the *Song of
the Sea,* Mara Lincoln's delivery, intimately tied to the sea, is nothing short
of a miracle. Mara too is a prophetess, an artist, and has a sisterly relationship with Moses. As a figure of Miriam, Mara Lincoln dies in her typological oasis of Kadesh, Orr's Island, and leaves her people to make their final
journey to salvation.

The dialogue of Stowe's novel strikes a similar chord to that of Mather's
providence, as well. Like the elect in Mather's tales, Stowe's characters are
never far from scripture. When Captain Pennel tucks in a sleeping child,
he "could n't help thinking: 'So he giveth his beloved sleep!'" (6:46). Ruey
is always prepared to sing a hymn appropriate to the occasion. Even Mrs.
Kittridge lends authority to her complaints of her husband with language
from the Rev. Cotton Mather. When scolding the Captain for excessive
levity, she compares his laugh to "the crackling of thorns under a pot," a
quotation from Mather's sermonic literature (6:129).[10]

With the 1862 publication of *The Pearl of Orr's Island,* Harriet Beecher
Stowe neither begins nor closes her novelistic experiment with the fictional form of the Puritan providence. In *The Minister's Wooing* (1859)
and *Sam Lawson's Oldtown Fireside Stories* (1872), she injects elements of
early American providence literature at all levels of narrative construction—plot, embedded tales, and characterization, as well as the language
of Mather's anecdotes.

10. In "The EPHEMERON," Mather writes, "Men are *Fools,* if they think, their *mirth* can last
any longer than *Sparks,* or than the *Crackling of thorns under a Pot*" (41). "The EPHEMERON.
Or, Tears Dropt on Dust and Ashes" is the second of three sermons by Cotton Mather collected
by Jonathan Edwards for publication as *The Words of Understanding* (Boston: Kneeland, 1724).
It appears most likely that Stowe was familiar with the other sermons in this collection as well.
The first, entitled "The PHILOMELA. With The Notes of Morning-Piety," encourages religious
devotion among the very young, such as Stowe's readers find in characters such as Mara Lincoln
and Mary Scudder. The third sermon, "JONAH: Or, the Dove in Safety," is grounded in the
images of a masculine rock and a feminine dove as metaphors of marital love. In *The Minister's
Wooing,* Mary figures prominently as a dove to Dr. Hopkins' rock. Additionally, the collection's
subtitle, "Occasioned by some EARLY DEATHS which require full Notice to be taken of them,"
is suggestive of the character of Mara Lincoln, whose early death also gives rise to religious
devotion.

The Female Minister

Examination of Calvinist doctrine informs Stowe's early novel, *The Minister's Wooing*, and, not surprisingly, the formulaic Puritan providence tale is central to its plot structure. Mary Scudder, the female protagonist of this novel, and Mara Lincoln, the heroine of *The Pearl of Orr's Island*, have much in common: youth, domestic accomplishments, and intense religious fervor. Both are also attracted to young men who, in the eyes of the community, are unregenerate and of questionable character. In the case of *The Minister's Wooing*, Stowe permits herself to complete the marriage plot, but not without securing the conversion of Mary's young man, James Marvyn, in order to exhibit that he is worthy of the saintly young lady. This she does within the framework of the providence tale following the pattern of the shipwreck at sea. Stowe's account tells of the supernatural strength of Marvyn who, with "the spirit of ten men in him," attempted to save his ship (5:238). At the final moment before capsizing, he makes an announcement that takes the form of a profession of faith, "Well, my boys, we're headin' right into eternity and our chances for this world ain't worth mentionin'. . . . I've tried to do my duty by you and the ship, but God's will be done" (5:238). At that very minute, the waves crush the boat and its crew against the rocks, and Marvyn alone is delivered to safety. Following the formula of Mather's tales in "Christus Super Aquas," Stowe's account demonstrates the exceptional physical prowess of the elect in extreme situations, and the author makes explicit that the physical strength is the result of "spirit" and not adrenaline. In providence tales, protagonists also exhibit foresight and complete understanding of their predicament, their final words—dramatically issued only seconds before catastrophe—expressing their faith in God and submission to His design. In conversation with Mary Scudder following his deliverance and return, Marvyn reveals that he was convinced of God's grace, if not of his deliverance, because he witnessed a vision of Jesus in his boat during the storm at sea, another motif from *Magnalia*.

Central to characterization in *The Minister's Wooing* is the singular importance of those who recognize the hand of God in quotidian events. As in *The Pearl of Orr's Island*, such wisdom is most often found in modest, traditionally undervalued, domestic women. A hired hand, Amaziah, is first to identify the wreck of the "Monsoon" as an "awful providence, that 'ar' is" (5:237). The Marvyn's black cook, Candace, who is convinced of the prophetic value of dreams, has a nocturnal vision of Jim Marvyn's deliverance that approximates his own account of the incident.

I dreamed I see Jim Marvyn a-sinkin' in de water, an' stretchin' up his hands. An' den I dreamed I see de Lord Jesus come a-walkin' on de water an' take hold ob his hand, an' says he, "O thou of little faith, wherefore didst thou doubt?" An' den he lifted him right out. (5:326)

When Candace is pressed to defend the veracity of the providence tale, she finds an ally in Miss Prissy, the local seamstress, who supports her interpretation and insists that the dream "may have reference to the state of his soul" (5:326).[11] In any event, both women agree not to disclose this remarkable occurrence to the minister. Like Rev. Sewell, Dr. Hopkins is not privileged to recognize and interpret providence. Moreover, Hopkins does not believe in providential signs. In the words of Candace, "de Doctor, he don't like to hab us talk much 'bout dese yer tings, 'cause he tinks it's kind o' heathenish" (5:326).

Were Stowe to craft her novel strictly according to Mather's conventions for the providence tale, the minister would record and interpret the events of Newport for his congregation. While Dr. Hopkins is intelligent, industrious, and well-meaning, his theology is rigid and his religious practice is austere to the extent that he himself is a remote figure. The very title of the novel may be read ironically because the minister does not actually "woo" Mary Scudder. Neither does he truly minister to his people. Candace consoles the grieving Mrs. Marvyn and convinces her of God's love, one of the ministerial roles at which Hopkins fails. Where Hopkins understands God's hand in the purported death of James Marvyn as a *terribilia Dei*, Candace's vision of the same event is that of God's great *magnalia* on behalf of James. Thus, once again, Stowe's fiction undermines the exclusive authority of the ministry, and instead asserts the agency of domestic women in establishing and maintaining community and in recording and interpreting the history of their communities.[12] Likewise,

11.   Nancy Schultz's important essay on the role of Prissy, "The Artist's Craftiness: Miss Prissy in *The Minister's Wooing*" in *Studies in American Fiction* 20.1 (1992), concludes that within the novel the woman as domestic artist "turns the tables on the voices of authority," familial, social, and religious (34).

12.   John R. Adams was the first to note the importance of Prissy and Candace in *The Minister's Wooing* in "Structure and Theme in the Novels of Harriet Beecher Stowe," *American Transcendental Quarterly* 24.1 (1974): 50–55. Although he does not identify these women with a female ministry of sorts, Adams rightly concludes that "notably the two wisest persons in the story are Miss Prissy, a gossipy dressmaker, and Candace, an Amazonian Negress of prophetic insight and practical wisdom who exerts overall influence second only to that of the saintly heroine" (53). In his essay "Making Declarations of Her Own: Harriet Beecher Stowe as New England Historian," *New England Quarterly* 71.1 (1998), Edward Tang argues that not only is Candace a female minister to Mrs. Marvin, but she effectively also "rewrites religious doctrine,"

their stories may be extraordinary, uncanny, and even eerie, after the fashion of the Reverend Cotton Mather's providence tales, but their role as the teller of tales truly disrupts the social order he envisioned.

Story and History

Published ten years after *The Pearl of Orr's Island,* Stowe's collection of short stories, *Sam Lawson's Oldtown Fireside Stories* (1872), continues to exhibit the author's fascination with the topoi of providential literature and, correspondingly, her convictions regarding divine intervention in the affairs of man. The venerable narrator, Sam Lawson, for whom storytelling is "an art and an accomplishment," is also a great believer in the remarkable providences in "Mister Cotton Marther's 'Magnilly'" (10:247, 263)—so much so that he borrows liberally from Mather's tales of Indian captivity, witchcraft, sea voyages, visions, and more.[13] Six of the fifteen stories in the collection, "The Ghost in the Mill," "The Sullivan Looking-Glass," "Mis' Elderkin's Pitcher," "The Ghost in the Cap'n Brown House," "Colonel Eph's Shoe-Buckles," and "A Student's Sea Story," are analogues of those found in book six of *Magnalia Christi Americana.* In each tale, the narrator uses either the term "providence" or "providential" to signal his working within this literary tradition. Moreover, in "The Ghost in the Mill," "The Sullivan Looking-Glass," and "The Ghost in the Cap'n Brown House," the narrator refers to the accounts of Cotton Mather in direct discussion of providential literature and its relation to the stories that he is in the process of narrating.[14] Each introduces a "remarkable occurrence" that is eventually understood within the framework of divine providence. Following Mather's formula, Lawson is "especially careful to impress an edifying moral" at the close of most tales (10:296).

As in *The Pearl of Orr's Island,* Stowe's characters in her short fiction are divided in their acceptance of God's agency in worldly events. Sam avers, "There's a providence in everything, . . . even down to shoe-buckles," and his opinion is shared by Granny Badger, a revered member of Oldtown society, who is devoted to the works of Cotton Mather (10:351). A young but loyal

---

although she "disavows any intention to contradict Dr. Hopkins" (81).

13. Charles H. Foster first noted Sam Lawson's affinity to the earlier storyteller, Cotton Mather (211).

14. One could also argue that tales such as "How to Fight the Devil" and "Tom Toothacre's Ghost Story" mirror providence tales from *Magnalia* although they contain no overt reference to the earlier text as other stories do.

member of Lawson's audience, Harry imbibes the stories with "very wide blue eyes, in which undoubting faith shone as in a mirror" (10:248). Within their circle, belief in God's omnipresence is fundamental, and relating stories about daily life is, therefore, a testimony to religious faith.

Unlike the characters of Aunt Roxy and Candace, however, Sam Lawson lacks the credibility of a sober, religious narrator. His tales, which he conjures for the village's little boys, are less religious or gothic than merely sensational. Lawrence Buell classifies his stories as "Yankee comic grotesque."[15] Children beg him for a story because they want "cold chills," not a glimpse of God's designs for his people (10:250). For his part, Lawson indulges himself in storytelling as a way to pass the time, avoid work, and earn himself a mug of cider. Lawson's comic posture as a narrator notwithstanding, he is entirely earnest in his faith in divine providence.

Stowe offers a counterexample to this belief in the character of Aunt Lois, an outspoken curmudgeon who is a rationalist to the point of obviating religious faith. According to Sam Lawson, she is "the very impersonation of that obstinate rationalism that grew up at the New England fireside, close alongside of the most undoubting faith in the supernatural" (10:262). Lois brings her austerity to her domestic activity as well, Stowe noting that she "knit severely" (10:260).

Interestingly, the character of Aunt Lois appears earlier in Stowe's fiction, in an embedded tale told by Ruey in *The Pearl of Orr's Island*. In Ruey's account, as in the *Fireside Stories*, Lois is confronted with evidence of divine intervention and refuses to recognize it as such. She finds a baby cradle washed up on shore after a storm, and takes it to her home. During gales, she observes that the cradle rocks itself, and she hears a baby cry, but ignores these critical signs. When her sister Cerinthy, providentially born with a veil over her face, sees the specter of a woman rocking the cradle one night, Lois cuts the cradle into kindling as if her physical action can resolve a supernatural problem. The resolution of this tale indicates otherwise (6:43–44).

In a mediate position between the superstitious Sam Lawson and the rational Aunt Lois is Granny Badger. Granny upholds the value of Mather's tales and attempts to mitigate Lawson's wild flights of fancy that compromise the integrity of providence tales. In the collection's opening tale, Lawson discloses his theory of historical narrative:

There's a putty consid'able sight o' things in this world that's true; and then

---

15. *New England Literary Culture from Revolution through Renaissance* (Cambridge: Cambridge University Press, 1986), 348.

ag'in there's a sight o' things that ain't true. Now, my old grand'ther used to say, "Boys," says he, "if ye want to lead a pleasant and prosperous life, ye must contrive allers to keep jest the *happy medium* between truth and falsehood." Now, that 'ere's my doctrine. (10:260)

It is questionable that Sam Lawson meets his objective in his *Fireside Stories* where he is extravagant and fanciful. As a true follower of Cotton Mather, he looks to his male ancestor as an exemplary historian, and would have never conceived of his grandmother in this role. Nonetheless, Stowe installs Granny in this august position.

In his *Oldtown Fireside Stories,* when Sam Lawson registers his disapproval of Aunt Lois, the excessively rational naysayer, he speaks to a larger issue:

You look at the folks that's allus tellin' you what they don't believe,—they don't believe this, and they don't believe that,—and what sort o' folks is they? Why, like yer Aunt Lois, sort o' stringy and dry. There ain't no 'sorption got out o' not believin' nothing. (10:330)

One could extend Lawson's comment to the issue of fiction in general, and argue that the literal-minded or obsessively rational reader will appreciate or "absorb" precious little from Lawson's fireside stories. On the other hand, those who are drawn to the fantastic or are willing to be seduced by the extraordinary will find in these accounts an experience that is palpable, full, and rich.

Stowe draws attention to this issue at the outset of the collection when she introduces the reader to Sam and his "chimney-corner story-telling" (10:247):

Society then was full of traditions and narratives which had all the uncertain glow and shifting mystery of the firelit hearth upon them. They were told to sympathetic audiences, by the rising and falling light of the solemn embers, with the hearth-crickets filling up every pause. Then the aged told their stories to the young,—tales of early life; tales of war and adventure, of forest days, of Indian captivities and escapes, of bears and wildcats and panthers, of rattlesnakes, of witches and wizards, and strange and wonderful dreams and appearances and providences. (10:247–48)

The narrator's traditional fireside stories approximate the subject matter of the providence tale, and the sequence of Lawson's tales roughly parallels the ordering of *Magnalia,* which begins in the early books with the history of the early colonists, their leadership, their adventures and wars, and ends with accounts of Indian captivity, New England witches, and "remarkable occurrences" of God's providence. Furthermore, the narrator takes great care to describe the fluid relationship between story and history. In this attempt at definition, Stowe employs the metaphor of the hearth that glows, albeit "uncertainly," against the dark, sooty backdrop of the fire-bricks. The "shifting mystery" of the flames dancing and dodging in the dark is a metaphor of the ambiguous relationship between fact and fantasy in Sam Lawson's tales. Lawson, like Cotton Mather, avows that his stories are grounded in truth. "Why, I know things, that ef I should tell,—why, people might say they wa'n't so; but then they *is* so for all that" (10:248). Consequently, when Lawson readies himself to tell a fireside tale, he picks up the tongs, and, in stern biblical language, "smote on the hickory fore-stick," tosses sparks, and sheds light on God's providence (10:248–49). Only Aunt Lois fusses about the mess of ashes and coals, the nuisance of physical reality; the others attend the stories, the blessings and wonders of providential events.

The intimate relationship between story and history expressed by Sam Lawson must figure in discussion of *The Pearl of Orr's Island* as well. E. Bruce Kirkham has carefully documented the factual basis for Stowe's novel, his study of Maine maritime history revealing that Maine suffered one of its worst shipwrecks in November 1849, just months before Harriet Beecher Stowe arrived for a stay at her home in Brunswick.[16] A written report of the disaster is unquestionably similar to the shipwreck Stowe describes at the outset of her novel. With this and other evidence, Kirkham puts forth a convincing argument that Stowe draws on specific, historical material within her novel. Important to this study is the way in which she, like Cotton Mather, finds meaning in historical detail. Mather's efforts as a historian are marked by his commitment to his ministry. His interpretation of historical events is determined by his attempt to understand singular events as part of the continuing history of God's people. Consequently, Mather's narrative framing of remarkable occurrences as providence tales issues from his concept of history as Christian epic. Likewise, in Stowe's novel, the history of the people of Orr's Island takes shape only as it is directed toward the story of their salvation. Although the novel begins and ends with the birth and death of Mara Lincoln, the scope of Stowe's novel

16. "The Source of the Shipwreck in *The Pearl of Orr's Island,*" *American Transcendental Quarterly* 40: 365–66.

is not the life of Mara, but the everlasting life of this woman and her community. Consonant with Stowe's theology, the novel's extraordinary events wrought by God and mundane events rendered by man can and ought to be viewed in terms of one's eternity. In her words, "the line of this present life seemed so to melt and lose itself" as it fuses with the larger reality of eternal life (6:331).

The Pearl of Orr's Island has been perhaps Stowe's most maligned novel. Admirers of the work frequently invoke John Greenleaf Whittier's accolade and Sarah Orne Jewett's qualified admiration of The Pearl because favorable reviews and critical evaluation have been rare. In a letter written to the author, Whittier described the novel as "the most charming New England idyl ever written," and Jewett wrote that The Pearl had "a divine touch here and there," although she found it to be "an incomplete piece of work."[17] Contemporary scholars fault Stowe primarily for clumsy, artificial plot devices and for the preposterous situations in which she places her characters. However, where critics lament the flawed construction of the novel, they fail to recognize Stowe's use of the literary form that she found so compelling in Cotton Mather's Magnalia Christi Americana. The form of the providence tale does not provide the verisimilitude that the modern reader demands of narrative. In particular, it ruptures the normal plotting patterns with unanticipated catastrophes and miraculous resolutions. The Pearl of Orr's Island also boldly defies the expected formula of the marriage plot common to nineteenth-century women's fiction. Granted, the novel opens and develops as a conventional tale of courtship and marriage, and does not radically depart from the conventional plot of the bourgeois novel until chapter thirty-six in a text of forty-four chapters. However, in the closing chapters of the novel, the narrator addresses the reader directly about questions of fiction forms and generic expectations.

> There are no doubt many, who have followed this history so long as it danced like a gay little boat over sunny waters, and who would have followed it gayly to the end, had it closed with ringing of marriage-bells, who turn from it indignantly, when they see that its course runs through the dark valley. This, they say, is an imposition, a trick upon our feelings. (6:364)

---

17. Whittier's letter is quoted in Charles Edward Stowe, Life of Harriet Beecher Stowe Compiled from Her Letters and Journals (Boston: Houghton Mifflin, 1889), 327. Jewett's statement is found in The Letters of Sarah Orne Jewett, ed. Annie Fields (Boston: Houghton Mifflin, 1911), 47.

In rhetorical response to the reader's unfulfilled expectations, the narrator simply asks, "Are we Christians or heathen?" (6:364). By way of explanation, the speaker notes that the figure of Christ offers a type for literature and for life. His early death and promise of eternal life offer another "form" and "style" in which the reader can frame and, therefore, understand fiction, and, ultimately, the human condition (6:365). Is not Mara's message for Moses the wisdom that her untimely death affords him a greater opportunity for salvation than her life might have? Thus, when Mara announces to her intended husband that God "sent you and gave you to me . . . to be mine in time and eternity," her devotion to Moses—as well as the plot of the novel—is clearly focused on their eternal life (6:322).

"Fate! there is no fate," Mara insists, when Moses mourns that their romance will not end happily ever after (6:378). In her rejection of fate is Mara's belief that the events of life are not random, unpredictable, or inexplicable. Neither are they predictable, determined by mortal beings, or easily explained by mortal beings. Between these opposing views of "fate" is Stowe's conviction regarding providential history and the ability of God's servants to perceive his strange workings in the lives of his people. In the introduction to book six, Mather issues a similar statement regarding his piety and his role as an author: "It is observ'd that the name . . . *Fortune* is not once used in all the works of Homer. We will now write a book of rare occurrences, wherein a blind *fortune* shall not once be acknowledged" (2:343). Consequently, *The Pearl of Orr's Island,* like *Magnalia Christi Americana,* relies on conventions of fiction that invoke spiritual belief to value appropriately events that often appear to be improbable and exceptional.

Stowe asks us to read *The Pearl of Orr's Island* as she read Mather's *Magnalia.* With her use of the topoi of the providence tale, she is working within the early American literary tradition, adopting its forms and, simultaneously, invoking its pieties. Foremost among those pieties is the desire of both Mather and Stowe for a society unified in its mission to march toward spiritual righteousness in this world, and salvation in the next. Leading this march, however, is the domestic woman of "faculty" as the minister and historian of her community. As such, *The Pearl of Orr's Island* represents Stowe's attempt to chronicle such a community, even if only in a "charming New England idyl," a work of the imagination.

Chapter 5

ᘓᘓ

Nathaniel Hawthorne and the "Singular Mind" of Cotton Mather[1]

Nathaniel Hawthorne's literary project was centrally involved with *res Americana,* well read as he was in the early and contemporary historical accounts of colonial and revolutionary America.[2] This is not to say that he fashioned himself as a professional historian. Michael J. Colacurcio cautions the reader that "he wrote tales and romances, not monographs and treatises."[3] Nonetheless, the argument of much of Hawthorne's imaginative work concerns itself centrally with the creation and reception of historical narrative. In the short fiction where Hawthorne confronts American history, he takes on one early historian more boldly than the others, and that historian is Cotton Mather. Hawthorne references Mather by name in *The House of the Seven Gables* and in seven short stories: "The Gray Champion," "Edward Randolph's Portrait," "Main-street," "Alice Doane's Appeal," "Time's Portraiture," "Dr. Bullivant," and "The Duston Family."

1. Hawthorne describes Mather as such in *The Whole History of Grandfather's Chair* in *The Centenary Edition of the Works of Nathaniel Hawthorne.* 23 vols. to date. Eds. Wm Charvat, Roy Harvey Pearce, Claude M. Simpson, Thomas Woodson (Columbus: The Ohio State University Press, 1984), 6:92. All references to Hawthorne's fiction and letters are to this edition, with the exception of references to "The Duston Family."

2. Marion L. Kessselring documents that the charge-books of the Salem Athenaeum record that Hawthorne is credited with borrowing Mather's *Magnalia Christi Americana* on June 19, 1827 and April 19, 1828. He also borrowed Increase Mather's *An Essay for the Recording of Illustrious Providences* in 1827, 1829, and 1834 as well as *The Proceedings of the Massachusetts General Court* many times throughout 1827 and 1830. In 1826, 1827, and 1829, he is listed as borrowing Francis Hutcheson's *An Historical Essay concerning Witchcraft* and Thomas Huchinson's *A Collection of Original Papers Relative to the History of the Colony of Massachusetts-Bay Boston* as well as his *The History of Massachusetts.* In addition, from 1828 through 1830 he is charged with many volumes of election sermons, lecture sermons, fast sermons, funeral sermons, ordination sermons, and occasional sermons. See *Hawthorne's Reading 1828–1850* (New York: The New York Public Library, 1949), 56, 53, 60–61.

3. *The Province of Piety: Moral History in Hawthorne's Early Tales* (Durham and London: Duke University Press, 1995), 1.

"The Prophetic Pictures" speaks of a Dr. Mather, although the story never clarifies which of the many Drs. Mather the author intends. Additionally, Hawthorne invokes Mather's father and fellow historian, Increase Mather, in "Sir William Phips" as well as his grandfather, John Cotton, who appears as a judge in "Mrs. Hutchinson."[4]

In many of these works, Hawthorne's characterization of Mather is pointedly critical and often brutal, Mather being depicted in "Alice Doane's Appeal" as "the representative of all the hateful features of his time" and in "The Duston Family" as "an old hard-hearted, pedantic bigot" (11:279, 17:235). Correspondence with Sophia Peabody on September 14, 1841 is equally derisive of the eighteenth-century historian; in this letter Hawthorne envisions

> old Cotton Mather, venerable in a three cornered hat and other antique attire, walking the streets of Boston, and lifting up his hands to bless the people, while they all revile him. An old dame should be seen flinging water or emptying some vials of medicine on his head, from the latticed window of an old-fashioned house; and all around must be tokens of pestilence and mourning—as a coffin borne along, a woman or children weeping on a door-step. (15:570)

The less harsh but equally denigrating depiction of Mather in Hawthorne's story "Edward Randolph's Portrait" is reminiscent of Harriet Beecher Stowe's statement on the Puritan historian as an "old New England grandmother." Hawthorne writes that "Dr. Cotton Mather . . . has filled our early history with old women's tales, as fanciful and extravagant as those of Greece or Rome" (9:262).

Had Cotton Mather's narratives of colonial America been relegated to the darkest corner of the dustiest archives, they would not trigger such a caustic response from Nathaniel Hawthorne. The continued republication of *Magnalia Christi Americana* in the nineteenth century may have rightly given Hawthorne cause to believe that this historical narrative—the foremost text in Mather's oeuvre—would become the received account

4. See *The House of the Seven Gables* (2:188), "The Gray Champion" (9:13), "Edward Randolph's Portrait" (9:262), "Main-street" (11:77), "Alice Doane's Appeal" (11:279), "Time's Portraiture" (11:331), "Dr. Bullivant" (23:80–81), "The Prophetic Pictures" (9:166), "Sir William Phips" (23:62–63), "Mrs. Hutchinson" (23:69–70), and "The Duston Family" in *The Complete Writings of Nathaniel Hawthorne, Old Manse Edition*, 22 vols. (Boston and New York: Houghton, Mifflin, 1900), 17:233, 235, 236. Additionally, in "The Haunted Quack," Hawthorne speaks directly about Glanvill's *History of the Witches, or the Wonders of the Invisible World Displayed*, a book that later served as source material for both Increase and Cotton Mather's work (11:252).

of seventeenth-century New England in his century. In fact, Reverend Thomas Robbins's introduction to the 1820 edition of *Magnalia* makes this very claim, and then extends the claim beyond both the nineteenth century and New England:

> *Magnalia* is a standard work with American Historians, and must ever continue to be such, especially respecting the affairs of New-England. To this portion of our country, always distinguished for emigrations, a great part of the population of New-York, the most important state in the American confederacy, and of all the western states north of Ohio, will always trace their origin. Nor will the lapse of ages, diminish their respect for the land of their forefathers. (v)

In his own work, Hawthorne challenges not the details of Mather's historical narratives as much as the conclusions that Mather draws from those details and the ideology that underpins his conclusions. This is to say that Hawthorne defies the historiographic principles of the earlier author. In particular, he questions Mather's insistence on providential history and the authority of the historian *cum* minister to determine God's judgment of every quotidian or exceptional event in the lives of men and women. Thus, when Hawthorne disparages Cotton Mather's "singular mind," he is concerned about the historian's singular goal of imposing the hand of God on the history of the United States, the implication of which is that the historian speaks on behalf of God.

Further, Hawthorne is also disquieted by Mather's dominant, singular voice amid the chorus of American voices on the subjects of our national history and identity. Because of his broad reading in early American history, Hawthorne was aware of the continuing presence of Mather's historiographic principles in the many, later historical narratives of early New England. Eighteenth-century historians Francis Hutcheson and Thomas Hutchinson, whose work was familiar to Hawthorne, both acknowledge Cotton Mather's influence on their scholarship. In prefatory remarks to *An Historical Essay Concerning Witchcraft*, Francis Hutcheson attempts to win his readers' confidence by claiming that he "uphold[s] the same notions" as those found in the works of "Mr. Increase and Mr. Cotton Mather's several Tracts."[5] Likewise, Thomas Hutchinson acknowledges, "I am obliged to no other person more than to my friend and brother the Reverend Mr. Mather."[6]

5. (London, 1718), a2.
6. See *The History of Massachusetts from the First Settlement Thereof in 1628, until the Year 1750.* 2 vols. (Salem, 1795), v.

Then, when George Bancroft, one of the early nineteenth century's fore-most historians, articulates his philosophy of historical inquiry, his voice likewise echoes that of Cotton Mather.[7] Bancroft, who like Mather was a Harvard-educated minister as well as historian, avows his belief in provi-dential design in the founding of New England and the development of the American nation. In the early pages of his *History of the United States,* he asserts that because "the fortunes of a nation are not under control of blind destiny," "it is the object of the present work to follow the steps by which a favoring Providence, calling our institutions into being, has conducted the country to its present happiness and glory."[8] This principle underpinning his historical narrative, Bancroft's plots and themes are crafted to evince the role of divine order in the continuing ascendant might and grandeur of the nation. As such, Bancroft's *History* is both backward looking and forward looking in that, as Susan L. Mizruchi points out, his dedication to providential history enables him to idealize the progressive program of Andrew Jackson.[9]

David Levin finds that Bancroft's deistic historiography and insistence on American exceptionalism is common to the work of many of his con-temporary historians.[10] The opening pages of James Thacher's 1835 *History of the Town of Plymouth, from its first settlement in 1620, to the present time* clearly characterizes the Puritan colonial enterprise as "an event in Divine

7. Kesselring documents that Bancroft's *History of the United States* was charged to Hawthorne's Athenaeum subscription in April 1837 (44). Additionally, Hawthorne's relationship with Bancroft was more than academic or literary. Hawthorne had a professional and personal relationship with George Bancroft that was sometimes contentious. Hawthorne was indebted to Bancroft for recommending him for the position in the Boston customs house, a post he was later happy to abandon. To more precisely characterize his position on his resignation, in January 1841 when Hawthorne left his position, he wrote to Longfellow, stating "I have broken my chain and escaped from the Custom-House" (15:508). Further, in a letter of 10 February 1840 to William Baker Pike, he bluntly refers to Bancroft as "an astounding liar" (15:410). See also Hawthorne's letter of 15 March 1840 (15:419).

8. *History of the United States.* 10 vols. (Boston: Little, Brown, 1834–1875), 1:14.

9. *The Power of Historical Knowledge: Narrating the Past in Hawthorne, James, and Dreiser* (Princeton: Princeton University Press, 1988), 47. Mizruchi cites the 1849–1852 publication of Richard Hildreth's *History of the United States* as the first attempt to remediate the celebratory, self-promotional tenor of American historical narrative (48–50).

10. *History as Romantic Art: Bancroft, Prescott, Motley, and Parkman* (Stanford, CA: Stanford University Press, 1959), 24–25. Jan Dawson and Harold Bush identify Bancroft as a leader in the nineteenth century's quest to identify Christian faith as the foundation of republicanism. See Dawson, *The Unusable Past: America's Puritan Tradition, 1830 to 1930* (Chico, CA: Scholar's Press, 1984), 27 and Bush, "Re-Inventing the Puritan Fathers: George Bancroft, Nathaniel Hawthorne, and the Birth of Endicott's Ghost" in *American Transcendental Quarterly* 9.2 (1995): 132–52.

Providence . . . worthy of particular and grateful commemoration."[11] In his study of early nineteenth-century historians, Levin concludes that they understood their obligation to be "both literary and moral" (27):

> The idea of a special New England mission was as old as New England itself, and the Jeffersonian philosophers had extended the obligation to the whole country. In nineteenth-century America as in seventeenth-century New England the writer's duty was based on the unusual moral purity of his country, on its unique situation as the country most nearly in harmony with divine (or natural) laws. (24–25)

Seemingly modern historical inquiry was tied to philosophical and religious principles that were remnants of an earlier day that was dominated by a "pedantic bigot" (17:235).

Hawthorne, who was a reader of both Bancroft and Thacher, would have uncovered the dogged consistency of historical narrative from the early eighteenth century to the early nineteenth century. He would have also seen in these works a patent refusal to follow Emerson's dictum that "each age, it is found, must write its own books; or rather, each generation for the next succeeding. The books of an older period will not fit this."[12] Although it is true that the early nineteenth century saw any number of new histories of the nation, the most notable among them evaded their responsibility to reconceptualize historical writing for their age and the succeeding generation. Instead, they relied on the vision of their forebears. Thacher's epigraph on the title page of his *History of the Town of Plymouth* is a clear indication of such: "Ask thy fathers and they will show thee; thy elders and they will tell thee." More than a testimony to the value of the study of history, Thacher argues the importance of retaining the voices of the past on the events of the past. As such, early nineteenth-century historians reprised providential historiography and replicated its themes

11. (Boston, 1835), 13. See also John O. Choules's preface to Daniel Neal's *The History of the Puritans, or Protestant Nonconformists* (New York, 1843) which identifies the providential historiographic platform for this work: "A thoughtful man is not only convinced that God has created this world, he is as deeply persuaded that God has a Church in it; that he planted it here, and waters and nourishes it, and exerts in its favor a heavenly influence" (v). In addition, Joseph Priestly's theoretical examination of the importance, creation, and use of historical narrative supports these historians' belief in providential history. See his *Lectures on History and General Policy*, 2 vols. (Philadelphia, 1803). Hawthorne's record at the Salem Athenaeum indicates that he borrowed both Thacher's and Neal's histories and Priestly's essays.

12. "The American Scholar," in *The Collected Works of Ralph Waldo Emerson*, 3 vols., ed. Alfred R. Ferguson (Cambridge: The Belknap Press of Harvard University Press, 1971), 1:56.

of English colonial conquest and Puritan dominance in the making of an ascendant America.

Hawthorne's investigation of his national history has long been a concern of his interpreters, most notably Michael J. Colacurcio, whose *The Province of Piety* is a thorough and insightful investigation of Hawthorne as a moral and intellectual historian.[13] While Colacurcio observes that "Hawthorne's early historical tales may not be, except in a very special sense, 'about' their [historical] sources," this study contends that they challenge the premises on which the sources are written (18).[14] Further, these tales address the way those sources have been received and eventually codified within our society. Indeed, Hawthorne is more concerned with the teller of historical narratives and the receiver of those accounts than with the specific details of the actual histories themselves. Consequently, he interrogates the ethos of the historian as a principle rhetorical feature of historical narrative. Likewise, he argues that the audience for our community's narratives ought to be critically aware of the nature of those oral tales and written documents. For Hawthorne, it is not a question of whether one should be a student of one's national history, but rather how one should understand the larger and ongoing project of constructing one's national history. Moreover, Hawthorne's fiction repeatedly emphasizes the responsibility of the community in revisiting and revising its story of nation with the object of refining one's story of self.

Hawthorne's inquiry into historical writing takes many fiction forms. While "The Duston Family" is historical narrative with interpolated commentary on Cotton Mather's earlier account of the same event, other stories such as "Main-street" examine history as an interpretive art, and "David Swan" and "Alice Doane's Appeal" offer mimetic representations of historical interpretation, the latter three tales offering a more distanced, theoretical perspective of the historian's task. Likewise, *The House of the Seven Gables*—rarely considered one of Hawthorne's finest works—takes on new coloring as a historiographical response to Mather's accounts of the Pyncheon and Maule families, and an imaginative enactment of the critical importance of historical narrative. These works stand beside many short stories and novels in which Hawthorne assumes the role of historiographer

---

13. Although George Dekker does not speak to the specific works that I address in this chapter, I wish also to acknowledge his critical framework for investigating Hawthorne's historical fiction in *The American Historical Romance* (Cambridge: Cambridge University Press, 1987): 129–85.

14. Colacurcio's analysis of Hawthorne's tale "Sir William Phips," in particular, directly takes up the subject of Hawthorne as historiographer (53–62).

as well as moral and intellectual historian. Although this chapter does not purport to be comprehensive, it argues that Hawthorne experimented with various fiction forms to explore his discontent with earlier and contemporary American historical narrative, and that his concern about American historical narrative became a thematic and structural focus of his fiction.

A Historiographical Primer

In addition to his fictional statements about American history, Hawthorne authored a history of New England from its early colonial settlement until the revolution; this text is entitled *The Whole History of Grandfather's Chair*.[15] That this book was written for children does not diminish its statement. Indeed, as Nina Baym observes, this 1850 collection contains Hawthorne's first assertion that history is a vital, ever present, and important part of human life.[16] *Grandfather's Chair* not only educates young people about key events in American history, but, more importantly, this book puts forth a philosophy of historical writing and inculcates in the next generation of citizens an ethic of reading and writing history. Furthermore, while much of Hawthorne's literary project centers on issues of history and historiography, *The Whole History of Grandfather's Chair* enacts the kinds of historical narratives that he advocates in his fiction. This text both models his historiography and provides exempla of the ethos of the historian.

Grandfather's Chair does so largely through the metonymic device of the great chair whose history Hawthorne follows from its provenance in the estate of the English Earl of Lincoln and its removal to the Massachusetts Bay Colony with Lady Arabella Johnson to its place in

15. There are three distinct sections to *The Whole History of Grandfather's Chair*: *Grandfather's Chair*, *Famous Old People*, and *Liberty Tree*, each of which was initially published separately in 1841. They were published together in 1850 under the title *The Whole History of Grandfather's Chair*. In referring to this work, I made no distinction regarding the three sections and refer to them by the abbreviated title, *Grandfather's Chair*.

16. *The Shape of Hawthorne's Career* (Ithaca and London: Cornell University Press, 1976), 90. Baym also counters the arguments of those who dismiss the importance of this work. She writes, "*The Whole History of Grandfather's Chair* is a genuine literary achievement, which is regularly overlooked or underplayed in the critical literature," a situation that she attributes to scholarly suspicion of children's literature in general" (86–87). See also Elizabeth Goodenough who concurs that *Grandfather's Chair* "reveals the value of historical consciousness and its origin in the moral imagination of the child." See "*Grandfather's Chair*: Hawthorne's 'Deeper History' of New England" in *The Lion and the Unicorn: A Critical Journal of Children's Literature* 15.1 (1991), 30.

various public and private colonial venues until its present location in the home of the wise grandfather to Laurence, Clara, Charley, and Alice. The great chair, a symbol of the authority of its occupant, is only currently and temporarily the seat of the grandfather who constructs the history of the nation through the story of this chair. Thus, at the level of the structure of his narrative, the narrator divests himself of the role of the exclusive authority on American history, giving voice to the many occupants of the chair. Moreover, the list of those who speak from the chair is exceptional because it is not limited to the dominant, public men of Puritan America. Beginning his tales with the woeful account of the fragile Arabella Johnson, Grandfather recounts the experience of private individuals as well as the public figures, the dissenters and outcasts as well as the political and religious orthodoxy. Each has his or her turn to hold forth from the chair. Implicit in the structure of *Grandfather's Chair* is Hawthorne's intellectual commitment to the plurality of historical voices. Similarly, Hawthorne exposes the plurality of narrative modes when Grandfather reveals the inglorious chapters of our national history, at one point confessing to these little children a time when "little negro babies . . . were offered to be given away like young kittens" as well as commending the proud events in the life of the nation (6:109).

Above all, the great chair grounds its authority in the dedication to "Justice, Truth, and Love," virtues that he claims are innate to humankind (6:209). Hawthorne's philosophical and ethical basis for his historical narratives stand in direct contrast to Cotton Mather's understanding that his authority as a historian derives from his ministerial insight into the designs of God. In this respect, Hawthorne's historiographic principles may appear equally naïve to the sophisticated reader. Nonetheless, although justice and truth are nigh impossible to ascertain completely, *Grandfather's Chair* enacts the narrator's charitable perspective on the people he attempts to characterize in each tale. Grandfather offers a sympathetic description of the nation's forefathers from John Winthrop to John Adams. He also extols the efforts of Roger Williams and Anne Hutchinson, and steps back from their individual accounts to observe more generally that "it often happens that the outcasts of one generation are those, who are reverenced as the wisest and best of men by the next" (6:27). As further evidence of the historian's dedication to the virtue of love, in his account of the Boston Massacre, Grandfather cautions the children to reject the idea that the colonists alone were men of integrity and honor. Speaking of the English loyalist, he asks,

> Do you see nothing admirable in a faithful adherence to an unpopular
> cause? Can you not respect that principle of loyalty, which made the roy-
> alists give up country, friends, fortune, everything, rather than be false
> to their king? It was a mistaken principle; but many of them cherished it
> honorably, and were martyrs to it. (6:177–78)

Neither does the historian excoriate King George, instead terming him
"honest and conscientious" as well as "the most unfortunate of persons
that ever lived" (6:178).

When respect figures as a historiographic principle, it manifests itself
in a nuanced and sympathetic treatment of every historical figure. That is,
under the guise of Hawthorne's fiction, when the narrator allows each individual to address the reader from the great chair, the reader is afforded the
unique perspective of that individual. The underlying assumption is that
people act as their best wisdom dictates, regardless of how their actions
are perceived by friends or foes. Thus, it behooves the historian to seek the
perspective of those individuals rather than issuing one's personal, definitive judgment of one's fellow men and women.

Even Cotton Mather, who asserted that he spoke God's judgment of
human events, is treated sympathetically in *Grandfather's Chair,* although
his assertions are contrary to Hawthorne's deeply held convictions. At
moments in the text, Hawthorne introduces Mather as one of the most
erudite men to ever occupy the great chair. Elsewhere, he issues faint praise
for his magnum opus. *Grandfather's Chair* describes *Magnalia Christi
Americana* as "a strange, pedantic history, in which true events and real
personages move before the reader, with the dreamy aspect which they
wore in Cotton Mather's singular mind" (6:92). Historical figures and
events are expressions of the "singular" and, in this case, "pedantic" visions
of the teller, rather than truth itself. In a later chapter, however, Hawthorne
illustrates how Mather fared at the hands of other individuals who evaluate the world "singularly." Hawthorne offers a sympathetic description of
Mather as a brilliant and altruistic scholar who investigated the smallpox
vaccine as a means to protect his community and, in particular, his young
son, Samuel. Hawthorne's assessment notwithstanding, he concedes that
Mather's fellow Bostonians constructed their estimation of him from the
kind of cruelty that originates in ignorance. Indeed, Mather was maligned
for his efforts to stem the epidemic, and even threatened with physical
harm. There is some irony in this unfortunate incident in that the minister
who consistently acts on his singular convictions is victimized by those

who are equally dogmatic in their views. Yet, in Hawthorne's historical narrative Mather is depicted as a courageous and intelligent individual.

The Historian's Ethos

When Hawthorne assumes the role of historian in *Grandfather's Chair,* his historiographic principles dictate that he would treat his subjects with "love." Thus, Mather fares well in the context of this collection. However, in his 1836 tale "The Duston Family," which is an exposé of the ways in which severely flawed historiography cripples our understanding of ourselves and our nation, Hawthorne is less charitable to the early historian. In "The Duston Family," Cotton Mather is cast as "an old hard-hearted, pedantic bigot" (17:235). Specifically, this story foregrounds the nineteenth-century author's discontent with the eighteenth-century historian's claim to objectivity. While Hawthorne explores his concerns through the example of Cotton Mather's narrative of the captivity of Hannah Duston, his larger argument is with the historian himself.[17]

One of the primary characteristics of Cotton Mather's providence tales, his account of the exploits of Hannah Duston being among them, is the tight, orderly construction that bears witness to the stability of the argument. Virtue is rewarded, vice punished. As part of the impracticable order of these accounts, providence tales exhibit exceptional consistency in their characterization of both saints and sinners. The saints generally have fine physiques, kindly expressions, and mild dispositions, their upright carriage portending their upright character. By contrast, sinners frequently display their malevolent natures by physical infirmity; they scowl and have unpleasant dispositions to match their evil nature. However, his tale of the captivity of Hannah Duston offers one challenge to Mather's otherwise uncomplicated construction of his characters in *Magnalia Christi Americana.* At the outset of the account, Hannah Duston is the archetypal female victim of an Indian raid who is lying in after the birth of her eighth

---

17. B. Bernard Cohen was the first scholar, to my knowledge, to identify and examine Hawthorne's historical sources for "The Duston Family." He looks to Samuel G. Goodrich, *Peter Parley's Method of Telling about the History of the World to Children* (Hartford: H. F. Sumner, 1832) and Benjamin L. Mirick, *The History of Haverill, Massachusetts* (Haverill:A. W. Thayer, 1832) in addition to Mather's *Magnalia.* See Cohen's "The Composition of Hawthorne's 'The Duston Family,'" *The New England Quarterly* 21.2 (1948): 236–41.

The surname Duston is rendered as Dustin and Dustan by various contemporary and subsequent historians. When I am not directly quoting the work of a specific historian or author, I use Hawthorne's spelling of the Duston name.

child. Yet, at the close of the narrative, she murders and scalps her captors—both adults and children—and encourages her nurse and a young English boy to abet her in murder. Testimony to Mather's skill as a rhetorician is his facility in fashioning a murderess as an exemplary Puritan goodwife.

Mather entitles his captivity narrative, "A Notable Exploit: *Dux Fœmina Facti*" (a woman the leader in the achievement), signaling his intent to valorize an exceptional woman. Consistent with the tropes of the genre, the tale begins with the captive's trauma: the raid itself, of course, but also the forced march without adequate food or rest, followed by other trials at the hands of the native Americans. After laying this background as motivation for retribution, Mather stalls the narrative of Hannah Duston's revenge by preliminarily presenting his own justification for the murderous acts. He first offers scriptural precedent for the murder; Duston is a typological Jael who murdered Sisera to save her people.[18] Then Mather cites a legal rationale: Duston found herself outside of the jurisdiction of English law that would protect her life, so she surmised that the life of her enemy was equally unprotected by law. With the motivation and justification in place, only then does Mather describe the actual murder.

Hannah Duston's murder of ten Indians, which is the dramatic center of the narrative, commands only a few sentences after which the author immediately turns to claims of public and private commendation for her action. Personal friends gave her "presents of congratulation," the General Assembly of the province rewarded her with fifty pounds, and the Governor of Maryland, a Catholic colony, sent a "very generous token of his favour" for her murder of Indians who, it should be noted, were converts to Catholicism (2:636). Cotton Mather concludes his narrative with these details of the universal approbation of the work of Hannah Duston to confirm indeed that *dux fœmina facti.*

Consistent with his historiographic platform, George Bancroft's nineteenth-century account of Hannah Duston's captivity substantially replicates the central elements of Mather's account. Most importantly, Bancroft perpetuates Mather's themes of Puritan triumph over the savages by casting Duston as a heroine. Echoing Mather's understanding of the providential design of history, Bancroft closes his narrative with a romantic implication of nature in God's plan for Hannah Duston:

18. Here I concur with Cynthia Brantley Johnson who finds that although Mather is no feminist, he nonetheless "seems to believe that women can and should be warriors in the service of America's establishment of New Jerusalem—and that means killing Indians the way the army led by Deborah killed Sisera's army." See "Hawthorne's Hannah Dustan and Her Troubling American Myth," *Nathaniel Hawthorne Review* 27.1 (2001), 22.

> The streams are the guides which God has set for the stranger in the wil-
> derness; in a bark canoe, the three descended the Merrimac to the English
> settlements, astonishing their friends by their escape, and filling the land
> with wonder at their successful daring. (188–89)

Benjamin Mirick's 1832 narrative of the Indian raid on Haverhill and
Hannah Duston's captivity echoes Bancroft's. In each account, romantic
thought inflects the author's deistic historiographic approach. Early in his
The History of Haverhill, Massachusetts, Mirick describes the founding
principles of the community. Foremost among them is the enhanced role
of the minister as "projector and leader" in the settlement of Haverhill
(11). When the community's founders looked upon the site that would
become their settlement, the minister instructed them that "they could
kneel in the forest, by the fountain, and the river, and He would be among
them" (12). Later, Mirick's treatment of the Duston family insists upon a
related point, that "it cannot but be confessed that the arm of the Almighty
was outstretched for their preservation" (88). Articulating his belief in the
role of divine providence in the founding of their community as well as the
role of the minister in discerning God's design, Mirick, much like Bancroft,
perpetuates Mather's theory of historical narrative.

Consistent with Mather's account, Mirick also depicts the native
Americans as "fierce savages." Furthermore, in a statement that reveals the
historian's awareness of the tradition of his profession, he writes

> Many writers have ascribed to this revengeful race, pure and lofty virtue,
> high and delicate principles of honor, and firm and devoted friendship to
> those who have granted them favors. To these assertions I am not prepared
> to subscribe. If valor be a virtue, then some of them surely possessed it;
> but even these were few, for the courage of a great majority only prompted
> them to murder woman and children, and attack men unawares, or while
> asleep. (4)

These actions, he argues, are "diabolical cruelties" (4). Especially notable
is the irony of Mirick's condemnation of murdering men, women, and
children in their sleep, a statement that prefaces his account of Hannah
Duston's praiseworthy murder of men, women, and children in their sleep.
Moreover, in a moment of self-reflection, Mirick reveals that he is aware of
the prospect of a contemporary reappraisal of the early American conflict
between the colonists and the native Americans. However, he elects to

stand with seventeenth- and eighteenth-century historians on this question.

Having read both Mather and Mirick, Hawthorne's objective for his response to Cotton Mather's "*Dux Fœmina Facti*" is signaled in the title of his 1836 story. "The Duston Family" concerns not only the actions of Mrs. Hannah Duston, but those of her husband and children as well. Thus, by broadening his focus, Hawthorne eschews the formula of the genre of the captivity narrative, which is largely a statement of God's protection of the individual, a protection that implies spiritual as well as physical redemption. Similarly, Hawthorne's narrative begins not with the raid, but with the life of an ordinary family in the Massachusetts Bay Colony.

Mrs. Duston appears to be Hawthorne's dark afterthought. She virtually disappears from the narrative until the midpoint of the tale when Hawthorne remarks, "We must not forget Mrs. Duston, in her distress" (17:233). At this juncture the reader might anticipate that the actual captivity narrative—the seizure and forced march of the victim—would begin. Yet, Hawthorne continues to foil our generic expectations by denying the authenticity and emotional tenor of the conventions of the genre. He notes briefly that the woman was recovering from childbirth, but undercuts the importance of this detail by informing the reader that "in nine cases out of ten" such victims have similarly newly given birth, and they survived these ordeals (17:233). Moreover, her husband felt secure that his wife, in particular, could withstand such trauma. Because he knew her well, Hawthorne tells us, he was assured that "she would hold her own, even in a contest with a whole tribe of Indians" (17:231).[19] In this way, Hawthorne prepares the reader for his historical perspective of Hannah Duston as a hard woman, and, ultimately, as a "blood old hag" (17:238).[20]

19. This detail is original to Hawthorne's tale. Mirick writes that Duston "tenderly and passionately loved" his wife (87).

20. Mirick terms Hannah Duston's murderous act a "heroic and unparalleled deed," but concedes that "various opinions are afloat concerning the justness of this certainly heroic deed." Ultimately, he concludes that "a wife in such a situation would not be apt to critically analyze the morality of the deed," a position that Hawthorne clearly rejects (91, 92, 93). Cynthia Brantley Johnson finds that Hawthorne's characterization of Hannah Duston is consistent with his derisive fictional representation of "aggressive, manly behavior" in women (22). She further cites T. Walter Herbert's observation that "womanly aggression was pictured as a misplaced manly trait" in Hawthorne's work. See *Dearest Beloved: The Hawthornes and the Making of the Middle-Class Family* (Berkeley: University of California Press, 1993), 11. Likewise, Ann-Marie Weis argues that this tale supports the Jacksonian ideology of benevolent paternity while it uncovers the tragic consequences of "menacing individualism" when practiced by a woman. See "The Murderous Mother and the Solicitous Father: Violence, Jacksonian Family Values, and Hannah Duston's Captivity," *American Studies International* 36.1 (1998): 46.

Likewise, Hawthorne is at odds with Mather's depiction of Goodman Duston, and again rejects the conventions of the genre in which men immediately assume the demeanor of the soldier when Indians attack their home. Because of the reversal of gender roles inherent in the plot—the wife is the warrior while the husband cares for the children—Cotton Mather himself might have had difficulty in constructing the character of the husband for an eighteenth-century audience. However, Mather is careful to assert the masculinity of this figure by insisting that he "manfully" walks with his children to the protection of the fort, and even casts the brood as a "*little army* of unarmed children" [Mather's emphasis] (2:635). To feminize Mr. Duston would suggest to Mather's readers that Mrs. Duston's power is emasculating. Avoiding this difficulty, Mather presents the husband as a soldier in his own right.

Hawthorne, too, takes special care in his portrait of the husband who leaves his wife to defend herself against the Indians, while he protects the children. In this story, Goodman Duston is the first to be apprised of the impending raid, and he responds to the crisis responsibly but also emotionally. He "tremble[s]," his "heart yearn[s]," and he is both "pale and breathless" when he arrives at his home (17:230, 231). Nonetheless, Mr. Duston is a horseman and a rifleman, and, as such, is coded as male. To draw attention to this depiction, in its original publication in *The American Magazine of Useful and Entertaining Knowledge,* the story is complemented by an illustration of a manly Mr. Duston astride his horse training his gun on a collection of native Americans. The plume of smoke trailing from his shotgun is impressive, and suggests that he already used the gun against his enemies, while Duston's pose indicates that he is prepared to exercise additional force. Yet, throughout the story, Mr. Duston's dominant feature is his intense, sentimental attachment to each of his children. Indeed, Hawthorne devotes several paragraphs to the man's special affection for his family and his loving care, rather than his fierce defense of them. However, far from constructing this man as a sentimental and thus ineffectual character, the author's final assessment is that his renown will be as a "tender-hearted yet valiant man" (17:238). In this way, Hawthorne is able to redefine a model of masculinity as having great sensitivity as well as bravery and physical prowess.

To close the tale Hawthorne predicts that Mrs. Duston will come to be known throughout history as an "awful woman," but his strongest approbation is for the early historian, Cotton Mather, whom he terms "an old hard-hearted, pedantic bigot" (17:235). Hawthorne's account argues that the historian defaults on his responsibility to the reader because in this case the historian is narrow-minded, cruel, and as such an unacceptable interpreter of these events. Hawthorne is especially appalled by the way that Mather revels in the death of the native Americans with his insensitive and gratuitous asides, and Hawthorne takes care to point to this unfortunate feature of Mather's prose with the example of a vicious pun: "But, a little before break of day, a deep, dead slumber fell upon the Indians. '[S]ee,' cries Cotton Mather triumphantly, 'if it prove not so!'" (17:236).[21] In this way, the historian resembles his historical subject. If Hannah Duston is a bloodthirsty tigress, Mather is equally savage.

To assert the ethos of the competing historian, Hawthorne's narrator, likewise, resembles the historical subject that he valorizes. Just as Hawthorne's historian celebrates Mr. Duston's resolve, courage, and compassion, so too he attempts to be resolute, courageous, and compassionate in his interpretation of this historical event, and that he is. The narrator is unafraid to call the native Americans "barbarians," "raging savages," and "skulking foe[s]" because men who attack civilian women and children should be seen as such (17:236, 229, 232). Nonetheless, unlike Mather, he is equally committed to depict the ways in which they are virtuous and repeatedly recognizes their Christianity. Similarly, Hawthorne understands that Hannah Duston is a victim in the account, but, in fairness, he acknowledges that even her husband knows her as a cruel woman who could "hold her own, even in a contest with a whole tribe of Indians" (17:231). Consistent with Hawthorne's thesis in *Grandfather's Chair*, the historian's ethos demands an even-handed, accurate approach to characterization.

Hawthorne's narrator is not only sympathetic to the "tender-hearted yet valliant" Mr. Duston, but he also resembles this figure in his great compassion and emotional engagement with the events. If Mr. Duston is at times "pale and breathless" in the face of tragedy, so too is the narrator who, for example, apostrophizes Mrs. Duston, and begs her to spare the life of the native babies: "But, O, the children! Their skins are red; yet spare them, Hannah Duston, spare those seven little ones, for the sake of the seven that have fed at your own breast" (17:237). The historian abandons his professional distance from his subject because, as Hawthorne suggests, this stance would compromise his ability to recognize and value the humanity of all the individuals in these accounts. The dispassionate historian would then rely too heavily on the abstract and often obfuscating predispositions of his nationality, race, social class, or religious convictions—as does the historian *cum* minister, Cotton Mather.

---

21. Hawthorne is quoting Mather, 2:636.

The title of his short story indicates that Hawthorne is interested in the life of the family that is ultimately the nation. When he insists that the account of the 1698 Indian raid on Haverhill "will be remembered as long as the deeds of old times are told round a New England fireside," he predicts that his evaluation of their actions will become the dominant narrative (17:238). More importantly, he asks us to contemplate the nature of the society that will form the readership for these historical accounts. Specifically, Hawthorne again locates his understanding of this issue in the wisdom of Mr. Duston whose finest achievement is securing the next generation of the American family. In his attempt to escape to the fortress, the "tender-hearted yet valiant" man cannot sacrifice even one of the seven children in his care. They are all different—one who is meek and another who is a little scrapper, one who resembles him and another who is the image of his wife, and so forth—but he calls them all "beloved," and proclaims, "We will live or die together!" (17:232).[22] Hawthorne's hero appreciates what Cotton Mather cannot fathom, that the country must be shared by peoples of all origins, dispositions, and inclinations, and that we must live together or we will be buried together. In this way, Hawthorne's tale works to transform our understanding of the ethos of the historian as well as the nation he addresses. This nation demands a plurality of sympathetic historical narratives to represent its plurality of sympathetic citizens.

The Historian's Protocol

In other works, Hawthorne retreats from responding to a specific historian and a specific historical account, and instead creates a fictional account of the American historian. Through the medium of fiction, Hawthorne can disclose his more universal, deep-seated anxiety about the professional historian and the specious nature of his trade. His 1849 short story, "Main-street," issues a particularly pointed critique in that it casts historical narrative as a carnival sideshow with crude cardboard puppets, artificial lighting, and "well-oiled" staging (11:49). The sideshow is composed of a sequence of tableaux, each depicting an era or an event in the history of Salem, the barker explicating each scene.

A cursory analysis of the show reveals that the historian's work is

---

22. Hawthorne's source for Mr. Duston's meditation on the unique qualities of each of his children is Sarah Josepha Hale's poem, "The Father's Choice," which celebrates Duston's special love for his children. Hale's poem is found in Mirick, 93–95.

"human art" which "has its limits" (11:52). Unfortunately, when a skeptical spectator queries the historian *cum* carnival barker on historical details, we learn that one of the fundamental and serious limits of the "art" of history is factual error. The narrative cannot withstand close scrutiny, and even the historian admits that his work is illusion. Yet, when Hawthorne sets the barker at odds with a man in the audience, this is not to say that Hawthorne champions the critical spectator while he derides the historian. Indeed, the critical spectator is too busy picking at nits in the historical accuracy of the presentation to appreciate its underlying themes. Yes, the historian's exhibition is "humbug," but so too is the critic's suggestion that perfect accuracy in the objective detail of the account is equivalent to perfect understanding of the event.

As Hayden White has argued, the details of historical events—whether they are disputed or not—may be value neutral, but historical narrative itself is surely otherwise. Thus, the carnival barker moralizes just as Puritan historians once did. At times, Hawthorne's historian rails against the severity and fanaticism of the nation's colonists, and celebrates the increasing distance between the Puritan mind and the character of his contemporaries. When the critical curmudgeon in his audience correctly identifies this aspect of the discourse as interpretation and evaluation rather than presentation, and objects that a "sermon" is not "in the bill," he assumes naively that sermonizing is not integral to historicizing, and as such, refuses to acknowledge that it is always "in the bill" (11:68).

However naive, the skeptic understands well enough the essential structural elements of historical narrative. When the carnival barker complains that his outbursts destroy the "illusion" of the show, the critic retorts,

> Illusion! What illusion? . . . I see nothing illusive in the wretchedly bedaubed sheet of canvass that forms your back-ground, or in these pasteboard slips that hitch and jerk along the front. The only illusion, permit me to say, is in the puppet-showman's tongue,—and that but a wretched one, into the bargain! (11:63)

The skeptic in the audience instinctively understands that there is no illusion inherent in the bald details of historical narrative. The facts of the events are plain to a fault. Furthermore, they alone have no rhythm or balance because, unemplotted, they are devoid of the grace of story. However, when the showman adds his voice or "tongue" to the details to create a narrative that is directed toward a political or moral end, therein lies the illusion. Ultimately, the cynic in the audience has not only identified this element of the story of Main Street, America, but he has also decided that he rejects the historian's interpretation of the historical events.

Nina Baym was one of the earliest scholars to identify the importance of the narrative frame of the exchanges between the barker and his critic, a feature that she finds "takes up some new aesthetic considerations" (*Shape of Hawthorne's Career*, 119). While it is true that the audience asks for realism, as Baym has argued, and then for compelling artistry, the complaints center on the barker's interpretation of his material, regardless of the form or tenor of its artful or artless presentation. Again, Hawthorne's fiction reveals that evaluation as well as description is always "in the bill."

As is characteristic of Hawthorne's tales, the narrator's rhetoric is subtle and often wily. In the case of the sideshow of "Main-street," the objectives of the historical narrative are both complex and seemingly contradictory. On one hand, the narrative sets out to discredit Puritan intolerance, each vignette testifying to their cruel behavior toward particular groups of men and women—native Americans, Quakers, petty criminals, and those suspected of witchcraft. Indeed, the showman repeatedly claims that modern man should be happy not to live under such conditions. The goal of this strain of the narrative is to put forth the ascendancy of the new Americans, the peoples who descend from the outcasts of Puritan society. Hawthorne suggests, then, that the very peoples who inhabited the metaphorical side streets and back alleys of the New English township become the denizens of the "main street" of nineteenth-century American life. At the close of the historical presentation, when the barker asks the audience to celebrate the "sunshine of the present" and presumably anticipate an even brighter future, he further predicts that the superior wisdom of the modern age will signal the end of all such barbarous activity (11:81). However, a competing theme of the narrative is that of the valor and righteousness of the Puritan errand in the new world. He praises their religious zeal and Anglo-Saxon energy, while simultaneously lamenting how such zeal and energies were utilized in the colonies. He offers a romantic portrait of the original beauty of these peoples, although he concedes that the loveliness faded quickly. Finally, in a flourish that suggests pulpit oratory, the narrator issues a progressive statement: "Let us thank God for having given us such ancestors; and let each successive generation thank him, not less fervently, for being one step further from them in the march of ages" (11:68).

Ultimately, does Hawthorne direct the reader to decide which historical interpretation of the selfsame material is superior? Further, does he coach the reader to determine whether the sideshow itself is authoritative or humbug? Not at all. Both views are valid. Similarly, the carnival show is both principled and suspect, just as the barker and his critic are both valuable and idiosyncratic. As in *The Whole History of Grandfather's Chair,* we learn that we need the voices of public and private men and women to construct and critique the stories that we create about ourselves as a nation. Likewise, the only stable argument in this tale is that of the instability of the historical account, which is always contested ground.

In his 1837 tale, "David Swan," Hawthorne speaks from yet another intellectual remove from his pointed inquiry into historical narrative to offer a mimetic representation of historical narration. Ultimately, the story enacts Hawthorne's deeply held historiographic principle of the plurality of historical narration.

"David Swan" has been passed over by critics and editors alike. It has received little scholarly notice, and is included in only the most complete collections of Hawthorne's short fiction. A brief tale of little more than two thousand words, "David Swan" is admittedly easily overlooked. The plot, too, seems insubstantial. David Swan falls asleep in the woods en route to Boston, where he will begin employment in his uncle's grocery. During his sleep, passersby notice Swan, speculate about him, and some of them momentarily fantasize about his future. One lady views him as her son, while a younger woman envisions him as her husband and the heir to her father's fortune. Some look kindly upon the sleeping man, and others plot to rob him. Finally he wakes—oblivious to those who have come upon him while sleeping—and continues his journey to Boston. The embedded narratives of the passersby, which are earnest and sometimes impassioned, decenter the otherwise mundane plot of an unexceptional trip, although they do nothing to alter the dénouement of the central plot.

"David Swan" explodes the security of historical narrative by creating alternate accounts based on information not often studied by historians. Hawthorne's narrative takes up the history of events that might have transpired in one's life, but were never realized. Within the context of the tale, the reality of what might have occurred is given equal footing with the reality of what took place, and thus allows the author to investigate the inexplicable vagaries of life, giving lie to the received notion of providential design as a fundamental historiographic principle.

Hawthorne teases the reader with the suggestion of divine order as a guiding principle for his narrative when, in the opening sentence, he speaks of the events of one's life that lead to a "final destiny" (9:183). He further suggests that Swan's sylvan bed appears to have been "planted on purpose for him." So too, one of the passersby, who acts as a commentator and a "historian" of Swan, observes that "Providence seems to have laid him here . . . and to have brought us hither to find him" (9:185). Nonetheless, contrary to early wonder stories that argue for divine order in the world, what appears to be providential in the eyes of the narrator or the eyewitnesses in "David Swan" never comes to pass. Hawthorne's story thus repeatedly invokes and defies the tight narrative structure of the early providence tale.

Definitive, moralizing closure being a feature of the tale of divine providence, Hawthorne's story similarly turns to the reader in the final paragraph to sermonize by extrapolating a larger truth from the non-events of his tale.

> Sleeping or waking, we hear not the airy footsteps of the strange things that almost happen. Does it not argue a superintending Providence, that, while viewless and unexpected events thrust themselves continually athwart our path, there should still be regularity enough, in mortal life, to render foresight even partially available? (9:190)

Here he broaches the concept of divine providence itself, and argues that we should first see the hand of the deity in the many quotidian and unexceptional features of man's life, which he terms "regularity." Whereas Cotton Mather chronicled remarkable occurrences as a sign of God's intervention in the mortal world, Hawthorne chooses to record the expected events in the average man's life as a statement of God's plan for man. In other words, Mather ironically looks to disorder and ruptures of normalcy as a sign of God's order, and Hawthorne views "regularity" as testimony to a "superintending Providence."[23] When an exceptional and even improbable event imposes itself on the narrative, it is not Mather's *deus ex machina,* but a dog *ex machina,* as in Poe's *Pym,* who in Hawthorne's tale interrupts the thieves who have designs on David Swan. Hawthorne's inversion of Mather's understanding of providential design addresses the alternate ways in which man can comprehend his life, alterneity itself not being a feature of the earlier morality tales.

Much like the abbreviated anecdotes in book six of Mather's *Magnalia,* Hawthorne's "David Swan" begins with a thumbnail sketch of the person

---

23. In making this statement about Mather's understanding of providential design, I am speaking only about the way in which he approaches this in the final books of *Magnalia Christi Americana.* In a larger sense, Mather clearly understood the regularity of nature as part of the exquisite order in God's design of the material world, and believed the beautiful order of this world to be a reflection of the mind of God and a prefiguration of the afterlife.

whose fate we are to follow. The reader is provided a sketch of the family of the individual, their station in life, and the person's current occupation, information that, in most of Mather's tales, predicts the individual's outcome in the narrative. Those of lowly rank, from a disreputable family, or having an unpleasant temperament will often not fare well under Mather's scrutiny. In Hawthorne's alternate history, however, this prefatory material does not anticipate resolution; it is simply without consequence.[24]

Likewise without consequence is each of the fantasies that Hawthorne records concerning the "secret history" of Swan (9:183). Of course, on one hand, they are inconsequential to the plot because they are simply daydreams and never actually occur. Moreover, attached to each event is an implied evaluation of Swan, which fundamentally has nothing to do with him. Each embedded tale represents merely the fantasy of another human being. Nonetheless, each of these individuals is a historian of sorts with an eyewitness account of David Swan. This grand parade of mankind comments on the sleeping man, each individual offering a distinct and sometimes contradictory version of what he or she perceives of the slumbering David Swan. One woman finds him "charming in his sleep," whereas the temperance lecturer is convinced that Swan is in a drunken stupor (9:184). Logically, these passersby *cum* historians cannot both be correct in their evaluations, although both are eyewitnesses to the same scene. Reluctant to draw a conclusion from the varied anecdotes, Hawthorne writes, "But, censure, praise, merriment, scorn, and indifference, were all one, or rather all nothing, to David Swan" (9:184). Truly, this is the only culminating statement one can make about the multiplicity of narratives that are generated in the forest. The perceptions of men about men are flawed, and lead to no material or spiritual end.[25] At the close of the tale, when Swan blithely boards a coach for Boston, none of these encounters has any impact on his mortal life or his "destiny." Ultimately, the narrator offers the reader no suggestion of the final disposition of this young man.

The subtitle of "David Swan" identifies the piece as "A Fantasy." Yet, in the opening paragraph "fantasy" is further defined as a "history," albeit a "secret history," thus complicating the notion of historical narrative. Swan's history is secret to the extent that this set of events never gains the attention

24. Indeed, the villains who conspire to steal from David Swan, who drink, make oaths, and threaten murder, escape unchastened. Although the "recording angel" duly notes their transgressions, God does not bring their wickedness to the attention of man, as one finds in providence tales.

25. This aspect of "David Swan" is reminiscent of Hawthorne's description of *Magnalia Christi Americana* as a "strange" history colored by the "dreamy aspect" of the historian's mind (*Grandfather's Chair*, 6:92).

of the larger world because they never actually occur. This history—secret or otherwise—is also fantasy because it attaches itself to erroneous interpretations of the man and the events. Nonetheless, although in each of the encounters with Swan in the forest, the story that each passerby creates about the young man has little to do with Swan, these same accounts have everything to do with the teller of the tale. The woman who lost her son sees the qualities of her son in Swan, the young girl sees in him the perfect lover, and the temperance lecturer sees the victim of demon rum. Consequently, for Hawthorne, the interpretive nature of historical narrative identifies history as more revealing of the historian than of the events the historian relates.

This is not to say that historical narrative has diminished value because it is not absolute. To the contrary, Hawthorne relates the accounts of each passerby because they have exceptional value in that they bespeak the most profound dreams and most fervent passions of men and women. Acknowledging that these tales are fantasies does not negate their importance or their power. Indeed, the structure of the tale argues that these dreams are sufficiently potent to derail the plot of what is factual and verifiable. Ultimately, Hawthorne's goal for "David Swan" is the reader's recognition that all historical accounts express the historian's deeply held personal ideals, however limited, flawed, or even perverse those persons and those ideals may be.

This point is crucial for Hawthorne because it underlies his commitment to a plurality of social narratives and a continual investigation of the story of the individual and the nation. Hawthorne's thinking is consonant with Emerson's call in "The American Scholar" for each age to "write its own books," on the grounds that the history of events and the history of ideas are neither definitive nor static. Because the tale is fundamentally dependent upon the teller, each generation of citizens has an obligation to create his or her own account of self and society.

Read from the perspective of Nathaniel Hawthorne's historiographic orientation, which was markedly distinct from earlier and even most contemporary approaches to the writing of historical narrative, many of his other works of historical fiction assume different coloring. While this chapter is intended to speak to the variety of narrative strategies that Hawthorne employs to address his concerns for American historiography in the aftermath of Mather's *Magnalia* and does not purport to be comprehensive, the analysis may suggest approaches to Hawthorne's other works of historical fiction.

The Claims of History

Critics have long been interested in the structure and argument of "Alice Doane's Appeal," one of his most self-conscious statements of metafiction.[26] Once again, in this tale, Hawthorne focuses on the ethos of the historian and the ethics of the citizen reader. "Alice Doane's Appeal" introduces the historian Cotton Mather in gothic figures as a "fiend" and a "blood-thirsty man" because he is "the representative of all the hateful features of his time" (11:279). Hawthorne terms him a "representative" because Mather claims to represent the singular Puritan ideology in his historical narrative for his generation and continued to do so for many succeeding generations of Americans. Likewise, Hawthorne queries his own generation's careless posture relative to its history, and the reader is invited to recoil at the idea of courtship rituals and mischief-making on the site of a once grim Gallows Hill. That frivolous scenes are played out on the physical founda-tion of our tragic past pointedly asks the reader to rethink the way the nation receives and uses its history. Stories of 1692 Gallows Hill told in the nineteenth century on Gallows Hill suggest, as Emily Budick puts it, "how future generations stand on the same perilous ground when they look back to the past and fail to recognize that its monsters inevitably reflect the pro-jected images of themselves" (100).

To compound this difficulty, the frame of "Alice Doane's Appeal"—by which the narrator tells the story of tragic love and sibling murder—embodies the difficulty of the narrator in reissuing the narrative of our past. From this perspective, the frame is less a metafictive device than a metahistorical statement about the hollowness of repeating earlier histori-cal accounts of the past when the narrator cannot endorse the principles upon which the earlier history was written. For this reason, the tragic tale is rendered as a gothic narrative rather than a Puritan morality tale, and

26. Michael Colacurcio offers an astute analysis of the theme of historiography in "Alice Doane's Appeal." See especially 78–93. Colacurcio also puts forward a provocative thesis that "Alice Doane's Appeal" takes up Robert Calef's cause against Cotton Mather on the subject of George Burroughs.

For arguments on narrative structure as an embodiment of Hawthorne's historical project, see Emily Miller Budick, *Fiction and Historical Consciousness: The American Romance Tradition* (New Haven and London: Yale University Press, 1989), 99–102; Michael Dunne, *Hawthorne's Narrative Strategies* (Jackson: University Press of Mississippi, 1995), 78–86; Charles Swann, *Nathaniel Hawthorne: Tradition and Revolution* (Cambridge: Cambridge University Press, 1991), 18–43; and G. R. Thompson, *The Art of Authorial Presence: Hawthorne's Provincial Tales* (Durham and London: Duke University Press, 1993), 161–201.

its effect is doubly terrifying. In yet another ironic twist, the gothic effect is to be understood as a victory within the context of the tale. When the narrator, who functions as the historian of a new age, has completed his macabre accounts of the past, he revels in the response to his narrative:

> ... their nerves were trembling; and sweeter victory still, I had reached the seldom trodden places of their hearts, and found the well-spring of their tears. And now the past had done all it could. (11:279–80)

An emotional reaction to historical narrative reveals that the account has impressed the audience with the importance of the text. In a telling gothic turn, the trembling nerves result in the welcome consequence of awakening a new generation to the importance of its own history.

Hawthorne's *The House of the Seven Gables* shares interesting historiographical features with "Alice Doane's Appeal." One feature common to both "Alice Doane's Appeal" and *The House of the Seven Gables* is, of course, an interest in the history of Gallow's Hill and the legacy of the accounts of witchcraft in nineteenth-century America. Many scholars have documented the author's knowledge of the early and contemporary historical accounts of the Pyncheon and Maule families, but once again Hawthorne's focus is not on the facts of seventeenth-century events.[27] Hawthorne's preface to the novel insists that "the personages of the Tale—though they give themselves out to be of ancient stability and considerable prominence—are really of the Author's own making" and that the entire work has "a great deal more to do with the clouds overhead, than with any portion of the actual soil of the County of Essex" (2:3). The opening chapter reprises this claim. "It is not our purpose to trace down the history of the Pyncheon family, in its unbroken connection with the House of the Seven Gables" (2:20). However, this is not to say that the novel's argument is unrelated to history when the opposite is clearly the case. As in "Alice Doane's Appeal," the author's objective is to interrogate the claims of historical tracts and the narrative structures that support those claims.

To underscore his dismissal of historicizing seventeenth-century occurrences within the novel, the narrator repeatedly destabilizes any confidence in accessing historical truth. In a series of negative absolutes, we are told that there exists "neither town-record, nor grave-stone, nor the

---

27. See especially Allan Emery, "Salem History and *The House of the Seven Gables*," in *Critical Essays on Hawthorne's* The House of the Seven Gables, ed. Bernard Rosenthal (New York: G. K. Hall, 1995), 129–49, and Deborah L. Madsen, "Hawthorne's Puritans: From Fact to Fiction," *Journal of American Studies* 33.3 (1999): 509–17.

directory, nor the knowledge or memory of man" that there exist heirs of Matthew Maule, a point that the novel itself refutes (2:25–26). Other documents that might aid the historian, such as maps of the Pyncheon property and deeds to the Pyncheon house, are hidden. Were one actually privy to such information, the novel nonetheless demands that the reader remain skeptical of such documents because the "cold, formal, and empty words of the chisel that inscribes, the voice that speaks, and the pen that writes for the public eye and for distant time . . . inevitably lose much of their truth and freedom by the fatal consciousness of doing so" (2:122). Throughout the novel, other forms of historical knowledge are cast variously as "gossip," "fable," "wild chimney-corner legend," and "long drama" (2:122, 123, 197, 316).[28] If, as the narrator claims, "life is made up of marble and mud," then representations of life are likewise made up of rigid public tracts and malleable private assertions, none of which alone may claim truth (2:41).

In their search for the historical texts—the "cold, formal, and empty words of the chisel"—that form the source material for *The House of the Seven Gables,* scholars look principally to Thomas Hutchinson's 1795 *The History of Massachusetts,* Rev. Charles W. Upham's *Lectures on Witchcraft, Comprising a History of The Delusion in Salem in 1692,* and Joseph B. Felt's 1849 *Annals of Salem.* Hawthorne's disclaimers on the historicity of his novel notwithstanding, there is undeniable interest in comparing these texts. However, consideration of Cotton Mather's *Magnalia Christi Americana* as a point of departure for Hawthorne's imaginative work enlarges our understanding of the structure and argument of Hawthorne's novel. Much like Harriet Beecher Stowe's *The Pearl of Orr's Island* and *The Minister's Wooing,* Hawthorne's *The House of the Seven Gables* lacks the kind of coherent plot that we anticipate from the novel. Nina Baym speaks for many critics when she argues that it "is a work whose plot is so often neglected or concealed by the narrator that at times the book seems to lack plot altogether."[29] Again, like Stowe's novels, the book's argument is found less in the plot than in the structure of the text as it responds to Cotton Mather's *Magnalia.*

---

28. Although the novel alerts the reader to the ways that "gossip" or "ancient superstitions" take on the authority of truth, the narrator nonetheless acknowledges that "it is often instructive to take the women's, the private and domestic view, of a public man" (2:122). Similar to Harriet Beecher Stowe's construction of the female minister *cum* historian in *The Pearl of Orr's Island* and *The Minister's Wooing,* this statement falls short of ascribing such full authority to women's "private and domestic view," which in Hawthorne's novel is deemed "instructive" but not essential.

29. "The Heroine of *The House of the Seven Gables;* or, Who Killed Jaffrey Pyncheon?" *New England Quarterly* 77.4 (2004): 607.

Cited only once in *The House of the Seven Gables,* Mather is mentioned in the context of our introduction to Matthew Maule, whose grandfather was executed in Salem for wizardry. Hawthorne identifies Cotton Mather as one of those who

> made such laudable efforts to weaken the great Enemy of souls, by sending a multitude of his adherents up the rocky pathway of Gallows-Hill. Since those days, no doubt, it had grown to be suspected, that, in consequence of an unfortunate overdoing of a work praiseworthy in itself, the proceedings against the witches had proved far less acceptable to the Beneficient Father, than to that very Arch-Enemy, whom they were intended to distress and utterly overwhelm. (2:188)

Hawthorne's bemused assessment of the unwitting effect of Cotton Mather's position on Salem witchcraft can also be read as the author's response to Mather's claims regarding the earliest of the Pyncheons in New England and the ancestors of young Matthew Maule and Holgrave. Hawthorne's irony, too, suggests his perspective on Mather's prose as well as the figure of Mather himself.

The opening books of *Magnalia Christi Americana* contain numerous albeit brief references to several Pyncheon men.[30] William Pyncheon is identified as one of the "persons of quality about London" who purchased a title from the king to settle a plantation in New England, which was later named Salem (1:67). Prominent figures, both he and John Pyncheon are listed as early magistrates in Massachusetts, Joseph Pyncheon figures on the roster of 1664 Harvard graduates, and a Major Pyncheon is noted as a member of the troops who successfully halted an Indian raid in Springfield in 1674 (1:141, 2:31, 2:565). In addition, Mather writes of the town they settled, "they called it Salem, for the *peace* which they had and hoped in it, and *so it is called unto this day*" (1:68). Although *The House of the Seven Gables* counters Mather's skeletal information about the Pyncheon entitlement to land, their position relative to the native Americans, and the peace that reigns in Salem, the novel is motivated more by Mather's extreme statements about Thomas Maule.[31]

---

30. Although Mather spells the surname as Pinchon and Pynchon, I use Hawthorne's spelling throughout.

31. Cotton Mather also provides the early Salem covenant with articles that call for charity toward native Americans and eschews "back-bitings" among Christian brethren, both of which are contradicted by Hawthorne's version of the Pyncheons of Salem. See *Magnalia* 1:71.

At the close of the section on the Indian wars and the beginning of his account of "Quakers Encountred," Cotton Mather maligns Tom Maule as a defender of the native Americans, and because of this, he is also cast as a traitor to New England, the enemy of true religion, a fool, and the worst liar in Salem. Mather writes,

[O]ne Tom Maule, at this time living in Salem, hath exposed unto the publick a volume of *nonsensical* blasphemies and heresies, wherein he sets himself to defend the Indians in their bloody villanies, and revile the country for defending it self against them. And that the *venom* of this pamphlet might be improved unto the *heighth* of *slanderouss wickedness,* there hath been since added unto it, in another pamphlet, a parcel of ingredients compounded for mischief, as if "by the art of the apothecary." None but he whom the Jews in their *"Talmuds"* call *Bentamalion,* could have inspired such a slanderer! Have the Quakers ever yet censured this their author for holding-forth in his *Alcoran,* (page 221,) "That the devil, sin, death, and hell, are but nothing, they are but a non-entity;" and (page 183,) that "all men who have a body of sin remaining in them, are *witches*"? I have cause to believe they never did! nor that they ever advised him to pull in his *horns,* from goring the sides of New-England with such passages as those in (page 195) the same horrible pamphlet: "God hath well rewarded the inhabitants of New-England for their unrighteous dealings towards the native Indians, whom now the Lord hath suffered to reward the inhabitants with a double measure of blood, by fire and sword," &c. And those "unrighteous dealings" he explains to be the killing of the Indians, (or murdering of them,) by the old planters of these colonies in their *first settlement.* Thus are the ashes of our *fathers* vilely *staled* upon by one who, perhaps, would not stick at the villany of doing as much upon their *baptism* it self. I must tell you, friends, that if you don't publickly "give forth a testimony" to defie Tom Maule, and "his works," it will be thought by some, (who it may be don't wish you so well as I do,) that you own this *bloody stuff;* which doubtless you'll not be so ill-advised as to do. But, certainly, if the good people of New-England now make it not a proverb for a *liar* of the first magnitude, "He is as very a liar as Tom Maule," they will deprive their language of one significant expression which now offers it self unto them.

Let us now leave our friend Maule's works as a fit volume to be an appendix unto the famous *"Tartaretus,"* and worthy of a room in Pantagruel's library. The fittest way to answer him, would be to send him to *Boston woods!* (2:644–45)

Within the text, Mather's invective is unexpected and unprompted, and its excessive theatricality surpasses that of his characteristically dramatic prose. In addition to his extreme proposition that Maule be executed in Boston woods, the site of the gallows, several features of Mather's argument are exceptional. In his flurry of charges against Tom Maule, Cotton Mather appears to know no limits and conflates Quakerism, Indian advocacy, theological heresy, and civic betrayal. Further evidence of Mather's fever-ish campaign against Maule is his desire to alter language to perpetually acknowledge Maule's purported sins. Finally, most disturbing is Mather's imperative that readers adopt his position at the risk of their reputation.

In *The House of the Seven Gables,* Hawthorne finds that Mather's call for execution of such individuals on Gallows-Hill is an "unfortunate overdoing" of his position, and constructs the plot to illustrate the ironic consequence of Mather's religious and civic zeal, just as he alerts us in his depiction of Mather in the novel. Although *The House of the Seven Gables* speaks at length about the deeds of the old and young Matthew Maules, Hawthorne mentions Thomas Maule only twice. In the first chapter, when Thomas Maule is identified as the "architect of the House of the Seven Gables," this attribution is to be read symbolically and points to Mather's portrayal of Tom Maule as providing the architecture of the fiction (2:10). The second reference is prompted by Mr. Pyncheon in the "Alice Pyncheon" chapter, who asks Matthew Maule if his name is Thomas or Matthew Maule and if he is son or grandson of the builder. Matthew replies forthrightly that he is "son of him who built the house—grandson of the rightful proprietor of the soil!," a statement that points to the novel's plot (2:194).

Although the goal of the novel is not revisionist history, Hawthorne creates a fictional account that fuses Mather's tale of the Pyncheons as early, prominent landowners and Indian fighters with that of Tom Maule, an outspoken, independent Quaker, and to underscore this, fuses the set-ting. Maule's Lane is also known as Pyncheon-street (2:11). Moreover, in his fiction, Hawthorne inverts Mather's depiction of Tom Maule, his demands on the citizenry, and even his call for a new maxim.

Ultimately, the novel reverses Mather's assessment of the Pyncheons and Tom Maule to prove that the Pyncheon men are liars and slanderers, and demonstrate that they are punished by death for their "unrighteous dealings" with both the native Americans and the Maules. Unlike Mather, however, Hawthorne will not suggest that this is divine providence, which is cast as "inexplicable" (2:149). If there exists a guiding providence, one honest man in Salem is willing to acknowledge that he is unable to decipher the hand of God, exclaiming "if we are to take it as the will of Providence, why, I can't exactly fathom it!" (2:318).

Cotton Mather was unable to popularize his new saying, "He is as very a liar as Tom Maule," but Nathaniel Hawthorne toys with Mather's aspiration to create a new commonplace that disparages his villain. Thus, in *The House of the Seven Gables,* when he reverses Mather's protagonist and antagonist, the Salem community regularly uses the adage, "He has Maule's blood to drink." Indeed, the novel plays on Mather's language that those who refuse to testify publicly against Maule will "own this *bloody stuff.*" Further, the Pyncheons who persist in the family lie and refuse to publicly acknowledge the Maule's right to their land die as Matthew Maule predicted—"God will give him blood to drink!" (2:8).

We find Hawthorne's reversal of Mather's caustic statement regarding Tom Maule at every level of narrative construction—language, characterization, and plot. The plot of *The House of the Seven Gables*—however erratic—suggests the repetition of motifs that one finds in typological literature such as Cotton Mather's *Magnalia* in which the good man is said to be a type of a scriptural hero while the sinner is typed as a scriptural villain. Jaffrey Pyncheon repeats the ill-doing of his forefathers just as young Matthew Maule practices the wizardry of old Matthew Maule, and the haughty Pyncheons will continue to defraud the long-suffering Maules. The Pyncheons and Maules of the present—Hepzibah, Clifford, and Holgrave included—persist in the ideologies of the past.[32] However, in this aspect of narrative construction, Hawthorne foils our expectation when the novel breaks with its typological structure and replaces repetition with reversal.[33] That is, the security of typological repetition that is a feature of the providence tale is trumped by the insecurity of Hawthorne's message of ruptured expectations.

Another feature common to "Alice Doane's Appeal" and *The House of the Seven Gables* is their use of the story-teller *cum* historian who is a young man looking at his community with new eyes. Distinct from the work's narrator, this character presents a manuscript with a tale that comments

32. Although Marc Amfreville comes to different conclusions about repetition of plot in this novel, he puts forth an interesting thesis that connects the text to the dramatic repetition found in Greek tragedy. See *"The House of the Seven Gables:* Une Tragédie Gothique," *Revue Française d'Études Américaines* 83 (2000): 113–28.

33. Michael Davitt Bell is one of the early critics who explore the repetition of plot and character in this novel. Although Bell arrives at different conclusions about this motif, he ties it in interesting ways to Hawthorne's theoretical concerns regarding history (215–36). See *Hawthorne and the Historical Romance of New England* (Princeton: Princeton University Press, 1971), 215–36.

on the larger narrative. In the case of "Alice Doane's Appeal, the young
man recounts a story of Gallows-Hill, while he is seated on this very place
in the fiction. His account also responds to the narrator's early statement
that "recently, indeed, an historian has treated the subject in a manner that
will keep his name alive."[34] Thus, the young man's metanarrative is on equal
footing with the narrator's tale and the work of the unnamed historian—
not because they are all equally legitimate, but because they are equally
fictive.[35] Likewise, in *The House of the Seven Gables*, when Holgrave pro-
duces his manuscript at the close of chapter twelve and announces, "I have
put an incident of the Pyncheon family-history, with which I happen to be
acquainted, into the form of a legend, and mean to publish it in a magazine," he proposes the importance of fiction in establishing the character of
the family and the larger community (2:281). Although he makes no claim
to undermine the legitimacy of historical narrative, when his "legend"
appears as chapter thirteen, it does just that. Michael Dunne notes that
when Hawthorne prints the legend without quotation marks to identify it
as Holgrave's invention, he signals that it holds "much the same authority
as the sections proceeding directly from the narrator" (124). Significantly,
this legend is the novel's only disclosure of the tragedy of Alice Pyncheon,
a critical part of the history of the animosity between the Pyncheons and
the Maules. Thus, history is cast as a fiction within a fiction.

Given this uncertainty, *The House of the Seven Gables* shies away from
definitive conclusion and, in the final chapter, offers no satisfying resolution that leads the reader to render judgment on the good fortune of the
proud Hepzibah Pyncheon and her simple brother, or the marriage of
Phoebe to the newly rich and newly conservative Holgrave. Emily Budick,
among other critics, raises concerns about the abrupt and mechanical
ending, and characterizes it as "painfully cheery and glib, reminiscent
of Clifford's insane statements about ascending spirals and transcenden-
talized realities" (121). Because the tone of the final chapter is at once
so oddly blithe and indeterminate, it appears to counter that of Cotton
Mather, whose diatribe on Tom Maule ends predictably with a call for his
execution, a singular, tragic conclusion. In this way, Hawthorne rejects

34. Colacurcio notes that this passage most likely refers to Charles Upham's 1831 *Lectures
on Witchcraft* (88, 552n102). However, Dunne proposes that "this sentence is intended to apply
equally to the author of the Salem history (whether Upham or a purely fictional historian), to the
fictional narrator of the metadiegetic tale and to the author of 'Alice Doane's Appeal'" (80). On
Hawthorne's use of Upham, see also Anne Henry Ehrenpreis, "Elizabeth Gaskell and Nathaniel
Hawthorne," *The Nathaniel Hawthorne Journal* (1973): 101–2, 105.

35. See Dunne's lucid commentary on the diegetic and metadiegetic narratives in "Alice
Doane's Appeal and *The House of the Seven Gables*," 79–86 and 118–28.

the rhetorical stance of Cotton Mather who insists upon a single response from his readers, and avoids any appearance of a legitimate closure, which Hayden White frames as the urge to moralize. Hawthorne's commitment to the malleability of historical narrative will not allow him to make such demands of his audience.

Likewise, Susan Mizruchi observes that within the framework of the novel's plot, not only do "all of the characters in *Seven Gables* exhibit uncertainty about their place in history," but also "the narrator shares the characters' anxiety about historical change" (89, 103). The reader, then, mirrors both the characters and the narrator. Anxiety about the historical indeterminacy can be understood in terms of the way that Hawthorne depicts the collection and dissemination of historical information in this novel.[36] At the center of *The House of the Seven Gables* is the assertion that historical narrative has been suppressed and distorted by a limited number of powerful individuals. These specific characters, Judge Pyncheon, in particular, believe that they control historical accounts and thus determine their own futures, but do not recognize that this very notion renders them insecure and ultimately vulnerable to those who threaten to disclose their duplicity. Indeed, such individuals lose their life because of their craven posture *vis-à-vis* history. Other characters, such as Hepzibah and Clifford Pyncheon, are denied access to their family history and are thus powerless victims of those who disseminate flawed historical accounts. These figures, in particular, are doubly victimized because, denied authority over their personal histories, they attempt to live in absurd fantasies of their past. Moreover, as in "Alice Doane," a house built on the site of historical deception can only be destructive to its inhabitants, and a nation built on a flawed historical identity cannot thrive.

When Michael Colacurcio mocks one of Hawthorne's narrators—light-heartedly, to be sure—for "having read too much Cotton Mather" (209), he suggests Hawthorne's rejection of the persistence of Mather's pedantic voice in present historical narratives. In Hawthorne's fiction, the unrelentingly singular focus of Cotton Mather's rhetorical appeals in his historical narrative come to represent the antithesis of responsible and productive history. History is not singular and static, and surely does not begin and

36. For additional statements on *The House of the Seven Gables* as an argument about historiography and the use of historical narrative as framed in this study, see Dunne, 118–28, Mizruchi, 83–135, and Swann, 96–117. Emily Budick's *Fiction and Historical Consciousness* (New Haven: Yale University Press, 1989) looks to the novel's propositions concerning historical "perception," a thesis that brings her to a different understanding of the novel than the one put forth here.

end with *Magnalia Christi Americana,* but demands to be re-envisioned and reinvented. This notion is underscored in the title of one of the author's collections, *Twice-told Tales.* Read from the perspective of Hawthorne's scrutiny of American historiography, this title signals much more than an interesting inventional strategy for fiction. It puts forth the author's ethical stance on writing and rewriting history, and further argues for the social imperative of twice-told tales and thrice-told tales and beyond.

Chapter 6

ॐ

"The story was in the gaps"[1]

CATHARINE MARIA SEDGWICK
AND EDITH WHARTON

In their fictional works, Catharine Maria Sedgwick and Edith Wharton, like Poe, Stowe, and Hawthorne, speak to contemporary anxiety regarding not the particularities of the received historical accounts, but to their larger, philosophical concerns about historiography and its implications for the individual citizen. In Sedgwick's *Hope Leslie* and Wharton's *Ethan Frome* and several of her New England tales, we are introduced to men and women who struggle to create a full and accurate narrative of their community. As the plot and the structure of these fictions reveal, their histories are invariably stunted. Both authors recognize that the fullest story of any society is often to be had in the gaps between the multiple accounts of the factual details rather than in any one definitive narrative.

Sedgwick's novel, *Hope Leslie,* is set in seventeenth-century New England and is populated with historical figures both prominent and obscure. Moreover, the characters in *Hope Leslie* tell and retell accounts of themselves and their community in their homes, courtrooms, and grave-yards, and they do so in various modes—conversation, lecture, letters, and courtroom testimony. One might surmise that the author was attempting to work through the din of private and public tales to discover the truth that would allow her to write a singular historical narrative of colonial New England. To the contrary, Sedgwick asks the reader to hear the cacophony of all the voices because the nation's history is noisy, frenzied, and conflicted. The author's objective within her fiction is to replicate the din, which, to her, represents the new democracy.

---

1. The narrator of Edith Wharton's *Ethan Frome* recognizes that when one character speaks, there are "perceptible gaps between his facts," and further determines that "the deeper meaning of the story was in the gaps." See Wharton's *New England: Seven Stories and Ethan Frome* (Hanover and London: University Press of New Hampshire, 1995), 101. All references to Wharton's fiction are from this edition.

Edith Wharton's statement on historical narrative is quieter. In the aftermath of her fictional accounts of illicit love affairs, murder, and tragic marriages, there is still no story to be had. Try though they may, the historians in "Bewitched" and *Ethan Frome* are at odds to establish a stable narrative concerning events of great importance to themselves and their community. By the admission of *Ethan Frome*'s frustrated narrator, "the deeper meaning of the story was in the gaps" (101). Despite competing and corroborating accounts and eyewitness testimony, a full, nuanced and authoritative historical narrative never emerges, and the supposed historian is silent. Contrary to Sedgwick's historiographical statement that invests confidence in the multiplicity of historical tales, Wharton looks with some disappointment to the interstices between the tales.

Sedgwick's Historical Romance

Catharine Maria Sedgwick was accustomed to hearing many voices on the history and mission of the nation. Much like Nathaniel Hawthorne, Sedgwick is a quintessential New England writer. The Sedgwick family, like the Hawthornes and Hathornes, has a recognized place in the history of the colonies and the new nation. In this way, the authors' relationship to their national history is personal as well as professional, and both draw on their particular attachment to the tales of New England as they fashion their own fictional narratives. Descended on both sides from the renowned ministers in the Connecticut Valley known collectively as the "River Gods," Catharine Maria Sedgwick is related to such notable figures as Jonathan Edwards and John Williams.[2] She was raised in a privileged home, dominated by her father, Theodore Sedgwick, a prominent man who served first in the Massachusetts legislature and then in the United States House of Representatives and Senate. Her father's staunch allegiance to Federalist principles in the political arena was matched by his adherence to orthodox Congregationalism in his religious life. An educated and independent woman, Sedgwick chose to support more democratic ideals in her public advocacy just as she rejected the Calvinist theology of her father.

Because she was raised in the conservative Congregational church, she

---

2. Karen Woods Weierman documents the genealogy of the Sedgwick family in "Reading and Writing *Hope Leslie*: Catharine Maria Sedgwick's Indian 'Connections,'" *The New England Quarterly* 75.3 (2002): 415–43. For biographical information on Catharine Maria Sedgwick and her family, I draw from Weierman's essay and Mary Kelley's introduction to Sedgwick's *The Power of Her Sympathy: The Autobiography and Journal of Catharine Maria Sedgwick* (Boston: Massachusetts Historical Society, 1993), 3–41. This book will be cited hereafter as *Power*.

was more than conversant in its Calvinist doctrines and practices, which figure in several of her historical novels. However, her relationship to her family's religion was vexed. She describes the Calvinist faith bluntly as "unscriptural," "unprofitable" and "demoralizing," and determines it to be a "gross violation of the religion of the Redeemer."[3] Moreover, she was able to see that nineteenth-century America was witnessing a shift in the church. In her autobiography, Sedgwick contrasts the conservative, backward-looking Dr. Stephen West with the liberal minister Henry Ward Beecher, and observes that their personal styles "fitly denote the past and present clerical dynasties" (*Power*, 96). She would also recognize that their theologies, too, speak to past and present religious thought.

Likewise, Sedgwick was exceptionally knowledgeable of the early histories of the nation's Puritan past. Her novel *Hope Leslie; or, Early Times in the Massachusetts* includes epigraphs and other direct quotations from William Bradford's *Of Plymouth Plantation*, William Hubbard's *The Present State of New England*, Edward Johnson's *Wonder-working Providence of Sions Savior in New England*, Roger Williams's *A Key into the Language of America*, and John Winthrop's *History of New England*—as well as Cotton Mather's *Magnalia Christi Americana*.[4] Indeed, in her preface to the novel, Sedgwick acknowledges her scholarly interest in colonial history and asserts that "the only merit claimed by the present writer, is that of a patient investigation of all the materials that could be obtained" (5). Placing additional value on the study of history, she adds that she would be "fully gratified if, by this work, any of our young countrymen should be stimulated to investigate the early history of their native land" (6).

Sedgwick's intellectual inquiry into the early history of her country is complemented by her personal attachment to figures in that history. Directly related to John Williams, a minister who was captured with several of his children during an Indian raid on Deerfield, Massachusetts, she was fascinated by the fate of his daughter—and her distant cousin—Eunice, who chose to remain with her captors. Eunice, a model for the character Faith Leslie, married a Roman Catholic Mohawk and lived out her life with her husband and children as a member of the Mohawk tribe.[5]

---

3. *Life and Letters of Catharine M. Sedgwick*, ed. Mary E. Dewey (New York: Harper & Brothers, 1871), 119. As testimony to her intellectual flexibility, Sedgwick's journal also reveals that she read the conservative, evangelical author Elizabeth Singer Rowe, whose work, she confesses, "had a strange charm for me" (*Power*, 83).

4. I am indebted to Mary Kelley's edition of the novel for its meticulous identification of Sedgwick's sources and allusions. See *Hope Leslie; or, Early Times in the Massachusetts* (New Brunswick and London: Rutgers University Press, 1990).

5. John Demos has brilliantly documented the life of Eunice Williams following her

Hope Leslie is a work of historical fiction, but according to the author, it is not "in any degree an historical narrative, or a relation of real events" (5). Yet, this does not imply that the novel makes no claims regarding the writing and reading of history. Indeed, its central theme directly addresses this issue, and the structure of the novel embodies Sedgwick's argument on the production and reception of historical narrative.

Because the novel reprises and revises accounts of historical events in seventeenth-century New England, and in doing so places an idealistic English young woman and a fearless Indian young woman at the center of the text, Hope Leslie can be clearly understood as counterplotting the received historical narratives of "early times in the Massachusetts." As Philip Gould has argued, "whether Hope Leslie contains, then, an invalidation of patriarchal history or an uncannily prescient exercise in historical dialogics, the line of continuity in these readings locates Catharine Sedgwick vis-à-vis seventeenth-century historiography."[6] Although critics attempt to situate Sedgwick in a stable position as a native American advocate, a proponent of feminist activism, or an heiress to republican virtue, Douglas Ford cautions the reader against a binary reading of her novel. Drawing on Foucault's "Truth and Power," Ford warns against "read[ing] the novel as subverting a single, monolithic ideology of a repressive mechanism, thus obstructing our view of the plurality of *discourses* which produce power."[7] Ford guides us instead

> to view how Hope Leslie represents individual discourses which produce conflicting versions of 'truth,' rather than a single over-arching ideology.

captivity in *The Unredeemed Captive: A Family Story From Early America* (New York: Vintage, 1994). Weierman offers interesting details about Catharine Maria Sedgwick's fascination with the story of Eunice Williams, including her attempt to meet Eleazar Williams, Eunice's great-grandson (419–21). See also Sedgwick's personal statement on the life of Eunice Williams in *Life and Letters*, 129–30.

6. "Catharine Sedgwick's 'Recital' of the Pequot War," *American Literature* 66.4 (1994), 642. For additional perspectives on Sedgwick's approach to and goals for an alternative history in this novel, see Kelley, "Introduction," *Hope Leslie*, xx–xxxv; Sandra A. Zagarell, "Expanding 'America': Lydia Sigourney's *Sketch of Connecticut*, Catharine Sedgwick's *Hope Leslie*," *Tulsa Studies in Women's Literature* 6 (1987), 235; Dana Nelson, "Sympathy as Strategy in Sedgwick's *Hope Leslie*" in *The Culture of Sentiment: Race, Gender, and Sentimentality in Nineteenth-Century America*, ed. Shirley Samuels (New York: Oxford University Press, 1992), 195; and Weierman, 416. Jeffrey Insko's provocative essay, "Anachronistic Imaginings: *Hope Leslie*'s Challenge to Historicism," *American Literary History* 16.2 (2004), 179–207, focuses on the novel's narrator, who offers a metacommentary on historical narrative by commenting on past historical accounts, creating a present document, and anticipating its response in the future.

7. "Inscribing the 'Impartial Observer' in Sedgwick's *Hope Leslie*," *Legacy: A Journal of American Women Writers* 14.2 (1997), 83.

Such a view reveals that the novel internalizes such conflict and engages in processes more problematic than the straightforward correction of injustices brought about by a monolithic form of power. (83–84)

Where Ford's observations on Sedgwick's representation of conflicting rhetorics in *Hope Leslie* lead him to an interesting analysis of the language of truth claims in the novel, his analysis also suggests ways to unravel the tangled structure of the novel. The plot of *Hope Leslie* may rightly be described as manic. With the exception of the tidy—if surprising—resolution of each major and minor plot, the action of the novel is as frenzied as that of Poe's *Pym*. The title character of the novel is a young woman who comes of age in seventeenth-century New England, befriends a young native American woman, Magawisca, falls in love with a suitable Puritan, Everell Fletcher, and tests herself and her society in the process. To this extent, it is a conventional marriage plot. However, many other threads vie for the reader's attention, and some of these are equally conventional captivity narratives and seduction plots. Others are simply wild. A closet Roman Catholic from England and his cross-dressing Spanish mistress figure in the novel, threatening to disrupt the marriage plot and forming a parallel seduction plot and captivity narrative of their own. The domestic situation of the Fletcher family could not be more unlikely. Their less-than-orderly Puritan family consists of William Fletcher and his wife and their children as well as Hope and Faith Leslie, the two orphaned daughters of his first love, Alice. In addition, the family includes two native American children who are captives and servants to the family, a variety of English servants, comic figures all, and the equally comic and frivolous Aunt Grafton from England. Outside of the Fletcher home, courtroom theatrics and jailhouse antics upset the purported order of the larger Puritan community. A simple attempt to cure a snakebite is construed as heresy, and unseemly midnight trysts are refashioned as sisterly reunions. Comedy is fused with history that is often represented as tragedy.

Michael Davitt Bell understands this "incredibly complicated plot" as testimony to the author's ingenuity, but also recognizes it as a "shortcoming." For Bell, it also expresses the development from history to romance, which he attaches to Northrop Frye's paradigm of the romantic or comic marriage plot in which the union of the hero and heroine "become the primary agents of the new society, of historical progress."[8] Using Frye's

8. See "History and Romance Convention in Catharine Sedgwick's *Hope Leslie*," *American Quarterly* 22.2 (1970): 213–21. Bell also argues that the plot—as a statement of American

approach to the resolution of a comic plot to understand *Hope Leslie* offers an interesting, but only partially satisfying, reading of the novel. From the perspective of an authorial resistance to early and contemporary historical writing, the manic plot signals another of Sedgwick's designs for her novel. Responding to the tidy plots of Mather's providence tales that lead to a singular, definitive conclusion, *Hope Leslie's* diffuse and often conflicting plots testify to the author's alternate understanding of the narratives that aspire to characterize a community.

Many scholars cite the novel's competing narratives of the 1637 Pequot War in chapter four as evidence of Sedgwick's revisionist history, and it is clear from this example that one of Sedgwick's goals for the text is to undermine the authority of colonial historical narrative. Young Everell Fletcher, who represents the future of the nation, is initiated into the foundational principles of America by way of its dramatic historical moments. The veteran Digby recounts his tale of the Pequot War, and the narrative both ennobles and terrifies Everell. Although we are not privy to Digby's account of his war experience, we infer that Digby strikes the conventional theme of the just cause, valor, and victory of the English soldiers. As Everell later claims, "as I have heard, our people had all the honour of the fight" (48). This is entirely consistent with the received histories of colonial New England that Sedgwick consulted for this novel. However, in the space of a few pages, when Magawisca offers her account of the same battles, the details of this war, the interpretation of those details, and the larger themes of the narrative are decidedly different and at times antithetical. In Sedgwick's vision of the future of the nation, the alternative history from the perspective of a native American woman is positioned as an important part of the education of the young white men who will become the leadership of the nation. From this point onward, the novel asks the reader to query every ostensibly official statement of any event, a move that the plot enacts by decentering dominant voices.

Moreover, if the reader is asked to use the example of these competing narratives to inform a reading of the remainder of the text, there are other lessons to be learned. Much like Hawthorne, Sedgwick insists that interrogating the ethos of the historian is an essential part of evaluating a historical account. Digby's credibility does not fare well under scrutiny. He may claim the authority of a soldier and eyewitness to the battles, but Sedgwick undercuts his claims by identifying him as one of those veterans who loves to recount his war stories especially in light of his having "brief military

---

values—embodies the move from artifice to liberty. Frye outlines his understanding of the marriage plot in *Anatomy of Criticism* (Princeton: Princeton University Press, 1957), 245.

experience" and presumably limited exposure to the reality of war. Thus, in the hands of Digby, history is immediately reduced to one old man's "tales of adventure, and danger" (43). Unfortunately, as Sedgwick reveals, Digby's tales are consonant with those of Mather, Bradford, Johnson, and other colonial historians. Subsequently in the novel when Sedgwick invokes the "chronicles of the times," "the history of the times," and "our early annals," the reader is asked to think of these documents as imaginative stories told among aging men of varying degrees of experience (47, 53, 56).

Like Harriet Beecher Stowe, Catharine Sedgwick challenges the white male historian by way of an undervalued woman. In *Hope Leslie*, Magawisca's historical narrative shows both attention to factual detail and sensitivity to her themes. At times, her account also surprises the reader by its impartiality. That is, she laments vicious behavior and moral failings among her own people in addition to vilifying the English. Most importantly, she is able to convince Everell that what he knows as victory visits death and numerous other forms of tragedy on her people. Finally, Magawisca's account inspires Everell with "sympathy and admiration of her heroic and suffering people" (54).

To argue that Sedgwick replaces the early providential histories authored by men with a native American history authored by a woman would deny the complexity of chapter four within the framework of the novel. Although the reader—like Everell—attends to Magawisca's narrative with "sympathy and admiration," we learn in the following chapter of *Hope Leslie* that our new historian is neither completely sympathetic nor admirable. That is, she is complicit in the murder of innocent people because she does not alert the Fletcher family to the impending raid on their home in Bethel. In this way, this complex character supports her father's murderous revenge, yet she also throws her arms around Mrs. Fletcher in an unsuccessful attempt to protect her from a warrior's knife. If the reader is looking for a binary vision of early American conflict or a clear signpost for the future, neither is to be found in the text. In Douglas Ford's words, *Hope Leslie* illustrates the "individual discourses which produce conflicting versions of 'truth,' rather than a single over-arching ideology" (83). Moreover, the individual discourses are themselves frequently compromised, irrespective of their origin.

Chapter five of the novel complicates the binary narratives of warring peoples in the previous chapter by introducing a third account of warfare. The raid on Bethel gives evidence of the tragic consequences of being seduced by any single statement of historical fact in the previous chapter. Digby is so convinced of the accuracy of his knowledge of the native American warriors that he ignores otherwise obvious signs of the impending attack. Likewise, Everell is so impressed with Magawisca's claims regarding native American honor and oppression that he is blind to her treachery. Because of the inability of these men to think with greater complexity about competing discourses, innocent people are slaughtered.

Sedgwick's account of the Indian raid on Bethel must also be read against the backdrop of both Magawisca's account of the English raid on Mononotto and his tribe and the received colonial histories of the Pequot War. In truth, it bears cruel resemblance to both. Multiple elements of the Bethel raid have parallels in Magawisca's earlier narrative, the most tragic of which is the death of women and children. Again, the victory of one people means the extermination of "defenceless families" of another people (54). In addition, the narrative of the Bethel raid offers an ironic, if comic, nod to the providential histories of New England. When Mr. Fletcher returns to his home, the site of Mononotto's revenge, and finds "not one—not one spared!," he is in error, and is quickly corrected by the foolish servant, Jennet:

> "Yes, one," spoke a trembling whining voice, which proved to be Jennet's, who had just emerged from her hiding-place covered with soot; "by the blessing of a kind Providence, I have been preserved for some wise end, but," she continued panting, "the fright has taken my breath away, besides being squeezed as flat as a pancake in the bed-room chimney." (66–67)

Self-absorbed to an extreme, Jennet is no help to Mr. Fletcher in understanding the events, discovering who might have survived, and recovering those living members of his family. "She was mainly occupied with her own remarkable preservation, not doubting that Providence has specially interposed to save the only life utterly insignificant in any eyes but her own" (68). The reader has already been schooled in the ills of preoccupation with one's own account of one's history. Moreover, in Sedgwick's novel, providential history itself is dealt a fatal blow. It is linked to self-interest and self-aggrandizement rather than any special disposition of God.

Chapters four and five clearly expose Sedgwick's argument regarding alternative histories, and identify the abusive way in which cultures use historical narrative to retain and wield power. However, it would be a mistake to find that these chapters bear the weight of Sedgwick's entire argument for alternative histories. Nonetheless, the triad of war tales reveals the architecture of the novel that embodies the author's argument. Sedgwick structures her novel such that many of the plot elements and motifs as well as characters have multiple analogues that complicate or otherwise contend with those elements, motifs, and characters.

To offer a relatively simple example, when Nelema extracts herbs from her deerskin pouch to concoct a medicinal liquor to cure Cradock's snakebite, she is indicted for witchcraft. At the close of the same chapter, Sedgwick includes Aunt Grafton's recommendation to Everell of an herbal cure for colds, one that she is proud to have received from a Lady Penyvere. The author juxtaposes these scenes for ironic purpose because Aunt Grafton would never recognize the similarity between her culture's herbal pharmacopoeia and native American medicine. Neither would she be charged with sorcery for brewing herbal tea. Once again, however, the novel does not slip into a facile binary comparison of these cultural conventions. Aunt Grafton acknowledges that Hope threw her pennyroyal tea out of the window and nonetheless recovered from her illness, and likewise predicts that Everell will reject her medical advice. Conflicting positions on a single issue such as herbal medicine are simultaneously cross-cultural, transatlantic, interdenominational, and cross-generational.

In related scenes that take place outside of domestic life, representations of legal proceedings are similarly cross-cultural, interdenominational, cross-generational, and gendered. When the native Americans put Everell Fletcher on trial, they fail to recognize him as one of their staunchest advocates in the Puritan community. This trial, which "they believed to be the execution of exact and necessary justice," is disclosed as Mononotto's attempt to avenge the murder of his son and repair his reputation as a stern leader within his tribe (91). The charge, trial, and sentence are further called into question when Mononotto's daughter, Magawisca, attempts to protect Everell from the executioner's hatchet and sacrifices her arm. In a second court case, Nelema is charged with sorcery, or, in Hope's words, "the crime of curing Cradock." When brought to trial, evidence against Nelema is produced by "Jennett and some of her gossips" (108). Thus, the crime, the process, and the sentence are challenged within the novel. In a third trial, that of Magawisca on the charge of spying for her people, the process is immediately undercut by Sedgwick's ironic observation that the magistrate speaks from a position of "soi-disant infallibility" (284).[9] As in Everell's trial, the Puritan community does not recognize

9. I am grateful to T. Gregory Garvey who drew my attention to Sedgwick's sequencing of legal trials. His study focuses on Nelema's and Magawisca's court appearances, which, according to Garvey, illustrate masculine authorities' failure to manage crisis within their communities and dramatize women's productive intervention in the legal process. See "Risking Reprisal: Catharine Sedgwick's *Hope Leslie*," *American Transcendental Quarterly* 8.4 (1994), 287–98.

Magawisca as their ally. In addition, Sir Philip Gardiner, as the fraudulent principal witness, compromises the process because he, like Mononotto, uses the trial to secure his civic standing. In the case of Gardiner, he needs to conceal his identity as a Roman Catholic and that of his page, who is actually his young Spanish mistress. With each legal trial, the novel asserts that the community must continually examine itself and the processes it installs to assert its authority. As with the historical narratives that societies perpetuate to codify their identity, the reader is asked to distrust all other public narratives that societies create to legitimize their understanding of themselves.

A triad of war stories followed by a triad of court scenes suggests the architecture and argument of *Hope Leslie*. Indeed, examples of the text's structural argument are found throughout the novel and concern topics from race and religious orthodoxy to the performance of gender and the dictates of fashion. In each case, *Hope Leslie* embodies its advocacy of the plurality of voices by virtue of its narrative construction that is otherwise perceived as manic. Although Sedgwick's novel contains many forceful and undeniably feminist statements, it avoids oversimplification in this respect as well. Thus, it would be a mistake to understand the title character exclusively as a woman who foils masculine abuse of power and redresses social wrong throughout the novel, and to view her as the exclusive heroine of the novel.[10] Like Magawisca, who is both heroic and treacherous, Hope is remarkably open-minded and limited, selfless and willful. She loves and admires her native American friend, but her resentment of her sister's marriage to Oneco is unsettling. She is relentless in pursuing her vision of what is right and good, but at times falls into dangerous error about what is worth pursuing and the means to accomplish her ends. While the modern reader may wish to find a proto-feminist heroine in the character of Hope Leslie, Sedgwick makes this difficult. Judith Fetterley has expressed her desire to study this novel in a way that balances the competing critical urges for hagiography of early women writers and criticism that they too are complicit in the ill-doing of the men of their age. Thus, she insists, "what is admirable about *Hope Leslie* cannot be separated from what is problematic."[11] Speaking to the construction of female identity in *Hope*

10. Erica R. Bauermeister alerts us that "Sedgwick creates a story that condemns numerous uses of authority, even in the ninety-five pages before Hope becomes a principal part of the action" in "*The Lamplighter, The Wide, Wide World*, and *Hope Leslie*: Reconsidering the Recipes for Nineteenth-Century American Women's Novels," *Legacy: A Journal of American Women Writers* 8.1 (1991), 20.

11. "'My Sister! My Sister!': The Rhetoric of Catharine Sedgwick's *Hope Leslie*," in *Catharine Maria Sedgwick: Critical Perspectives*, ed. Lucinda L. Damon-Bach and Victoria Clements

Leslie, Fetterley concludes that Hope's questionable stance on race and her misspent independence provide examples of the rhetorical complexity of the novel and evidence of Sedgwick's "hopelessly" realistic vision of America.

Yet, from the perspective of the author's argument concerning historiography, this novel puts forth a decidedly nuanced understanding of humanity, which is neither definitively hopeful nor hopeless. Unlike the saints and sinners in Mather's providence tales who either enjoy *magnalia Dei* or suffer *terribilia Dei* but never both, Sedgwick's characters are capable of greatness in their public and private lives, but invariably, these same individuals are also at times weak and limited. Moreover, the qualities that we most admire in her characters are frequently those that compromise them, such as Hope's willingness to act, and Everell's unbiased view of his fellow men and women. Thus, at the level of characterization, *Hope Leslie* departs from the formula of the providence tale—whether in the form of the captivity narrative or the marriage plot—to underscore the author's commitment to a fuller expression of humanity and historical reality.

Rather than expressing a "hopelessly" realistic nation, the novel asserts its optimism from the earliest pages where Sedgwick casts the colonial past as the "preceding twilight" that she contrasts with the "glory of our risen day" (16). In the terms of this novel, the distinction between the twilight of the past and the current daylight is a liberal understanding of self and society, informed by a plurality of historical accounts. That Everell Fletcher is educated by Digby, Magawisca, and the English schoolmasters and becomes the father of "many generations" in America indicates the breadth of intellectual and social experience required by republican leadership (349).

Sedgwick's argument regarding historiography is similarly nuanced. While the novel critiques the definitive nature of early histories, any move to put forth a singular counternarrative would be a move to commit the same error. Interestingly, Sedgwick's representation of providential history is analytic, but not cynical or even dismissive. Although she undermines its exclusive claim to truth, especially in the example of Digby's retelling of the Pequot War, she gives credence to the rhetoric of divine providence when invoked in the service of humanity. In the trial of Magawisca, Reverend Eliot is invited to open the proceedings and does so by acknowledging that the wonder-working providence of God "mak[es] their enemies to be at peace with them" and demands that Christian people "show their light" to

---

(Boston: Northeastern University Press, 2003), 79.

the native Americans, arguments that call for mercy for the accused. Once again, the novel eschews a binary understanding of history by acknowledging the value of the very historiographical theories that it critiques. As Hawthorne has argued, historiography is always contested ground. Thus, society demands a plurality of historical statements that it looks to for affirmation and definition. Much like the structure of Hawthorne's "David Swan," *Hope Leslie* gives voice to a wide range of histories with the understanding that a plurality of statements on medicine, law, womanhood, virtue, and the national identity is welcome, necessary, valuable, and, finally, inevitable. Similarly, *Hope Leslie* refuses an orderly representation of historical events because such is the product of the imagination, and a limited imagination at that. As Hayden White has shown, neatly plotted representations of reality, like those of providential historians, are fictions that artfully establish coherence from a collection of disparate, conflicting, and ambiguous events. These narratives work to mitigate the terrifying experience of the chaos of life, and instead create a plot that contrives wholeness and meaning out of disorder and uncertainty (*Content,* 21). Unlike Poe's *Pym,* which unmasks historical tracts to reveal their terrifying chaos, *Hope Leslie*'s use of the cultural and gendered construction of history is enlightening and empowering, and heralds the "glory of our risen day" (16).

Another testament to Sedgwick's historiographical argument is the dizzying array of source materials that resembles Mather's compendium of early and contemporary materials for *Magnalia. Hope Leslie* defies this comparison only in the range of materials that Sedgwick draws from. To speak exclusively of the chapter epigraphs, she hallmarks the words of Puritan minister Cotton Mather and Anglican minister William Morrell as well as the dissenter Roger Williams. Quotations from their work stand alongside those from the poetry of Americans Felicia Hemans and William Cullen Bryant, and Europeans Shakespeare, Milton, Gray, Burns, LaRochfoucauld, and Metastasio.[12] The novel does not locate truth in any one sect, generation, nationality, language, gender, or genre. All must be heard. In this respect, the novel also resembles Hawthorne's *The Whole History of the Grandfather's Chair* in which individuals of divergent

---

12. Suzanne Gossett and Barbara Ann Bardes make a related claim in their essay, "Women and Political Power in the Republic: Two Early American Novels," *Legacy: A Journal of American Women Writers* 2.2 (1985), 20, in which they characterize *Hope Leslie* as "cosmopolitan." In comparison to contemporary novels, including those by Sedgwick herself, the landscape of *Hope Leslie* is populated with Europeans of different origins as well as native Americans. As part of her education, Hope is instructed in multiple foreign languages.

perspectives have an equal opportunity to hold forth from the distinguished chair.

Nonetheless, Sedgwick's structural emphasis on multiple conflicting perspectives on virtually every account should not be understood as advocating a valueless approach to truth or human motivation. *Hope Leslie* is a highly charged moralistic novel that clearly rewards virtuous behavior and does not hesitate to denigrate the actions of abusive men as well as those of the heroes and heroines, when necessary. As Maria Karafilis has recognized, the novel does not "elide difference and valorize a homogeneous society."[13] Its disposition of characters suggests the opposite. Those individuals who are rigidly ethnocentric or sectarian—such as Jennet or Mrs. Fletcher—die violently in the text, and those who shift allegiance from one culture to another—such as Magawisca and Faith—are maimed or infantilized. Sedgwick's model citizen attends to heterogeneity, negotiates difference, and acts for the common good on conflicted responsibilities to self and society. From the disparate, coherent historical fictions that compete for her attention, Hope Leslie, of all the novel's characters, has learned to decode the disparate, incoherent current events that demand her response. Similarly, from the manic, diffuse plot of *Hope Leslie,* the reader is asked to hear multiple, divergent narratives simultaneously as a lesson in how to construct a narrative of a democratic nation.

Wharton's Gothic History

Edith Wharton is not often associated with the themes and tropes of early American Calvinist literature. Indeed, her reputation rests largely on her insights into the high society of early twentieth-century New York rather than the struggling Puritan townships of seventeenth-century New England. Nonetheless, Wharton reminds the reader in *A Backward Glance* that she descends from Massachusetts colonial stock that relocated to New York because, she posits, they were "more interested in making money and acquiring property than in Predestination and witch-burning."[14] Moreover, in several short stories and in longer works such as *Ethan Frome* and *Summer,* Wharton returns to Massachusetts to interrogate her nation's

---

13. "Catharine Maria Sedgwick's *Hope Leslie:* The Crisis Between Ethical Political Action and US Literary Nationalism in the New Republic," *American Transcendental Quarterly* 12.4 (1998), 133. Karafilis's essay offers an astute analysis of the novel's "grammar of socio-political behavior."

14. (New York: Charles Scribner's Sons, 1933), 9.

New England Puritan origins, and expresses her interest in election, predestination, and even witch-hunting. More important to this study, in a
number of these texts, she examines the selection and education of the
community's historian.

Edith Wharton's 1925 short story, "Bewitched," is constructed much
like Cotton Mather's narratives that investigate the satanic possession of
a woman in the community. Wharton, like Mather, meticulously sets out
the protocol for documenting this remarkable occurrence and identifies
something of a tribunal that has been summoned to the investigation.
This group is naturally composed of the principals in this dilemma—Saul
Rutledge, who has regular assignations with a dead woman, Ora Brand;
his wife, who seeks an end to her husband's alleged affair; and Sylvester
Brand, father of the deceased Ora. In the tradition of Mather's invocation
of the disinterested, authoritative members of society who witness his
remarkables, Wharton includes two additional members of the investiga-
tory party—Deacon Hibben, and a young farmer and town selectman
named Orrin Bosworth—representing the religious and civil order of the
community.

Mrs. Rutledge, the aggrieved wife, begins laying out the case in a
definitive manner that sets the assertive tone for the remainder of her
narrative: "We're in trouble here, and that's the fact" (211). Both she and
her husband have witnessed the peculiar events that she divulges to her
audience, but she alone claims the authority to speak the purported fact of
her husband's being "bewitched." As Mrs. Rutledge puts forth the details
of the case, she allows no debate or equivocation on her testimony. When
queried about her facts, her response is blunt: "I don't think—I know"
(214); "I seen 'em" (214); and again "Don't I tell you I seen 'em?" (215).
To her mind, that she is an eyewitness to her husband's assignations is
both necessary and sufficient authority to understand and narrate these
events. However, situating fact as the exclusive purview of this querulous
and relentlessly domineering woman calls into question the very nature of
her truth. As Wharton writes in another story, "The Triumph of Night,"
"Oh, facts—what *are* facts? Just the way a thing happens to look at a given
minute . . ." (193).

As one might anticipate, the woman with the facts claims the right to
propose the resolution to the case. Mrs. Rutledge determines that the men
put an end to her and her husband's difficulty by driving a stake through
the dead woman's breast. She is as definitive in her method to resolve the
situation as she is in her narration of the events. "A stake through the
breast! That's the old way; and it's the only way!" she insists (219). Again

in the tradition of Mather, she invokes both scripture and history to secure her argument. Mrs. Rutledge quotes the proscription from Exodus that "Thou shalt not suffer a witch to live," and cites the historical precedent from within their very community, that is, a similar occurrence in which Lefforts Nash was cured of his spell when "they" put a stake through Hannah Corey's heart. In short order, Mrs. Rutledge is able to make her case and marshal support for the next step in the inquiry when the men would attempt to sight Ora Brand and Saul Rutledge at their next encounter. Thus, in controlling the story of the occurrence and in selecting her audience for the story, Mrs. Rutledge is able to determine the outcome of her tale.

Like many accomplished storytellers, in the process of constructing her narrative, Mrs. Rutledge trains her audience in the way she wishes them to "read." In this case, she first predisposes them to see what she wants them to see; then, as eyewitnesses to the events, they would issue reports that are consonant with hers. Moreover, this woman knows her audience well— with one exception. Clearly experienced in speaking to her husband, she also has insight into orchestrating an appeal to the deacon and Sylvester Brand, both long-standing members of the community. However, Orrin Bosworth is less well known. He was raised in neighboring Lonetop and is now a member of North Ashmore's town council, so we are led to believe that he has a certain prominence in the community. At the same time, he represents the next generation, and, as Wharton puts it, "had had more contact with the modern world" (220). Much of the drama of "Bewitched" circles around Mrs. Rutledge's selecting Bosworth as a member of her "audience" and her subsequent training of this man to serve her goals.

The ostensible primary plot of "Bewitched," of course, concerns the resolution of Saul Rutledge's purported relationship with the dead Ora Brand. This is only one of the ways in which we can understand the tale as gothic. The development of the character of Bosworth is also at the center of the story's argument, this aspect contributing to the gothic mode of this tale. Initially Bosworth "follows" the rest, doesn't understand why they have been called, and fails to appreciate Mrs. Rutledge's hand in the gathering. "Queer, our all meeting here this way," he says (209). Contemplating his position among the four people around the table, he can think only of the ways in which he is distinct from the others. He is young, advanced, successful, and, in fact, he and his friends laugh at the superstitious nonsense—such as this—they hear in the village.

However, in the setting of the Rutledge's parlor, Bosworth performs the duties of an official of the township. He attempts to establish a reasonable protocol for the investigation and even takes a deposition of sorts. He questions the "witnesses," requests independent statements, and asks for "proof." He does so although he has not been called upon for his independence, reason, and impartiality. To the contrary, he has been enlisted because he is naïve and compromised, and for these reasons, he may be trained to speak on behalf of the equally compromised community.

Wharton tells us that Bosworth "listened with a sense of suffocation; he felt as if he were wrestling with long-armed horrors in a dream (213)." This statement anticipates the embedded narrative that reveals Bosworth's relationship to the community and the grotesque occurrences that bind him to the people of North Ashmore. Bosworth's "long-armed horrors" include his insane Aunt Cressy, the story of whom he was advised to suppress lest "the shame of it would kill" his family (221). Yet, at this moment, the past has never seemed so present in his life, and he likewise recalls the related history of the others in the room. Deacon Hibben is a descendant of Mistress Hibben, one of the witches who were convicted in Salem in 1692.[15] Sylvester Brand has a similar family disgrace in the death of his wife who is also his first cousin. They share in superstition and shame.

The Hibbens, Brands, and Bosworths, we learn, have resided in Hemlock County "ever since the white men had come here" (221). Orrin, whose name means "white man," takes his place in the community as the next generation of white, male historians. Further, as he remembers his personal history, he allies himself more fully with his fellow men. More specifically, he takes on the responsibilities that are required by men in Hemlock County. When Mrs. Rutledge insists that they kill the witch, Ora Brand, she forces her point by tying the task to the performance of their masculinity. "Ain't any of you folks got the grit—?," she asks (222). Sylvester Brand ultimately kills his living daughter Venny at the scene of the assignation, and Bosworth participates by accompanying the party and taking Brand's gun after he fires his shot. His role is to witness and remember. Ironically, when Mrs. Rutledge attaches masculinity to the mandate to murder, she effectively emasculates those whom she has called to do her bidding. If Bosworth's primary role as a historian is to witness and remember, he does so because he has first submitted to the will of a woman.

The nature and function of history are complex and remain illusive in "Bewitched." The tale of rumored incest, adultery, and murder is never

---

15. Gerard M. Sweeney has identified "pathology" in Deacon Hibben himself and argues that the description of his face as "queerly blotched and moldy looking" is consistent with the symptoms presented by syphilitic patients. See "Wharton's 'Bewitched,'" *Explicator* 56.4 (1998): 198–201.

fully disclosed. The new historian himself "was never quite sure in which order the events that succeeded took place," and his vision was compromised by extremes of both light and darkness (226). Ultimately the history that he witnesses remains unspoken. When Bosworth's sister asks him if he had heard the news of Venny Brand, he tersely asks, "What news?" (227). The role that binds him to the men of the community alienates him from his own sister who now seems "miles away" although they inhabit the same kitchen (227). By the close of the story, he literally and metaphorically carries his societal load, the funeral bier. He shoulders the responsibility for the community's identity, which is both moribund and inextricably bound to the past. Because the past is never fully investigated and understood, there is no future in North Ashmore. In the absence of an honest narrative of the community—which may demand atonement and reform—there can be no future. Life in this New England community is relegated to replicating the past if only because its citizens intimidate subsequent generations, forcing them to reprise the behaviors of the past. To paraphrase the dictum of the dominant Mrs. Rutledge, "The old way is the only way!" (219).

Early in her novella *Ethan Frome,* Edith Wharton signals that this narrative is related to "Bewitched." She identifies *Ethan Frome*'s setting in Starkfield as lying just to the south of the short story's setting in North Ashmore.[16] The two works being both geographically and thematically related, it is productive to read Edith Wharton's *Ethan Frome* from the historiographic perspective found in "Bewitched" and center the narrative on the emerging voice of the narrator, the new member of the community.

Unlike Orrin Bosworth, who initially doesn't know that he has been tapped to witness extraordinary events, the narrator of *Ethan Frome* begins his tale with an assertive voice. In the opening four words of the novella, he claims, "I had the story" (99). He immediately checks his assertion with a statement of his two methods of acquiring and evaluating the story. The narrator first learns "bits" of his information from a variety of individuals whom he calls "informants" (99). He later becomes an eyewitness to current events that bear on his story, further solidifying his claim on the narrative.

A responsible historiographic protocol in place, the narrator nonetheless reveals as much about himself as his does about his subject matter. Like Orrin in "Bewitched," this narrator counts himself an outsider in Starkfield,

---

16. There are two bleak references to Starkfield in "Bewitched." First, Orrin Bosworth's mother threatens him to silence concerning his Aunt Cressie's condition under penalty of having her sent to the Starkfield asylum. Second, Ora Brand attends a Starkfield school to learn bookkeeping. She never practices her trade, but "when Ora came back she sickened and died" (221).

Massachusetts, unlike the other men in the town. Gradually he learns that
this is not entirely true. Primarily, he discloses—again in "bits"—the many
ways in which he resembles Ethan Frome, the man whose story he tells. As
Cynthia Griffin Wolfe has pointed out, the narrator discovers "disconcert-
ing and unexpected similarities": both are interested in technology, both
have spent time in Florida.[17] Describing Frome as "stiffened and grizzled"
by his harsh and confined life in Starkfield, the narrator admits that he, too,
is becoming habituated to his sorely limited life in the town. He recounts,
"I chafed at first, and then, under the hypnotizing effect of routine, gradually began to find a grim satisfaction in the life" (101). Dulled by routine
and content with a grim disposition, the narrator begins to understand
more fully the condition of Ethan Frome.

By the close of the novella, when Wharton returns to the frame, it
is unsettling to realize that the narrator is not making plans to leave
Starkfield. Harmon Gow claimed early in the tale that "Most of the smart
ones get away," causing the narrator to wonder why Frome has not extri-
cated himself from the town (100). However, he, too, is not going any-
where. He is "anchored" in Starkfield because of his work, but temporarily
without work because of a labor strike (101).[18] Moreover, like Frome, he
has been domesticated. Both men live with two women, Frome with Zeena
and Mattie, and the narrator with Mrs. Ned Hale and her mother, Mrs.
Varnum. Ruth Hale laments that Ethan, Zeena, and Mattie are "all shut up
there'n that one kitchen," but fails to see that the narrator, her daughter,
and she herself are sitting "in the austere seclusion of the horsehair parlor," the only difference being that of Hale's relative affluence (180, 179).
Similarly, her claims of being pained by Ethan's suffering might be matched
by the narrator's horror of her tale.

Most importantly, because of his stasis and domestication, he has lost
control of the story of Ethan Frome and has relinquished his authority to
Ruth Hale. He opens the novella with his claim of owning the story—"I
had the story"—but cannot close the tale. Despite the substantial information that he has acquired throughout the novella, the narrator is reduced

17. *A Feast of Words: The Triumph of Edith Wharton* (New York: Oxford University Press,
1977). 166. See also 167–68.

18. Jennifer Travis has pointed out the interesting relationship between the male characters
and work, and speaks to the labor crisis in Massachusetts townships in 1910 as the context for
Wharton's concern about the many psychological and social adversities caused by rural poverty.
See "Pain and Recompense: The Trouble with *Ethan Frome*," *Arizona Quarterly* 53.3 (1997): 37–
64. I would add that the want of work and the rewards of work contribute to the emasculation
of both Ethan Frome and the narrator and their consequent inability to speak in the presence of
assertive women.

to silence and can only ask a few limited questions. In this he resembles Orrin Bosworth of "Bewitched," who is depicted initially as "the youngest and most communicative" of men, but later speaks tersely and evasively. Likewise, much like Mrs. Rutledge's control in constructing the narrative of her husband and Ora Brand, Ruth Hale dominates the telling of her community's tale and has the final words on Ethan Frome and in *Ethan Frome*. His voice has been drowned out by the woman's tongue.

The narrator has the makings of a fine historian. He is young, analytical, disinterested, and evinces a natural curiosity about life. However, the trajectory of the novella suggests that these qualities are insufficient. Full historical narrative is not created by a dispassionate outsider, but is a volatile composite of the personal and public, engaged and disinterested. It is unclear that Ruth Hale's personal, longstanding relationship with the Fromes affords her greater truth about Ethan Frome than the narrator holds. It is equally uncertain that the narrator approaches the truth with greater clarity because he has no prior relationship with these individuals and can claim greater objectivity. Indeed, Wharton argues that the narrator may gather all the requisite facts to construct his account, but will never succeed in filling in the gaps. The lacunae in his tale result not from a lack of knowledge about the individuals and events, but from a lack of understanding about his relationship with these individuals, their past, and his present. The objective, authoritative historian is a flawed historian.

There are many ironies in Wharton's novella, most of which center on the suffering in the Frome household. However, another central irony concerns the development of the narrator. While he may command certain facts about the life of Ethan Frome, he cannot fill in the gaps by interpreting those facts. Much like Poe's narrators, Wharton's young historian finds that his attempt to understand and chronicle the community leads to fragmentary knowledge devoid of conclusion.[19] Only when he gets close to the Starkfield community can he possibly understand their history and the story of the Fromes. However, at the point that he becomes a member of their community, he will also resemble the men of Starkfield in their

19. In her introduction to *Ethan Frome* (New York: Charles Scribner's Sons, 1911), Wharton writes "Each of my chroniclers contributes to the narrative *just so much as he or she is capable of understanding* of what, to them, is a complicated and mysterious case; and only the narrator of the tale has scope enough to see it all, to resolve it back into simplicity, and to put it in its rightful place among his larger categories" (ix). I disagree with the author's perception of her work because the text closes without answering many questions about the individuals who form the Frome household and the narrator himself. I am also compelled by the final scene in which the narrator relates the emotional testimony of Ruth Hale, but lacks the resources to weave her statements into his own account. He has no full narrative, and he himself is silent.

incoherent understanding of themselves, their faltering language, and their personal stasis. He will be silenced by the voice of women.

Unlike Stowe and Hawthorne, Wharton does not set her fiction in the seventeenth- and eighteenth-century New English colonies. A twentieth-century writer, she fashions these fictive accounts as contemporary to her readers, and does this for many reasons, one of which is that her reader will not lose sight of his or her relationship to the argument of Wharton's fiction. At the same time, "Bewitched" and *Ethan Frome* are stories of rural New England whose landscape is populated by characters with solidly New English names who consistently invoke their individual, familial, and community history in rural New England. The backward gaze of these characters is not incidental, but fully central to Wharton's fiction. This narrative feature implies a continuity of human character and communal experience from the Puritan past to the American present. Likewise, Wharton's prefatory description of her characters in *Ethan Frome* as "*granite outcroppings*" signals their endurance in the nature of American men and women. This depiction suggests more than stability and resilience, for these outcroppings are "half-emerged from the soil, and scarcely more articulate" ("Introduction," vi). Both *Ethan Frome* and "Bewitched" enact the ways in which men and women struggle to repress or reckon with their personal and communal narratives and meet with little success. Wharton's fiction demands that the reader wrestle with the ways in which the past informs the present and shapes the identity of the nation and the private and public identities of its citizens.

Although Edith Wharton's fiction offers no directive as to the specific themes of historical narrative, her work offers a consistent argument concerning the role of the historian. She insists that the historian is never disinterested in his role as narrator of public events. Even when Orrin Bosworth of "Bewitched" and the narrator of *Ethan Frome* believe themselves to be removed from their community and their subject matter, they learn that they are intimately related to the tales that they are called upon to recount or repress. Their history informs their narration of the community's history, and conversely their accounts of the community are telling of their self-understanding.

Authors such as Edgar Allan Poe, Harriet Beecher Stowe, Nathaniel Hawthorne, and Catharine Maria Sedgwick would concur that the invention of history is wedded to the ethos of the historian. This principle is at the center of their discussion of historical narration within their fiction. Moreover, in their construction of the historian, they take issue with the authority of the historian as established by earlier authors, in particular

Cotton Mather, who speaks at length about his belief in the sacred role of the historian. Indeed he opens book six of *Magnalia Christi Americana* with a statement to this effect:

> To *regard* the illustrious displays of that PROVIDENCE wherewith our Lord Christ governs the world, is a work, than which there is none more *needful* or *useful* for a Christian: to *record* them is a work, than which, none more proper for a minister. (2:341)

While Cotton Mather insists that his ministerial standing constitutes authority for his role as historian, he also emphasizes the importance of witnessing historical events as playing a significant part in legitimizing his role. For this reason, he informs the readers when he himself experienced or observed the "remarkable occurrences" that he recounts. In instances where he cannot make this assertion, he is careful to document the identity of the eyewitness. "One of my honest neighbours, whose name is Christopher Monk, brought me this account of what had befallen himself," he writes (2:352). And, "our venerable old Mr. Wilson saw one man to be extreamly perverse above the rest" (2:397). At the close of a tale of sea deliverance, Mather insists that "[t]hence they came to Barbadoes, and there they made oath to the truth of this narrative" (2:467). Most frequently, the eyewitnesses are themselves ministers. In each case, actual observation of an event cannot be overestimated in establishing the credibility of the account.[20] Mather's insistence upon observation of an event should not be confused with experience of that event. The historian *cum* minister remains disengaged from the actual experience, and, further, does not seek to understand the saint or sinner and thus sympathize with them. His role is first to document historical events and then, in his ministerial interpretation of those events, determine them to be either *magnalia Dei* or *terribilia Dei*, and, in this way, issue God's judgment of the actions of man. In this way, Mather aligns himself more closely with God than with man.

Wharton's "Bewitched" and *Ethan Frome* expose the limitations of the eyewitness account, and identify its weakness in the character and disposition of the witness as well as in the limited relationship of the historian to his subject. These texts also expose the weakness of a sympathetic relationship to the historical subject. Damaging to the ethos of the

---

20. In the absence of personal experience or knowledge of eyewitnesses, at times Mather offers scholarly evidence of the authenticity of the tale. For example, he prefaces "The Wonderful Story of Major Gibbons" with the note that "no less than three several writers have published that wherein Major Edward Gibbons of Boston in New-England was concerned" (2:345).

eyewitness historian is Orrin Bosworth's candid confession that although he was present at critical events, he cannot be sure of what he saw or heard. From a different perspective altogether, the historiographic fiction of Edgar Allan Poe, such as "The Black Cat," "William Wilson," and *The Narrative of Arthur Gordon Pym*, push Mather's insistence upon eyewitness knowledge of the recounted events to its extreme conclusion in that his narrator has experienced the events more fully and intensely than any other individual because he recounts his own story. In "The Black Cat" and "William Wilson," the narrative is given over to the criminal's own voice. Likewise, Pym tells his own story. In this way, Poe purports to subscribe to Mather's historiographic principles, but inverts them to reveal the very voice that is suppressed in Mather's accounts. Poe will not allow the minister's statement—or the statement of any other authority—to supplant the statement of the individuals who are truly at the center of Poe's remarkable occurrences. In this way, his narrators claim sole authority for their understanding of the self and their world. They also acknowledge the absolute individuality of such understanding. In addition to negating the religious platform of the narratives of remarkable occurrences, Poe's gothic fiction undermines Cotton Mather's commitment to shared experience and principles.

David S. Reynolds notes that Poe is similar to Charles Brockden Brown in severing the ties between fantastic plots and religious didacticism, and instead "places it in an extracreedal realm of terror," thus "connect[ing] reverie and supernatural visitation with psychology rather than with doctrinal commentary or religious comfort."[21] Poe's objective is neither to evaluate the actions of man nor even to understand them, but to offer the reader an opportunity to participate in the experience of those actions. Moreover, through narrative fissures, lacunae, and rejection of resolution, Poe's fiction denies Cotton Mather's commitment to represent the world as coherent and ordered. In place of divine providence, Poe asks the reader to face the contingency of this world and acknowledge the self as other.

Harriet Beecher Stowe shares Cotton Mather's commitment to the belief that the one who is charged with interpreting the important and mundane events of life must above all be mindful of the spiritual significance of those events. However, she is unwilling to suggest that this individual be a dispassionate observer. Stowe's historians—Roxy and Candace, among others—are characters who wield the authority of both spirituality

---

21. *Faith in Fiction: The Emergence of Religious Literature in America* (Cambridge and London: Harvard University Press, 1981), 45.

and sentimental attachment to her fellow men and women. It is not coin-
cidental that this is the same as Stowe's authorial ethos. In the construction of her fiction, Stowe frequently speaks directly to her readers, queries
them, and invites them to participate in a conversation of sorts with the
text.[22] She is in sympathetic relation to her reader just as her characters,
when they serve as textual narrators, are in sympathetic relation to their
subjects and their textual audience. Further, Stowe taps characters to serve
as textual narrators only when they are allied to their textual audience.
Equally important, Stowe does not invest this authority exclusively in the
minister, and more frequently, elects a wide range of characters for this role
and specifically excludes the minister from this calling.

David S. Reynolds speaks to the blurred boundaries between religious
tracts and fiction in the mid-nineteenth century, noting that Stowe was
aware of the religious appeals that issue from fiction, a popular phenomenon that went far beyond her individual contributions (*Faith in Fiction*,
208–11). The fusion of religious tract and historical narrative is, of course,
evident in *Magnalia Christi Americana*, which employs the forms and
devices of fiction to realize its objectives. While Stowe surely recognized
the religious and historical value of Mather's accounts, she also identified
them as "wonderful stories" (11:122). In her own century, she recognized
that novels and short stories authored by the lay writer that promulgated
religious ideals and interpretation were found in ministers' libraries, in
sectarian magazines, and in Sunday school classrooms as well as in the
home. In this way, contemporary writing and publishing practices mir-
rored and supported her commitment to the shared, communal authority
for religious interpretation and indoctrination.[23] Likewise, in terms of historical narrative, in *The Minister's Wooing* a young, sensitive woman offers
the fullest account of the life of Aaron Burr, and in *The Pearl of Orr's Island*
the spinster seamstress has the most acute understanding of the history of
Orr's Island.

Like Stowe, Nathaniel Hawthorne invests authority in the historian
on the basis of his or her humanity. As a corollary to this notion, his fiction rests on the author's suspicion of every claim of objectivity and any

22. See Dorothy Z. Baker, "Harriet Beecher Stowe's 'Conversation' with the *Atlantic Monthly*:
The Construction of *The Minister's Wooing*," *Studies in American Fiction* 28.1 (2000): 27, which
argues that the novel is constructed as a dialogue with both the reader and the other writers in
the *Atlantic Monthly*, the magazine in which the novel was serialized.

23. Reynolds also reveals that Stowe recognized the influence of fiction on homiletic style
and made a humorous statement that clergymen would soon feel obliged to include a serial story
in the weekly sermon (*Faith in Fiction*, 209).

suggestion of a definitive historical record. As "David Swan" illustrates, the fluidity and subjectivity of historical narrative do not compromise its validity for Hawthorne. To the contrary, it asserts the humanity of the enterprise and attests to its vital importance. The showman in "Main-street" stages a carnival sideshow of American history because he is aware of our desire to know who we are. Further, the audience dispute his presentation and interpretation of history because they, too, are emotionally invested in determining the national identity. In this tale as in *Grandfather's Chair,* Hawthorne makes clear that the individual desires to know what the nation represents because—for better or ill—the individual is intricately bound to the communal.

In addition to the ethos of the narrator, another structural feature of these texts must figure in a discussion of fictional responses to Cotton Mather's historical narrative, that of the embedded narrative. In many of the texts examined in this book, the gothic element is contained in or centrally related to embedded narratives. Stowe's Aunt Roxy speaks of the otherworld in the stories that issue from her long life on Orr's Island, and Candace reveals her vivid dreams of other places and other times that are accurate to the letter. In the dead of night, Sedgwick's characters recount grim tales of Indian raids that appear to interrupt the central plot, and revelations of herbal sorcery and witchcraft trials are recounted in transatlantic epistles. Orrin Bosworth of Wharton's "Bewitched" recalls the grotesque behavior of his Aunt Cressy only in the periphery of his experience of equally grotesque dealings in Hemlock County. The literary manuscripts of Holgrave in *The House of the Seven Gables* and the narrator in "Alice Doane's Appeal" are read to a fictional audience within the frame of the larger work, while the series of otherwise random stories spun by the passersby in "David Swan" overtakes the limited central plot. In general, the embedded narrative mirrors or otherwise reflects on the central plot, yet in these works the implications of this structural device on the literature are pointedly subversive. In several instances, the embedded narrative derails the received literary form of the fiction. Roxy's account of her vision of Mara Lincoln in a funereal white dress defies the marriage plot of this novel just as Candace's dream of James Marvyn's deliverance spells the end to the minister's wooing. This is to say that the seemingly ancillary anecdotes overtake the dominant form and argument, which is precisely Stowe's objective. Likewise, the sequence of embedded captivity narratives and tales of Indian raids in *Hope Leslie* destabilize this formulaic fiction and render all such later accounts in the novel suspect. Holgrave's magazine story is given equal footing with Salem history in *The House of the Seven Gables,* and thus confounds readerly confidence in historical narrative. An extreme example, Hawthorne's "David Swan" is composed almost entirely of embedded narratives, none of which is definitive. The value is in the structure itself that argues for the insecurity of all narrative, especially the dominant, framing account that is the real fiction.

Once again, the use of the embedded narratives as a central device comments on the literary form as Cotton Mather employed them. Puritan ministers regularly used homely anecdotes—providence tales among them—in their sermons to secure the larger, spiritual message. Likewise, the providence tales in book six of *Magnalia Christi Americana* are, in a sense, all embedded narratives in that they do not contribute to a larger plot, but serve individually as examples of Mather's argument that God intervenes in the lives of His people to demonstrate His will. There is an explicit consonance between the framing argument and the embedded narratives in this text. However, in the fiction studied in this book, the embedded narratives do not support, but actually undermine, what might be understood as the dominant fiction form of the text. They trump the formulaic plots and received structures of providence literature and rupture confidence in design—providential or otherwise. The gothic structure of these texts is built on the fissures between the purported argument of the fiction and that of its interpolated stories, and speaks once again to authorial distrust of the philosophical underpinning of the providence tale.

It would be gross exaggeration to claim that the emphasis on historical fiction in nineteenth-century America results exclusively from a crisis in American religious practice or historiography. There is a complex constellation of reasons why authors choose to write fiction in a historical mode as do Poe and Hawthorne, and fictional accounts of historical events as do Sedgwick, Stowe, and Hawthorne. Moreover, these authors—as well as many twentieth-century writers—are among many who explore our nation's history within imaginative literature. These individuals take the dramatic step of contesting the dominant voices on the American past, Cotton Mather and the nineteenth-century historians who reprise and romanticize his accounts. By challenging Mather's historical accounts, Poe, Stowe, Hawthorne, Sedgwick, and Wharton also reveal their distrust of the nature of historical narrative as he conceives it, and invite the reader to consider such accounts as tentative, plastic, and fictive. Their work suggests, as Hayden White observes, that in the stories of our past

reality wears the mask of a meaning, the completeness and fullness of which we can only imagine, never experience. Insofar as historical stories can be completed, can be given narrative closure, can be shown to have had a plot all along, they give to reality the odor of the ideal. This is why the plot of a historical narrative is always an embarrassment and has to be presented as "found" in the events rather than put there by narrative techniques. (*Content,* 21)

Because fiction has no essential claim to truth, the authority of the text rests on the authority of its narrator (*Content,* 19). Similarly, the argument of fiction—inherent in its emplotment—reveals the vision of its author. When later authors train their eyes on the mission and responsibilities of the individual historian and narrator, they do so with an awareness of the process by which history is shaped, proffered, and consumed. If *Magnalia Christi Americana* lends "the odor of the ideal" to the American past, Poe, Stowe, Hawthorne, Sedgwick, and Wharton reject Mather's vision of the ideal. Instead, they put forth an alternate vision that occasionally expresses their ideal and more frequently confesses their notion of what is merely imperfect, human, and true.

Works Cited

 infin

Adams, John R. "Structure and Theme in the Novels of Harriet Beecher Stowe." *American Transcendental Quarterly* 24.1 (1974): 50–55.

Amfreville, Marc. "*The House of the Seven Gables:* Une Tragédie gothique." *Revue Française d'Etudes Américaines* 83 (2000): 113–28.

Arac, Jonathan. *The Emergence of American Literary Narrative, 1820–1960.* Cambridge and London: Harvard University Press, 2005.

Arch, Stephen Carl. *Authorizing the Past: The Rhetoric of History in Seventeenth-Century New England.* DeKalb, IL: Northern Illinois University Press, 1994.

———. "Romancing the Puritans: American Historical Fiction in the 1820s." *ESQ: A Journal of the American Renaissance* 39.2 (1993): 107–32.

Arner, Robert D. "The Story of Hannah Duston: Cotton Mather to Thoreau." *American Transcendental Quarterly* 18.1 (1973): 19–23.

Baker, Dorothy Z. "Harriet Beecher Stowe's 'Conversation' with the *Atlantic Monthly:* The Construction of *The Minister's Wooing.*" *Studies in American Fiction* 28.1 (2000): 27–38.

———. "Puritan Providences in *The Pearl of Orr's Island:* The Legacy of Cotton Mather." *Studies in American Fiction* 22.1 (1994): 61–79.

Bancroft, George. *History of the United States.* 10 vols. Boston: Little, Brown, 1834–1875.

Bauermeister, Erica. "*The Lamplighter, The Wide, Wide World,* and *Hope Leslie:* Reconsidering the Recipes for Nineteenth-Century American Women's Novels." *Legacy: A Journal of American Women Writers* 8.1 (1991): 17–29.

Baym, Nina. "The Heroine of *The House of the Seven Gables:* or, Who Killed Jaffrey Pyncheon?" *New England Quarterly* 77.4 (2004): 607–18.

———. *The Shape of Hawthorne's Career.* Ithaca and London: Cornell University Press, 1976.

Bell, Michael Davitt. *Hawthorne and the Historical Romance of New England.* Princeton: Princeton University Press, 1971.

———. "History and Romance Convention in Catharine Sedgwick's *Hope Leslie.*" *American Quarterly* 22.2 (1970): 213–21.

Bell, Susan Cherry. "History and Artistry in Cotton Mather's *Magnalia Christi Americana,*" diss., SUNY Binghamton, 1991.

Bercovitch, Sacvan. "Cotton Mather," in *Major Writers of Early American Literature.* Ed. Everett Emerson. Madison: University of Wisconsin Press, 1972.

———. "'Delightful Examples of Surprising Prosperity': Cotton Mather and the American Success Story." *English Studies* 51.1 (1970): 40–43.

———. "The Historiography of Johnson's *Wonder-Working Providence.*" *Essex Institute Historical Collections* 54 (1968): 138–61.

———. *New England Epic: A Literary Study of Cotton Mather's "Magnalia Christi Americana,"* diss., Claremont Graduate School and University Center, 1965.

———. *The Puritan Origins of the American Self.* New Haven: Yale University Press, 1975.

Berens, John F. *Providence and Patriotism in Early America 1640–1815.* Charlottesville: University Press of Virginia, 1978.

Berkson, Dorothy. "Millennial Politics and the Feminine Fiction of Harriet Beecher Stowe." *Critical Essays on Harriet Beecher Stowe.* Ed. Elizabeth Ammons. Boston: G. K. Hall, 1980. 244–58.

Bradford, William. *Of Plymouth Plantation, 1620–1647.* Ed. Samuel Eliot Morison. New York: Knopf, 1953.

Budick, Emily. *Fiction and Historical Consciousness.* New Haven: Yale University Press, 1989.

Buell, Lawrence. "Calvinism Romanticized: Harriet Beecher Stowe, Samuel Hopkins, and *The Minister's Wooing.*" *ESQ: A Journal of the American Renaissance* 24 (1978): 119–32.

———. *New England Literary Culture from Revolution through Renaissance.* Cambridge: Cambridge University Press, 1986.

Bush, Harold K. "Re-Inventing the Puritan Fathers: George Bancroft, Nathaniel Hawthorne, and the Birth of Endicott's Ghost." *American Transcendental Quarterly* 9.2 (1995): 132–52.

Callinicos, Alex. *Theories and Narratives: Reflections on the Philosophy of History.* Durham: Duke University Press, 1995.

Carey, George. "John Greenleaf Whittier and Folklore: The Search for a Traditional American Past." *New York Folklore Quarterly* 27.1 (1971): 113–29.

Clark, Michael. "Witches and Wall Street: Possession is Nine-Tenths of the Law." *Texas Studies in Literature and Language* 25.1 (1983): 55–76.

Clarke, Samuel. *A mirrour or looking-glasse both for saints and sinners.* London, 1646.

Clery, E. J. *The Rise of Supernatural Fiction 1762–1800.* Cambridge Studies in Romanticism 12. Cambridge: Cambridge University Press, 1995.

Cohen, B. Bernard. "The Composition of Hawthorne's 'The Duston Family.'" *The New England Quarterly* 21.2 (1948): 236–41.

Cohen, Daniel A. *Pillars of Salt, Monuments of Grace: New England Crime Literature and the Origins of American Popular Culture, 1674–1860.* New York and Oxford: Oxford University Press, 1993.

Colacurcio, Michael J. *The Province of Piety: Moral History in Hawthorne's Early Tales.* Durham and London: Duke University Press, 1995.

Crozier, Alice C. *The Novels of Harriet Beecher Stowe.* New York: Oxford University Press, 1969.

Crumpacker, Laurie. "Four Novels of Harriet Beecher Stowe: A Study in Nineteenth-

Century Androgyny." *American Novelists Revisited: Essays in Feminist Criticism.* Ed. Fritz Fleischmann. Boston: G. K. Hall, 1982.

Daly, Robert. "William Bradford's Vision of History." *American Literature* 44.4 (1973): 557–69.

Davidson, Cathy. *Revolution and the Word: The Rise of the Novel in America.* New York and Oxford: Oxford University Press, 1986.

Davidson, Frank. "Melville, Thoreau, and 'The Apple-Tree Table.'" *American Literature* 25.4 (1954): 479–88.

Dawson, Jan. *The Unusable Past: America's Puritan Tradition, 1830–1930.* Chico, CA: Scholars' Press, 1984.

Dekker, George. *The American Historical Romance.* Cambridge: Cambridge University Press, 1987.

Demos, John. *The Unredeemed Captive: A Family Story From Early America.* New York: Vintage, 1994.

Dunne, Michael. *Hawthorne's Narrative Strategies.* Jackson: University Press of Mississippi, 1995.

Eakin, Paul John. "Poe's Sense of an Ending." *American Literature* 45.1 (1973): 1–22.

Eberwein, Jane Donahue. "Fishers of Metaphor: Mather and Melville on the Whale." *American Transcendental Quarterly* 26.1 (1975): 30–31.

———. "'Indistinct Lustre': Biographical Miniatures in the *Magnalia Christi Americana.*" *Biography: An Interdisciplinary Quarterly* 4.3 (1981): 195–207.

Ehrenpreis, Anne Henry. "Elizabeth Gaskell and Nathaniel Hawthorne." *The Nathaniel Hawthorne Journal* (1973): 89–119.

Elbert, Monika M. "Bourgeois Sexuality and the Gothic Plot in Wharton and Hawthorne." Ed. John L. Idol, Jr. In *Hawthorne and Women: Engendering and Expanding the Hawthorne Tradition.* Amherst: University of Massachusetts Press, 1999. 258–70.

Elliott, Emory, ed. *Puritan Influences in American Literature.* Urbana: University of Illinois Press, 1979.

Emerson, Ralph Waldo. *The Collected Works of Ralph Waldo Emerson.* 3 vols. Ed. Alfred R. Ferguson. Cambridge: The Belknap Press of Harvard University Press, 1971.

Emery, Allan. "Salem History and *The House of the Seven Gables.*" In *Critical Essays on Hawthorne's* The House of the Seven Gables. Ed. Bernard Rosenthal. New York: G. K. Hall, 1995. 129–49.

Engler, Bernd. "The Dismemberment of Clio: Fictionality, Narrativity, and the Construction of Historical Reality in Historiographic Metafiction." In *Historiographic Metafiction in Modern American and Canadian Literature.* Eds. Bernd Engler and Kurt Müller. Paderborn: Ferdinand Schönigh, 1994. 13–34.

Engler, Bernd and Oliver Scheiding, eds. *Re-Visioning the Past: Historical Self-Reflexivity in American Short Fiction.* Trier: Wissenschaftlicher Verlag Trier, 1998.

Felker, Christopher P. *Reinventing Cotton Mather in the American Renaissance:* Magnalia Christi Americana *in Hawthorne, Stowe, and Stoddard.* Boston: Northeastern University Press, 1993.

Felt, Joseph B. *Annals of Salem.* 2 vols. Salem: W. and S.B. Ives, 1845, 1849.

Fetterley, Judith. "Only a Story, Not a Romance: Harriet Beecher Stowe's *The Pearl of Orr's Island.*" *The (Other) American Traditions: Nineteenth-Century Women*

Writers. Ed. Joyce W. Warren. New Brunswick: Rutgers University Press, 1993. 108–25.

———, ed. *Provisions: A Reader from 19th-Century American Women.* Bloomington: Indiana University Press, 1985.

———. "'My Sister! My Sister!': The Rhetoric of Catharine Sedgwick's *Hope Leslie.*" In *Catharine Maria Sedgwick: Critical Perspectives.* Ed. Lucinda L. Damon-Bach and Victoria Clements. Boston: Northeastern University Press, 2003. 78–99.

Fiedler, Leslie. *Love and Death in the American Novel.* 1960. New York: Stein and Day, 1982.

Fields, Annie. *Life and Letters of Harriet Beecher Stowe.* Boston: Houghton, Mifflin, 1898.

Fisher, Marvin. "Bug and Humbug in Melville's 'Apple-Tree Table.'" *Studies in Short Fiction* 8.3 (1971): 459–66.

———. "Seeing New Englandly: Anthropology, Ecology, and Theology in Thoreau's *A Week on the Concord and Merrimack Rivers.*" *Centennial Review* 34.3 (1990): 381–94.

Ford, Douglas. "Inscribing the 'Impartial Observer' in Sedgwick's *Hope Leslie.*" *Legacy: A Journal of American Women Writers* 14.2 (1997): 81–92.

Forrest, William Mentzel. *Biblical Allusions in Poe.* New York: Macmillan, 1928.

Foster, Charles H. *The Rungless Ladder: Harriet Beecher Stowe and New England Puritanism.* 1954. Rpt. New York: Cooper Square, 1970.

Franklin, Benjamin. *The Autobiography of Benjamin Franklin: A Genetic Text.* Ed. J. A. Leo Lemay and P. M. Zall. Knoxville: University of Tennessee Press, 1981.

———. "Mss. of Benjamin Franklin: A Lecture on the Providence of God in the Government of the World." *Southern Literary Messenger* 2.5 (1836): 293–95.

Frye, Northrop. *The Anatomy of Criticism.* Princeton: Princeton University Press, 1957.

Fukuchi, Curtis. "Poe's Providential *Narrative of Arthur Gordon Pym.*" *Emerson Society Quarterly* 27.3 (1981): 148–56.

Garvey, T. Gregory. "Risking Reprisal: Catharine Sedgwick's *Hope Leslie* and the Legitimation of Public Action by Women." *American Transcendental Quarterly* 8.4 (1994): 287–98.

Gay, Peter. *A Loss of Mastery: Puritan Historians in Colonial America.* Berkeley and Los Angeles: University of California Press, 1966.

Gilmore, Michael T. *The Middle Way: Puritanism and Ideology in American Romantic Fiction.* New Brunswick: Rutgers University Press, 1977.

Gitelman, Lisa. "Arthur Gordon Pym and the Novel Narrative of Edgar Allan Poe." *Nineteenth-Century Literature* 47.3 (1992): 349–61.

Goddu, Teresa A. *Gothic America: Narrative, History, and Nation.* New York: Columbia University Press, 1997.

Goodenough, Elizabeth. "*Grandfather's Chair:* Hawthorne's 'Deeper History' of New England." *The Lion and the Unicorn: A Critical Journal of Children's Literature* 15.1 (1991): 27–42.

Goodrich, Samuel G. *Peter Parley's Method of Telling About the History of the World to Children.* Hartford: H.F. Sumner, 1832.

Gossett, Suzanne and Barbara Ann Bardes. "Women and Political Power in the

Republic: Two Early American Novels." *Legacy: A Journal of American Women Writers* 2.2 (1985): 13–30.

Gould, Philip. "Catharine Sedgwick's 'Recital' of the Pequot War." *American Literature* 66.4 (1994): 641–62.

Gross, Louis S. *Redefining the American Gothic from Wieland to Day of the Dead*. Ann Arbor and London: AMI Research Press, 1989.

Gura, Philip F. *The Wisdom of Words: Language, Theology, and Literature in the New England Renaissance*. Middletown: Wesleyan University Press, 1981.

Hall, David D. *Worlds of Wonder, Days of Judgment: Popular Religious Belief in Early New England*. Cambridge: Harvard University Press, 1990.

Hall, Michael G. *The Last American Puritan: The Life of Increase Mather 1639–1723*. Middletown, CT: Wesleyan University Press, 1988.

Hartman, James D. *Providence Tales and the Birth of American Literature*. Baltimore and London: Johns Hopkins University Press, 1999.

Hawks, Francis L. *Contributions to the Ecclesiastical History of the United States of America—Virginia*. New York: Harper & Brothers, 1836.

Hawthorne, Nathaniel. *The Centenary Edition of the Works of Nathaniel Hawthorne*. 23 vols. Ed. Wm. Charvat, Roy Harvey Pearce, Claude M. Simpson, Thomas Woodson. Columbus: The Ohio State University Press, 1984–1994.

———. "The Duston Family." *The Complete Writings of Nathaniel Hawthorne, Old Manse Edition*. 22 vols. Boston and New York: Houghton, Mifflin, 1900. 17: 229–38.

Hedges, William L. *Washington Irving: An American Study, 1802–1832*. Baltimore: Johns Hopkins University Press, 1965.

Hedrick, Joan D. "'Peaceable Fruits': The Ministry of Harriet Beecher Stowe." *American Quarterly* 40.3 (1988): 307–22.

Herbert, T. Walter. *Dearest Beloved: The Hawthornes and the Making of the Middle Class Family*. Berkeley: University of California Press, 1993.

———. *Moby Dick and Calvinism: A World Dismantled*. New Brunswick: Rutgers University Press, 1977.

Hoffman, Daniel. *Poe Poe Poe Poe Poe*. 1972. New York: Paragon House, 1990.

Hovey, Kenneth Alan. "The Theology of History in *Of Plymouth Plantation* and Its Predecessors." *Early American Literature* 10.1 (1975): 47–66.

Hubbard, William. *The Present State of New-England. Being a Narrative of the Troubles with the Indians in New-England, from the first planting thereof in the year 1607, to this present year 1677*. London, 1677.

Hutcheson, Francis. *An Historical Essay concerning Witchcraft*. London, 1718.

Hutchinson, Thomas. *The History of Massachusetts from the First Settlement Thereof in 1628, until the Year 1750*. 2 vols. Salem, 1795.

Insko, Jeffrey. "Anachronistic Imaginings: *Hope Leslie*'s Challenge to Historicism." *American Literary History* 16.2 (2004): 179–207.

Irving, Washington. *Journals and Notebooks*. Vol. II. 1807–1822. Ed. Walter A. Reichart and Lillian Schlissel. Boston: Twayne, 1981.

———. *The Sketch Book of Geoffrey Crayon, Gent.* Ed. Haskell Springer. Boston: Twayne, 1978.

Irwin, John T. *The Mystery to a Solution: Poe, Borges, and the Analytic Detective Story*. Baltimore and London: Johns Hopkins University Press, 1994.

Janeway, James. *Mr. James Janeway's Legacy to his Friends: Containing Twenty Seven Famous Instances of Gods Providences in and about Sea-Dangers and Deliverances.* London, 1674.

Jewett, Sarah Orne. *The Letters of Sarah Orne Jewett.* Ed. Annie Fields. Boston: Houghton Mifflin, 1911.

Johnson, Cynthia Brantley. "Hawthorne's Hannah Dustan and Her Troubling American Myth." *Nathaniel Hawthorne Review* 27.1 (2001): 17–35.

Johnson, Edward. *Johnson's Wonder-working Providence of Sions Saviour in New England 1628–1651.* 1654. Ed. J. Franklin Jameson. New York: Barnes and Noble, 1946.

Johnson, Parker H. "Humiliation Followed by Deliverance: Metaphor and Plot in Cotton Mather's *Magnalia*." *Early American Literature* 15.3 (1980/81): 237–46.

Karafilis, Maria. "Catharine Maria Sedgwick's *Hope Leslie*: The Crisis Between Ethical Political Action and US Literary Nationalism in the New Republic." *American Transcendental Quarterly* 12.4 (1998): 327–44.

Kelley, Mary. *Private Woman, Public Stage: Literary Domesticity in Nineteenth-Century America.* New York: Oxford University Press, 1984.

——. "A Woman Alone: Catharine Maria Sedgwick's Spinsterhood in Nineteenth-Century America." *New England Quarterly* 51.2 (1978): 209–25.

Kennedy, J. Gerald. *The Narrative of Arthur Gordon Pym and the Abyss of Interpretation.* New York: Twayne, 1995.

——. *Poe, Death, and the Life of Writing.* New Haven: Yale University Press, 1987.

Kessselring, Marion L. *Hawthorne's Reading 1828–1850: A Transcription and Identification of Titles Recorded in the Charge-Books of the Salem Athenaeum.* New York: The New York Public Library, 1949.

Kilgour, Maggie. *The Rise of the Gothic Novel.* London and New York: Routledge, 1995.

Kimball, William J. "Two Views of History." *Studies in Short Fiction* 8 (1971): 637–39.

Kirkham, E. Bruce. "The Source of the Shipwreck in *The Pearl of Orr's Island*." *American Transcendental Quarterly* 40: 365, 66.

Knight, Janice. *Orthodoxies in Massachusetts: Rereading American Puritanism.* Cambridge and London: Harvard University Press, 1994.

Laffrado, Laura. *Hawthorne's Literature for Children.* Athens and London: University of Georgia Press, 1992.

Levin, David. *Cotton Mather: The Young Life of the Lord's Remembrancer, 1663–1703.* Cambridge, MA and London, England: Harvard University Press, 1978.

——. *History as Romantic Art: Bancroft, Prescott, Motley, and Parkman.* Stanford: Stanford University Press, 1959.

——. *In Defense of Historical Literature: Essays on American History, Autobiography, Drama, and Fiction.* New York: Hill and Wang, 1967.

——. "William Bradford: The Value of Puritan Historiography." *Major Writers of Early American Literature.* Ed. Everett Emerson. Madison: University of Wisconsin Press, 1972. 11–31.

Levin, Harry. *The Power of Blackness: Hawthorne, Melville, Poe.* New York: Alfred A. Knopf, 1958.

Lowance, Mason I. "Typology and the New England Way: Cotton Mather and the Exegesis of Biblical Types." *Early American Literature* 4.1 (1970): 15–37.

Lowell, James Russell. "Reviews and Literary Notices." *The Atlantic Monthly* 6.37 (1860): 637–39.

Madsen, Deborah L. "Hawthorne's Puritans: From Fact to Fiction." *Journal of American Studies* 33.3 (1999): 509–17.

Martin, Robert K. "Haunted by Jim Crow: Gothic Fictions by Hawthorne and Faulkner." In *American Gothic: New Inventions in a National Narrative*. Ed. Robert K. Martin and Eric Savoy. Iowa City: University of Iowa Press, 1998. 129–42.

Mather, Cotton. *Bonifacius. An essay upon the good, that is to be devised and designed, by those who desire to answer the great end of life, and to do good while they live.* Boston, 1710.

———. *Diary of Cotton Mather 1681–1709.* 2 vols. New York: Frederick Ungar, 1957.

———. *Magnalia Christi Americana; or, The Ecclesiastical History of New-England; From its First Planting, in the Year 1620, unto the Year of Our Lord 1689.* 1702. Introduction and occasional notes by Thomas Robbins. 1852 edition. 2 vols. Reproduction of 1820 edition. New York: Russell and Russell, 1967.

———. *Memorable providences, relating to witchcrafts and possessions.* Boston, 1689.

———. *Mirabilia Dei. An Essay On the very Seasonable and Remarkable Interpositions of the Divine Providence, to Rescue & Relieve Disstressed People, Brought unto the very Point of Perishing.* Boston, 1719.

———. *Parentator: Memoirs of Remarkables in the Life and the Death of the Ever-Memorable Dr. Increase Mather Who Expired, August 23, 1723.* In *Two Mather Biographies. Life & Death and Parentator.* Ed. William J. Scheick. Bethlehem, PA: Lehigh University Press, 1989.

———. *Pillars of Salt. An History of Some Criminals Executed in this Land, For Capital Crimes.* Boston, 1699.

———. *The Religious Mariner.* Boston, 1700.

———. *Selected Letters of Cotton Mather.* Ed. Kenneth Silverman. Baton Rouge: Louisiana State University Press, 1971.

———. *Silentiarius. A brief essay on the holy silence and godly patience, that sad things are to be entertained withal.* Boston, 1721.

———. *Terribilia Dei. Remarkable judgments of God, on several sorts of offenders, in several scores of instances; among the people of New-England.* Boston, 1697.

———. *The wonderful works of God commemorated. Praises bespoke for the God in heaven in a thanksgiving sermon.* Boston, 1690.

———. *Wonders of the Invisible World. Being an Account of the Tryals of Several Witches Lately Executed in New England. To Which is Added, A Further Account of the Tryals of the New England Witches, by Increase Mather.* Boston, 1693.

———. *The Words of Understanding.* Boston, 1724.

Mather, Increase. *A Call from Heaven To the Present and Succeeding Generations.* Boston, 1679.

———. *A doctrine of divine providence open and applied.* Boston, 1684.

———. *Remarkable Providences Illustrative of the Earlier Days of American Colonisation.* 1684. London, 1890.

Matheson, T. J. "Poe's 'The Black Cat' as a Critique of Temperance Literature." *Mosaic* 19.3 (1986): 69–80.

Miller, Perry. *The New England Mind: From Colony to Province.* 1953. Cambridge: Belknap Press of Harvard University Press, 1981.

———. *The New England Mind: The Seventeenth Century.* 1939. Cambridge: Belknap Press of Harvard University Press, 1981.

Mirick, Benjamin L. *The History of Haverill, Massachusetts.* Haverill: A. W. Thayer, 1832.

Mizruchi, Susan L. *The Power of Historical Knowledge: Narrating the Past in Hawthorne, James, and Dreiser.* Princeton: Princeton University Press, 1988.

Morton, Nathaniel. *New Englands memoriall.* 1669. Ed. Howard J. Hall. New York: Scholars' Facsimiles and Reprints, 1937.

Murdock, Kenneth Ballard. *Increase Mather: The Foremost American Puritan.* Cambridge: Harvard University Press, 1926.

Neal, Daniel. *The History of the Puritans, or Protestant Nonconformists; from the Reformation in 1517, to the Revolution in 1688.* 2 vols. New York, 1843.

Nelson, Dana. "Sympathy as Strategy in Sedgwick's *Hope Leslie.*" In *The Culture of Sentiment: Race, Gender, and Sentimentality in Nineteenth-Century America.* Ed. Shirley Samuels. New York: Oxford University Press, 1992. 191–202.

Onishi, Naoki. "Melville's *Moby Dick.*" *Explicator* 50.3 (1992): 148–50.

Parrington, Vernon Louis. "Harriet Beecher Stowe: A Daughter of Puritanism." *Main Currents in American Thought.* Vol. 1. New York: Harcourt, Brace, Jovanovich, 1930. 371–78.

Poe, Edgar Allan. *Collected Writings of Edgar Allan Poe. Vol I: The Imaginary Voyages.* Ed. Burton R. Pollin. Boston: Twayne, 1981.

———. *Tales and Sketches.* Ed. Thomas Ollive Mabbott. 2 vols. Urbana and Chicago: University of Illinois Press, 2000.

Pollin, Burton R. *Discoveries in Poe.* Notre Dame and London: University of Notre Dame Press, 1970.

Porte, Joel. *The Romance in America: Studies in Cooper, Poe, Hawthorne, Melville, and James.* Middletown, CT: Wesleyan University Press, 1969.

Pribek, Thomas. "'Between Democritus and Cotton Mather': Narrative Irony in 'The Apple-Tree Table.'" *Studies in the American Renaissance.* Ed. Joel Myerson. Charlottesville: University Press of Virginia, 1989. 241–55.

Priestly, Joseph. *Lectures on History and General Policy.* 2 vols. Philadelphia, 1803.

Rachman, Stephen. "'Es lässt sich nicht schreiben': Plagiarism and 'The Man of the Crowd'" in *The American Face of Edgar Allan Poe.* Ed. Shawn Rosenheim and Stephen Rachman. Baltimore and London: Johns Hopkins University Press, 1995, 49–87.

Read, David. "Silent Partners: Historical Representation in William Bradford's *Of Plymouth Plantation.*" *Early American Literature* 33.3 (1998): 291–314.

Reilly, John E. "A Source for the Immuration in 'The Black Cat,'" *Nineteenth-Century Literature* 48.1 (1993): 93–95.

Reynolds, David S. *Beneath the American Renaissance: The Subversive Imagination in the Age of Emerson and Melville.* Cambridge: Harvard University Press, 1989.

———. *Faith in Fiction: The Emergence of Religious Literature in America.* Cambridge and London: Harvard University Press, 1981.

———. "Poe's Art of Transformation: 'The Cask of Amontillado' in Its Cultural Context."

In *New Essays on Poe's Major Tales.* Ed. Kenneth Silverman. New York and London: Cambridge University Press, 1993.

Ridgely, J. V. "Tragical-Mythical-Satirical-Hoaxical: Problems of Genre in *Pym. American Transcendental Quarterly* 24.1 (1974): 4–9.

Ringe, Donald A. *American Gothic: Imagination and Reason in Nineteenth-Century Fiction.* Lexington: University Press of Kentucky, 1982.

Romines, Ann. *The Home Plot: Women, Writing, and Domestic Ritual.* Amherst: University of Massachusetts Press, 1992.

Rosenzweig, Paul. "'Dust Within the Rock': The Phantasm of Meaning in *The Narrative of Arthur Gordon Pym. Studies in the Novel* 14.2 (1982): 137–51.

Royot, Daniel. "Franklin as Founding Father of American Humor." In *Reappraising Benjamin Franklin: A Bicentennial Perspective.* Ed. J. A. Leo Lemay. Newark: University of Delaware Press, 1993. 388–95.

Rubin-Dorsky, Jeffrey. *Adrift in the Old World: The Psychological Pilgrimage of Washington Irving.* Chicago and London: University of Chicago Press, 1988.

Scheick, William J., ed. *Two Mather Biographies:* Life & Death *and* Parentator. Bethlehem, PA: Lehigh University Press, 1989.

Scheiding, Oliver. "Subversions of Providential Historiography in Herman Melville's 'Benito Cereno.'" *Re-Visioning the Past: Historical Self-Reflexivity in American Short Fiction.* Ed. Bernd Engler and Oliver Scheiding. Trier: Wissenschaftlicher Verlag Trier, 1998. 121–40.

Schultz, Nancy Lusignan. "The Artist's Craftiness: Miss Prissy in *The Minister's Wooing. Studies in American Fiction* 20.1 (1992). 33–44.

Sage, Victor. *Horror Fiction in the Protestant Tradition.* New York: St. Martin's Press, 1988.

Sedgwick, Catharine Maria. *Hope Leslie.* New Brunswick and London: Rutgers University Press, 1990.

———. *Life and Letters of Catharine M. Sedgwick.* Ed. Mary E. Dewey. New York: Harper & Brothers, 1871.

———. *The Power of Her Sympathy: The Autobiography and Journal of Catharine Maria Sedgwick.* Ed. Mary Kelley. Boston: Massachusetts Historical Society, 1993.

Sedgwick, Eve Kosofsky. *The Coherence of Gothic Conventions.* New York and London: Methuen, 1986.

Silverman, Kenneth. *Edgar A. Poe: Mournful and Never-ending Remembrance.* New York: HarperCollins, 1991.

———. *The Life and Times of Cotton Mather.* New York: Columbia University Press, 1985.

Spengemann, William C. *The Adventurous Muse.* New Haven: Yale University Press, 1977.

Stanton, Rev. E. F. "Manual Labor Schools." *Southern Literary Messenger* 2.4 (1836): 244–52.

Stewart, E. Kate. "Another Source for 'The Black Cat.'" *Poe Studies* 18.2 (1985): 25.

Stievermann, Jan. "Writing 'To Conquer All Things': Cotton Mather's *Magnalia Christi Americana* and the Quandary of *Copia.*" *Early American Literature* 39.2 (2004): 263–97.

Stowe, Charles Edward. *Life of Harriet Beecher Stowe Compiled from Her Letters and Journals.* Boston: Houghton Mifflin, 1889.

Stowe, Harriet Beecher. *The Writings of Harriet Beecher Stowe.* 16 vols. New York: AMS, 1967.

—— and Catherine E. Beecher. *The American Woman's Home or, Principles of Domestic Science.* 1869. Rpt. Hartford, CT: The Stowe-Day Foundation, 1991.

Swann, Charles. *Nathaniel Hawthorne: Tradition and Revolution.* Cambridge Studies in American Literature and Culture, 52. Cambridge: Cambridge University Press, 1991.

Swartzlander, Susan. "'Appealing to the Heart': The Use of History and the Role of Fiction in 'Alice Doane's Appeal.'" *Studies in Short Fiction* 25.2 (1988): 121–28.

Sweeney, Gerard M. "Wharton's 'Bewitched.'" *Explicator* 56.4 (1998): 198–201.

Tang, Edward. "Making Declarations of Her Own: Harriet Beecher Stowe as New England Historian." *New England Quarterly* 71.1 (1998): 77–96.

Thacher, James. *History of the Town of Plymouth, from its first settlement in 1620, to the present time.* Boston, 1835.

Thompson, G. R. *The Art of Authorial Presence: Hawthorne's Provincial Tales.* Durham and London: Duke University Press, 1993.

Travis, Jennifer. "Pain and Recompense: The Trouble with *Ethan Frome.*" *Arizona Quarterly* 53.3 (1997): 37–64.

Upham, Charles W. *Lectures on Witchcraft, Comprising a History of the Delusion of Salem in 1692.* Boston: Carter, Hendee and Babcock, 1831.

Van Cromphout, Gustaaf. "Cotton Mather: The Puritan Historian as Renaissance Humanist." *Early American Literature* 49.3 (1977): 327–37.

Van Horne, John C. "Collective Benevolence and the Common Good in Franklin's Philosophy." In *Reappraising Benjamin Franklin: A Bicentennial Perspective.* Ed. J. A. Leo Lemay. Newark: University of Delaware Press, 1993. 435–40.

Ware, Tracy. "'A Descent into the Maelström': The Status of Scientific Rhetoric in a Perverse Romance." *Studies in Short Fiction* 29.1 (1992): 77–84.

Warren, Austin. "Grandfather Mather and His Wonder Book." *Sewanee Review* 72.1 (1964): 96–116.

Weber, Alfred. "Die Anfänge des Kurzen Erzählens im Amerika des 17. und 18. Jahrhunderts: Die 'Providences' der Amerikanischen Puritaner." *Mythos und Aufklärung in der Amerikanischen Literatur.* Ed. Dieter Meindl and Friedrich W. Horlacher. Erlangen: Erlanger Forschungen, 1985, 55–70.

Weierman, Karen Woods. "Reading and Writing *Hope Leslie:* Catharine Maria Sedgwick's Indian 'Connections.'" *The New England Quarterly* 75.3 (2002): 415–43.

Weis, Ann-Marie. "The Murderous Mother and the Solicitous Father: Violence, Jacksonian Family Values, and Hannah Duston's Captivity." *American Studies International* 36.1 (1998): 46–65.

Wenska, Walter P. "Bradford's Two Histories: Pattern and Paradigm in *Of Plymouth Plantation.*" *Early American Literature* 13.2 (1978): 151–64.

Wharton, Edith. *A Backward Glance.* New York: Charles Scribner's Sons, 1933.

——. *Ethan Frome.* New York: Charles Scribner's Sons, 1911.

——. *Wharton's New England: Seven Stories and* Ethan Frome. Ed. Barbara A. White. Hanover and London: University Press of New Hampshire, 1995.

White, Hayden. *The Content of the Form: Narrative Discourse and Historical Representation.* Baltimore and London: The Johns Hopkins University Press, 1987.

———. *Metahistory: The Historical Imagination in Nineteenth-Century Europe.* Baltimore: Johns Hopkins University Press, 1973.

———. *Tropics of Discourse: Essays in Cultural Criticism.* Baltimore and London: The Johns Hopkins University Press, 1978.

———. "The Value of Narrativity in the Representation of Reality." *Critical Inquiry* 7 (1980): 5–27.

Whittier, John Greenleaf. *Leaves from Margaret Smith's Journal.* 1849. Upper Saddle River, NJ: Literature House, 1970.

———. *Legends of New England.* 1831. Ed. John B. Pickard. Gainesville: Scholars' Facsimiles, 1965.

———. *The Supernaturalism of New England.* 1847. Ed. Edward Wagenknecht. Norman: University of Oklahoma Press, 1969.

Williams, Daniel E. *Pillars of Salt: An Anthology of Early American Criminal Narratives.* Madison, WI: Madison House, 1993.

———. "Puritans and Pirates: A Confrontation Between Cotton Mather and William Fly in 1726." *Early American Literature* 22.3: 233–51.

Williams, Roger. *A Key into the Language of America.* Providence: Publications of the Narragansett Club, 1866.

Winship, Michael P. *Seers of God: Puritan Providentialism in the Restoration and Early Enlightenment.* Baltimore: Johns Hopkins University Press, 1996.

Winthrop, John. *Winthrop's Journal 1630–1649.* 1825–26. Ed. James Kendall Hosmer. New York: Barnes and Noble, 1959.

———. *History of New England.* New York: Scribner's, 1908.

Wolff, Cynthia Griffin. *A Feast of Words: The Triumph of Edith Wharton.* New York: Oxford University Press, 1977.

Wolstenholme, Susan. *Gothic (Re)Visions: Writing Women as Readers.* Albany: State University of New York Press, 1993.

Wood, Gordon S. *The Americanization of Benjamin Franklin.* New York: Penguin, 2004.

Zagarell, Sandra A. "Expanding 'America': Lydia Sigourney's *Sketch of Connecticut,* Catharine Sedgwick's *Hope Leslie.*" *Tulsa Studies in Women's Literature* 6 (1987): 225–45.

Zanger, Jules. "Poe's 'The Pit and the Pendulum' and American Revivalism." *Religion in Life* 49 (1980): 96–105.

Ziff, Larzer. *Puritanism in America: New Culture in a New World.* New York: Viking, 1973.

———. "Upon What Pretext? The Book and Literary History." *Publications of the American Antiquarian Society* 95.2 (1985): 297–315.

Index

౭ఌౣ